Y0-BQH-737

Electronics in Communication

ELECTRONIC TECHNOLOGY SERIES

SERIES EDITOR
Irving L. Kosow Ph.D

Electronics In Communications

Sol Lapatine

Department of Electrical Technology
College of Staten Island
City University of New York

John Wiley & Sons

New York
Santa Barbara
Chichester
Brisbane
Toronto

Library of Congress Cataloging in Publication Data:

Lapatine, Sol, 1918-
  Electronics in communication.

  (Electronic technology series)
  Includes index
  1. Telecommunication. 2. Electronics. I. Title.
TK5101. L32   621.38′0413   77-17573
ISBN 0-471-01842-2

Printed in the United States of America

10 9 8 7 6 5 4 3 2 1

Preface

This book derives from the class notes I wrote to supplement the textbook I was then using. It is intended for a one semester course in electronic communications at the community college technical level.

There are many excellent books available dealing with radio frequency (RF) systems and a lesser number of similarly fine books stressing microwaves. However, it appears that no books are available that place equal emphasis on RF and microwaves. In addition, no book is available that is intended to cover the subject in one semester.

Even this book has grown beyond my original intentions and presents somewhat more material than I have been able to utilize in my lectures. On the other hand, this surplus permits the individual instructor the freedom to select topics considered more relevant to the needs of a particular one semester course.

The book includes much emphasis on analytic troubleshooting of RF systems. I found this emphasis to be very useful and a source of great satisfaction to the student. Also included are many problems and questions. The problems have already been tested in class assignments and have been refined with use. The technique of self-evaluation questions has also been incorporated. The book is written to present a course structured to stimulate reading and self-study. The text should be used in conjunction with a laboratory course that includes the testing and troubleshooting of various receivers, UHF systems, and microwave systems.

The specific material this book deals with is well-defined by the table of contents. The technical depth of the material is appropriate for the community college student in electronic technology. I have departed from the usual custom of packing in as much detail as possible. On the contrary I have included only *limited* highlights that can reasonably be covered in one semester; these will serve as an introduction to further in-depth study of communications in subsequent courses.

My thanks to Dr. Irving L. Kosow of Wiley for his patient and expert guidance, and to Jean Johnson for typing and proofreading.

Sol Lapatine

To my beloved and beautiful Beatrice

Contents

Chapter 1 Introduction to and Limitations of Communications

1-1
Objectives To learn:

1. The basic components of a communications system.
2. Various types of communications systems.
3. Noise limitations on a communications system.
4. Various forms of external noise.
5. Various forms of internal noise.
6. Significance of noise figure.

1-2
Self-Evaluation Questions Test your prior knowledge of the information in this chapter by answering the following questions. Watch for the answers to these questions as you read the chapter. Your final evaluation of whether you understand the material is measured by your ability to answer these questions. When you have completed the chapter, return to this section and answer the questions again.

1. Define the basic components of an electronic communications system.
2. List five examples of natural external noise.
3. List ten examples of man-made external noise.
4. Define Johnson noise.
5. Explain why noise is a limitation on the use of a receiver.
6. Define partition noise.
7. Define shot noise.
8. Explain the significance of signal-to-noise ratio.
9. Define noise figure.
10. Define microphonic noise.

1

**1-3
Basic Components of
a Communications
System**

Communication is the transfer of intelligence from a source to a recipient. The most common communication is person-to-person speech across a few feet of air as the separating medium. A flirting wink of the eye is undoubtedly communication. Likewise the menacing approach of a protagonist. Some primitive and early forms of communication are Indian smoke signals and tribal jungle drums. A slightly more sophisticated system has two children speaking into round cereal boxes that are connected by a string and held taut. Who would take exception to the fact that a skunk is communicating when it sprays an enemy? The famous blind and deaf author Helen Keller learned to communicate by applying appropriate touch. The legendary dragon made a lot of sense by snorting flame.

These examples suggest that the source of communication may be sound or motion or touch or heat radiation. Similarly the recipient of a communication may be using hearing or sight or touch or smell.

**1-4
Various Types of
Communications
Systems**

A study of *electronic* communications, the purpose of this text, extends from the basic telegraph set through telephone, radio, television, radar, laser, to sophisticated satellite communications. As communications technology developed, a complex industrial society required an ever-expanding frequency spectrum. Recent developments have pushed the usable frequency spectrum into the visible light region with the advent of lasers and associated flexible light-conducting cable.

Every communications system has a beginning and an end. The most common electronic communication system is the *telephone*, discussed in the next paragraph. This starts with a human voice that sets air into motion. In a true sense the vocal chords and mouth are the most basic *transducer*. (A transducer is a device for converting energy from one form to another.) In speech, vocal chord vibrations are translated to air motion. There are many transducers used in modern society. A partial listing is: conversion of the studio scene to television signals, cloud formation to radar weather signals, barometric pressure to electric signals, wind velocity and direction to electric signals, amount of rain to electric signals, acceleration to electric signals, altitude to electric signals, light intensity to electric signals, ocean depth to electric signals, and a multitude of other applica-

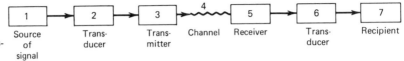

Figure 1-1 Basic communications system.

tions. The basic communications system is shown in Fig. 1-1.

The simplified direct-wired *telephone* system includes a mouthpiece or microphone that converts the air waves to electric signals. This signal is amplified in the transmitter section. It is next sent over *wire* to a receiver that passes the signal to the output transducer or *earpiece*. This converts the electrical signal to air pressure waves that strike the eardrum. In practice, the modern telephone system is a maze of switching circuitry, amplifiers, repeaters, and cables. The *channel* of Fig. 1-1 occasionally includes RF and even satellite stations for international telephone calls.

The simple system of Fig. 1-1 has its counterpart in any modern communications system, (radio, television, radar, computer, facsimile, sonar) including the many military communication systems. The channel (block 4) of Fig. 1-1 may also be used to carry a number of *simultaneous* information signals. This involves a process called *multiplexing* where signals are mixed together either on a sequential time basis or on different frequencies.

The range of usable frequencies for transmission of intelligence is called the *frequency spectrum*. The FCC (Federal Communications Commision) allocates the spectrum in *decade* ranges, called *bands*. The *very-low frequency* (VLF) band from 3 to 30 kHz is used for audio systems. The *low frequency* (LF) band from 30 to 300 kHz is used for *long-distance* radio, and navigation. The *medium frequency* (MF) band from 0.3 to 3 MHz is used for AM radio. The *high frequency* (HF) band from 3 to 30 MHz covers the *citizens band* (CB). The *very-high frequency* (VHF) band from 30 to 300 MHz includes television (TV) and FM. The *ultra-high frequency* (UHF) band from 0.3 to 3 GHz covers the balance of TV bands and lower microwave regions. The last two bands, *super-high frequency* (SHF), 3 to 30 GHz and *extreme-high frequency* (EHF), 30 to 300 GHz, are both in the microwave region and are used for radar and satellites. In Ch. 10 on microwaves we shall see that the last two microwave bands are further subdivided into (a dozen) subbands designated by letters, such as *L, C, X*, etc.

Communications systems operating *under* 30 MHz may have signals radiated from and reflected back to earth by the *ionosphere* layer. In this way by a series of ground and sky reflections, a radio signal may travel around the world. Systems operating above 30 MHz are limited to *line-of-sight* transmissions. Of course, a line-of-sight transmission that includes a satellite still enables around-the-world communications.

Communications usually require transmission of intelligence through *space*. This, in turn, dictates need for a *transmission line* and an *antenna*. It is the space transmission segment of any communications system (channel block 4 of Fig. 1-1) that is *most susceptible* to degeneration. This is the result of two distinct features of *space*. One is the natural *attenuation* of signal strength in space as the transmission distance increases. The second is the super-imposition of *noise* on the signal. Noise is always present in any earthbound space.

1-5 Noise Limitations on a Communications System *Noise* is the natural enemy of any communications system. Noise is any *undesired* signal; whether two broadcast stations tuned in simultaneously, children at play when you're trying to fall asleep, or a rock concert when you are trying to do income tax returns. A signal that in itself may be entirely enjoyable at one time is noise at the wrong time. Allegedly, one of the most effective methods of protecting a conversation from electronic surveillance is to converse during a bustling energetic cocktail party. The din of the other conversations makes it impossible to be heard even with most modern eavesdropping equipment. The other extreme of secrecy in conversation, which is to hold the talk in an open meadow away from people, does *not* provide protection from a highly directive, extremely sensitive microphone because of the absense of noise. Having concluded that noise is undesirable, the next step is to catalog noise as *external* or *internal*.

1-6 Forms of External Noise External noise can be classified as either *natural* or *man-made*. Natural noise includes static that results from thunder storms. *Outerspace* noise, another form of natural noise, has *many* sources. Our own sun is the greatest offender. The sun's contribution of noise varies in many ways: day to night, seasonal variation, a seven year cyclic variation, and finally a hundred year cyclic variation. The earth also receives *cosmic* noise from the suns (stars) of many distant galaxies. Also falling into the category of outerspace noise are signals from *quasars* (starlike objects with both visible and radio-frequency emission) and *pulsars* (very short-period galactic radio sources). Very little can be done about outerspace noise other than an impractical move to a more remote and quiet galaxy.

Man-made noise, depending on circumstances, may be equally unavoidable. Special types of communication such as radio telescopes, military systems, and space stations may be located remote from civilization so as to minimize the effect of man-made noise. In this context man-made noise includes motors, fluorescent lamps, automobiles, subways, aircraft, shavers, hair dryers, egg beaters, and especially citizen's band radio transmitters. The average home includes 27 motor-driven devices. Even the neighbors' AM, FM or TV receivers may act as a source of electrical noise to your receiver.

1-7
Forms of
Internal Noise

Obviously we have more specific control over the sources of noise generated *within* the communications system. Nevertheless, there are types of *internal* noise (within any electronic device) that can be only *minimized* but not eliminated. For proper hearing, the signal imposed on a loudspeaker should be many times greater than the noise.

There are various types of noise generated internally. Each of these is amplified in subsequent stages of the system and eventually appear in amplified form at the output. The noise generated at the very input to a system is the most troublesome noise because it is then amplified (along with the intelligence) throughout the system.

1-7.1
Johnson Noise

The most basic limitation on the sensitivity of a broadcast receiver is the *Johnson* noise. This relates to the fact that the temperature of any electrical device is a measure of the random motion of its atoms and electrons. This results in the radiation of electromagnetic energy that appears at the terminals as a *noise voltage*. This voltage is related to the absolute temperature

(°K) of the device. This noise voltage is a form of *white* noise, meaning that it occurs at *all* frequencies. For this reason it is desirable to reduce the bandwidth of the system to the minimum required for communication. This relationship of noise voltage and bandwidth is independent of the bandwidth center frequency. Therefore a 10 kHz bandwidth at 3 MHz will present the same noise voltage as a 10 kHz bandwidth at 300 MHz. Finally, the noise voltage is related to the resistive component of the impedance of the electronic component. Because this noise voltage is generated by the input component of a system as well as every other resistive component, it is the *most* troublesome of the internal noises. It is called *thermal agitation* noise, or *Johnson* noise or *white* noise. The relationships are summarized in Eq. (1-1).

$$E_n = \sqrt{4kT(BW)R} \qquad \text{rms volts (V)} \qquad (1\text{-}1)$$

where: k = Boltzmann's constant, 1.38×10^{-23} joules per degree Kelvin (J/°K)

T = absolute temperature (°K = 273 + °C)

BW = bandwidth of receiver, Hz

R = resistance of component, ohms (Ω)

Example 1-1

A receiver is operating at a temperature of 27 °C. The transistors used in the receiver average an input resistance of 1 kΩ. Calculate Johnson noise voltage for a receiver with a bandwidth of:

a. 15 kHz

b. 200 kHz

c. 6 MHz and a temperature of 77 °C

(Assume an ambient temperature of 27 °C if not otherwise specified.)

Solution

a. $E_n = (4kT(BW)R)^{1/2}$ (1-1)

$$= \left(4 \times 1.38 \times 10^{-23} \frac{J}{°K} \times (273 + 27) \ °K \times 15 \times 10^3 \ Hz \times 10^3 \Omega\right)^{1/2}$$

$$= 4.98 \times 10^{-7} \ V = \mathbf{0.4984 \ \mu V}$$

b. $.4984 \ \mu V \left(\dfrac{200 \ kHz}{15 \ kHz}\right)^{1/2} = \mathbf{1.82 \ \mu V}$

c. $.4984 \ \mu V \left(\dfrac{6000 \ kHz}{15 \ kHz} \times \dfrac{350}{300}\right)^{1/2} = \mathbf{10.77 \ \mu V}$

It can be seen from Ex. 1-1 that the three ways to minimize white noise effects is to use a method of communications that can be accomplished with a *narrower bandwidth*, keep the receiver input circuit *cool*, and design the circuit to have a *low resistance*. Depending on the system, one or more of these features may be accomplished. Note the actual frequency of operation does not enter into the calculations of Ex. 1-1 using Eq. (1-1). This is shown in Ex. 1-2.

Example 1-2

A TV receiver has a 4 kΩ input resistance and operates on channel 2 (frequency range of 54 to 60 MHz). Determine the rms noise voltage at the input. (Assume an ambient temperature of 27 °C if not otherwise specified.)

Solution

$$E_n = \sqrt{4kTR\,(BW)} \tag{1-1}$$

$$= \sqrt{4 \times 1.38 \times 10^{-23} \times (273 + 27) \times 4 \times 10^3 \times (60 - 54) \times 10^6}$$

$$= 19.94 \times 10^{-6} = \mathbf{19.94\ \mu V}$$

Note in Ex. 1-2 the specific frequencies do not enter into the equation for internal noise.

1-7.2
Shot Noise
There are various other types of noise generated within a communications system. *Shot effect* is one of the more troublesome. It refers to the fact that even though the bias on a transistor or vacuum tube is supposed to *maintain* the dc current *constant*, there are tiny variations in the amount of current arriving at the transistor collector or plate of a tube from moment to moment. These variations constitute an (ac) current that must also be considered noise, since it is undesired.

1-7.3
Partition
Noise
Partition noise refers to the fact that the bias is supposed to maintain a constant dc current *split between* collector and base, or between plate and screen grid. There is in fact a continuously varying *division of the current* among the elements. Again, this variation in partition of current constitutes an ac signal that results in noise.

**1-7.4
Transit-Time
Noise** At ultra-high frequencies (UHF), the time required for an electron to travel from emitter to collector, or cathode to plate is comparable to the time of the period of the controlling signal. The resulting confusion is called *transit-time* noise.

**1-7.5
Miscellaneous
Internal Noise** Another form of noise results when a strong signal and a weak signal are combined in a transistor or vacuum tube. This is called *mixer noise*. This effect can be minimized if the mixing is done at a second stage rather than the input stage of a receiver.

Microphonic noise results if the circuit elements (vacuum tube grids) are not mechanically rigid. The resulting vibrations as you walk across the room are reflected in the varying sound.

There are many other causes of noise. The *power supply* may contribute *hum noise* if the filtering is inadequate. Any coil, (such as power supply transformer, filter chokes, RF chokes, RF or IF transformers) may contribute undesired magnetic field coupling. Any high impedance circuit in a communications system may be the reluctant recipient of stray electric field coupling.

There are more exotic types of noise, such as *harmonic distortion, cross-modulation, intermodulation*. The specifications of any good quality (expensive) receiver include the details of these and various other types of noise.

**1-8
Noise
Figure (NF)** For purposes of noise calculation, the manufacturer of transistors or vacuum tubes provides an equivalent noise resistance value as part of their specifications. This defines the amount of resistance at the input that would create an equal amount of noise.

If the received signal is *very* strong, the many noises generated within a receiver are negligibly small in comparison. In a real sense it is the *ratio* of the *signal* strength to the *noise* strength that is always important. At the input this *signal-to-noise ratio* is expressed S_i/N_i. If no (internal) noise is generated in succeeding stages of the receiver, the same ratio prevails ideally at the output, as shown in Eq. (1-2).

Input S/N ratio $=$ Output S/N ratio, or

$$\frac{S_i}{N_i} = \frac{S_o}{N_o} \qquad \text{(dimensionless)} \qquad (1\text{-}2)$$

where: S_i = input signal (μV)

S_o = output signal (μV)

N_i = internal noise at input (μV)

N_o = internal noise at output (μV)

The *noise figure* (*NF*) is a measure of the degradation caused by the receiving system. In practice, some noise must be generated in each stage of the receiver. Therefore, the ratios of Eq. (1-2) usually are *not* equal. The signal-to-noise ratio is frequently expressed in dB, where $S/N = 10 \log_{10} S/N$ (dB). The *noise figure* (*NF*) is defined as the comparison of the two ratios.

$$NF = \frac{S_i/N_i}{S_o/N_o} \tag{1-3}$$

The closer the value of noise figure is to unity, the more noise-free the receiver. A perfect receiver would have a noise figure of zero dB.

Example 1-3

The input signal to a receiver is 50 μV and the internal noise at the input is 5 μV. After amplification, the signal at the output is 2 V and the noise at the output is 0.4 V. Determine the noise figure.

Solution

$$NF = \frac{S_i/N_i}{S_o/N_o}$$

$$= \frac{50/5}{2/0.4} = \frac{10}{5} = 2 \tag{1-3}$$

The *NF* in Ex. 1-3 is not quite the ideal value of unity, but it is an acceptably low *NF* value. Note that since S_o/S_i is the voltage gain (*G*) of the system, Eq. (1-3) can also be expressed

$$NF = \frac{N_o}{GN_i} \tag{1-4}$$

Example 1-4

The input noise to an amplifier is 5 μV and the output noise is 200 mV. The system gain is 5000. Calculate the system noise figure.

Solution

$$NF = N_o / GN_i$$

$$NF = \frac{200 \times 10^{-3}}{5000 \times 5 \times 10^{-6}} = 8 \qquad (1\text{-}4)$$

For a system that is not generating internal noise after the input circuit, Eq. (1-4) reduces to unity. Noise figure is also frequently expressed in dB, in which case $NF = 10 \log_{10}(NF)$(dB).

For cascaded amplifiers the overall noise figure becomes Eq. (1-5).

$$NF = NF_1 + \frac{NF_2 - 1}{G_1} + \frac{NF_3 - 1}{G_1 G_2} + \frac{NF_4 - 1}{G_1 G_2 G_3} + \cdots \qquad (1\text{-}5)$$

where: NF_1, NF_2, NF_3 and NF_4 are noise figures for cascaded stages 1, 2, 3, 4.

G_1, G_2, G_3 are gains for cascaded stages 1, 2, and 3.

Example 1-5
Given 4 amplifier stages cascaded with the following data: $NF_1 = 10$, $NF_2 = 5$, $NF_3 = 8$, $NF_4 = 12$, $G_1 = 50$, $G_2 = 20$, and $G_3 = 10$. Calculate the overall noise figure.

Solution

$$NF = NF_1 + \frac{NF_2 - 1}{G_1} + \frac{NF_3 - 1}{G_1 G_2} + \frac{NF_4 - 1}{G_1 G_2 G_3}$$

$$= 10 + \frac{5 - 1}{50} + \frac{8 - 1}{50 \times 20} + \frac{12 - 1}{50 \times 20 \times 10}$$

$$= 10 + 0.08 + 0.007 + 0.0011 = \mathbf{10.0881} \qquad (1\text{-}5)$$

Note the noise contribution of succeeding stages is minimal.

**1-9
Summary**   Each communications system must have a *sender* and a *recipient*. The sender may initiate the signal by voice, picture, tape, tele-typewriter, or any number of other devices. This input must be converted by an appropriate input *transducer* for activating the *transmitter*. The transmitter operates on the signal and sends the signal through a *channel* to the *receiver*. Here the signal is operated upon once again and trans-

ferred by an *output transducer* to an appropriate output. During transit the transmitted signal is subjected to various *natural* and *man-made noises*. Within the *receiver* the minimum receivable signal is determined by the *internally generated noises*. The *noise figure* is an indication of noise generated within the receiver.

Now return to the objectives and self-evaluation questions at the beginning of this chapter and see how well you can answer them. If you cannot answer certain questions, place a check next to each of them and review appropriate parts of the text. Then answer the questions and solve the problems below.

**1-10
Questions**

Q1-1 List 10 examples of electronic communications systems.

Q1-2 What is the distinction between natural and man-made (external) noise?

Q1-3 Explain why noise is a limitation on the use of a receiver.

Q1-4 List three methods of minimizing Johnson noise.

Q1-5 How do the input and output signal-to-noise ratios compare in an ideal receiver that does not generate noise after the input stage?

Q1-6 Define transit-time noise.

Q1-7 Define mixer noise.

Q1-8 Define the basic elements of a telephone communications system.

Q1-9 List four miscellaneous types of internal noise.

Q1-10 Define a transducer.

Q1-11 List four types of transducers.

Q1-12 Define frequency spectrum.

Q1-13 Define the frequency range for:
    a. VLF
    b. UHF
    c. EHF

Q1-14 What is the highest frequency that will be reflected by the ionosphere?

Q1-15 Which parameters of space tend to degenerate a signal?

Q1-16 List three parameters of Johnson noise.

**1-11
Problems**

P1-1 An RF amplifier has an input resistance of 600 Ω and is operating in the FM band from 90.2 to 90.4 MHz. Calculate the Johnson rms noise voltage.

P1-2 Calculate the Johnson rms noise voltage of an RF amplifier having a 5 kΩ input resistance operating in the AM band from 870 to 890 kHz at a temperature of 55 °C.

P1-3 A TV receiver has a 2 kΩ input resistance and a 6 MHz bandwidth. Determine the Johnson rms noise voltage.

P1-4 Given an input S_i/N_i of 10 and an output S_o/N_o of 8, calculate the noise figure.

P1-5 Given three cascaded amplifier stages with the following data: $NF_1 = 7$, $NF_2 = 5$, $NF_3 = 4$, $G_1 = 100$, $G_2 = 30$, and $G_3 = 20$. Calculate the overall noise figure in dB.

P1-6 Given an input noise of 8 μV, an output noise of 500 μV and a system gain of 300. Calculate the noise figure.

Chapter 2

**RF
Coupling
and
Filters**

**2-1
Objectives**

To learn:

1. The characteristics of a series-resonant circuit.
2. The characteristics of a parallel-resonant circuit.
3. The effect of loading on resonant circuits.
4. Methods of coupling RF circuits.
5. Characteristics of RF coupling circuits.
6. Frequency characteristics of various RF filters.

**2-2
Self-Evaluation
Questions**

Test your prior knowledge of the information in this chapter by answering the following questions. Watch for the answers to these questions as you read the chapter. Your final evaluation of whether you understand the material is measured by your ability to answer these questions. When you have completed the chapter, return to this section and answer the questions again.

1. What is the significance of the Q of a resonant tank?
2. What is meant by the skirt of a resonance curve?
3. How would you lower the Q of a parallel-resonant circuit?
4. What is the significance of the L/C ratio in a parallel resonant circuit?
5. Explain the effect on the primary caused by drawing current from the secondary winding of a transformer.
6. Why are powdered iron cores used in RF transformers?
7. What change in the physical location of the windings of a transformer would you make, to *reduce* the coefficient of coupling?
8. What are the advantages of *link* coupling?
9. For the double-tuned circuit, if the overcoupling is excessive, what disadvantages may result?
10. Given a single-tuned circuit with the source feeding a tap on the coil, what kind of impedance matching is being accomplished?

11. What characteristics besides frequency response would you specify for a RF filter?

12. Describe the frequency response characteristic of a bandstop filter.

2-3 Resonant Circuits It is assumed that the reader has taken a fundamentals course that included theory of resonant circuits, inductance, inductive coupling, and basic transformer action. On this assumption, these subjects are given a quick review and the more significant equations are listed for ready reference.

Radio frequency (RF) circuits operate on principles involving resonance theory. In practice, parallel-resonant circuits are more commonly used than series-resonant circuits. However, this statement is not meant to minimize the importance of series-resonant circuits. Besides, it is simpler to introduce parallel-resonant theory via series resonance, and convention usually follows this approach.

2-4 Series Resonance The basic series-resonant circuit consists of a coil and a capacitor with the only resistance being the resistance of the coil (R_S). We thus have an L inductance (henries), C capacitance (farads), and R_S resistance (ohms) all considered to be in series, as shown in Fig. 2-1.

The fundamental theory of series resonance occurs when the inductive reactance ($X_L = 2\pi f L = \omega L$) is equal to the capacitive reactance ($X_C = 1/2\pi f c = 1/\omega C$) at a specific frequency called the resonant frequency (f_0). The vector addition of the two reactance terms cause them to cancel leaving only R at resonance. This results in a total circuit impedance ($Z = R$) that is a minimum impedance at resonance. Consequently the following conditions occur at resonance. Note that the significant values when measured at resonance are indicated by the subscript "0".

1. $f_0 = \dfrac{1}{2\pi\sqrt{LC}}$ hertz (Hz)   (2-1)

where: f_0 is the series-resonant frequency in hertz (Hz)
L is inductance, henries (H)
C is capacitance, farads (F)

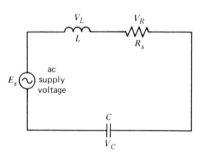

Figure 2-1 Series resonant circuit.

2. $X_L = 2\pi f L$ ohms (Ω)   (2-2a)

$X_C = \dfrac{1}{2\pi f C}$ ohms (Ω)   (2-2b)

where: X_L is inductive reactance, ohms (Ω)
X_C is capacitive reactance, ohms (Ω)

3. $X_L = X_C$ at resonance   (2-3)

This relationship results in the resonant frequency formula Eq. (2-1).

4. $Z_0 = R_s$ (minimum value)   ohms (Ω)   (2-4)

where: Z_0 is the total impedance of the circuit at resonance, ohms (Ω)
R_s is the resistance in the circuit, ohms (Ω)

5. $E_s = V_{R_0}$ volts (V)   (2-5)

where: E_s is the source voltage, volts (V)
V_{R_0} is the voltage drop across the resistor at resonance, volts (V)

6. $I_0 = E_s / R_s$ (maximum value)   amperes (A)   (2-6)

where: I_0 is the circuit current at resonance, amperes (A)

7. $Q = X_L / R_s = X_c / R_s$ (no units)   (2-7)

where: Q is the figure of merit of the coil, no units

8. $V_{L_0} = V_{c_0} = I_0 X_L = \dfrac{E_s}{R_s} X_L = Q E_s$ (2-8)

where: V_{L_0} is voltage drop across L at resonance, (V)
V_{c_0} is voltage drop across C at resonance, (V)

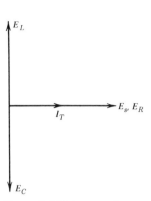

Figure 2-2 Voltage and current relationships of a series-resonant circuit at resonance.

Note: The circuit is resistive at resonance and the current is in phase with the source voltage.

The voltage/current phase relationships of a series-resonant circuit at resonance is shown in Fig. 2-2.

Note: For the *ideal* series-resonant circuit indicated in Fig. 2-2 the current is in phase with the source voltage. The voltage drop across the resistor is equal to and in phase with the source voltage. The reactive voltages are $\pm 90°$ with respect to source voltage and Q times as large.

In general the sharpness of the current response curve depends on the Q. There are a number of ways of defining the Q of a circuit. One definition that is valid at all frequencies and for all components relates to energy. Refer to Eq. (2-9).

$$Q = \frac{\text{energy stored in a circuit}}{\text{energy dissipated per cycle}} \qquad (2\text{-}9)$$

A more common expression for Q is the *figure of merit* of a coil. Mathematically it relates the resistance of the coil, the operating frequency, and the inductance. Refer to Eq. (2-10).

$$Q = \frac{2\pi f_0 L}{R_s} \qquad (2\text{-}10)$$

The *bandwidth* (BW) of a circuit is the range of frequencies that a circuit will pass without serious amplitude deterioration (attenuation). The commonly accepted definition of a passed signal is whether the amplitude of the output at a particular frequency is no less than 70.7% of the output peak value. Figure 2-3 shows frequencies f_1 and f_2 that correspond to the 70.7% points, or $0.707 \times$ peak current. The 0.707 point corresponds to the *half-power* condition. It is also the 3 *dB down* from the peak point.

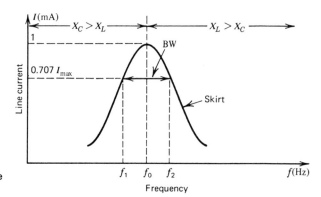

Figure 2-3 Universal series-resonance curve.

The bandwidth is thus defined as $f_2 - f_1$, and is expressed in hertz (Hz). *BW* is also related to Q and f_0, as indicated by Eq. 2-11.

$$BW = \frac{f_0}{Q} \qquad \text{hertz (H}_z\text{)} \qquad (2\text{-}11)$$

As Q is increased the BW decreases and the resonance curve becomes sharper. The *skirt* or falloff of the curve becomes steeper (Fig. 2-4).

The curves of Fig. 2-4 indicate that BW is varying inversely with Q. If the BW is not sufficiently wide, the Q must be lowered and the curve flattened. At RF frequencies a Q of from 100 to 200 may be readily achieved. For purposes of our discussion, it is assumed that the curve on either side of resonance is symmetrical with uniform skirts. The Q can be lowered

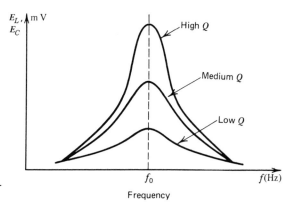

Figure 2-4 Effect of Q on series-resonant circuit.

by adding a resistor (R) in series with the series-resonant circuit. The total resistance is then the sum of R and R_s.

Off resonant frequency the circuit impedance reverts back to Eq. (2-12).

$$Z = \sqrt{(R_s)^2 + (X_L - X_C)^2} \qquad \text{ohms } (\Omega) \qquad (2\text{-}12)$$

where Z is the total impedance of the series circuit, ohms (Ω)

Likewise, off resonance the phase angle is no longer zero. At frequencies below f_0, X_L is smaller than X_c. The circuit is capacitive and I leads the source voltage, (E_s). Above f_0, $X_L > X_c$ and I lags E_s.

The resonant frequency formula, Eq. (2-1), relates f_0 to the product of L and C. As a result, the same f_0 can be accomplished by increasing L and decreasing C or vice versa. This changes the L/C ratio. A high ratio results in a low C. This in turn makes the circuit more susceptible to stray capacitance effects and results in a less stable circuit.

Example 2-1

A series circuit consists of $L = 2$ mH, $C = 0.2$ μF, $R = 5$ Ω, and a source voltage $E_T = 15$ V. At the resonant frequency, calculate:

a. f_0 d. V_{R_s}
b. I_0 e. Q rise in voltage across C and L.
c. Q

Solution

a. $f_0 = \dfrac{1}{2\pi\sqrt{LC}}$ (2-1)

$ = \dfrac{0.159}{\sqrt{2 \times 10^{-3} \times 0.2 \times 10^{-6}}} = \dfrac{0.159}{\sqrt{4 \times 10^{-10}}}$

$ = \dfrac{0.159}{2 \times 10^{-5}} = \textbf{7950 Hz}$

b. $I_0 = E_T / R_s$ (2-6)

$ = 15 \text{ V} / 5 \text{ }\Omega = \textbf{3A}$

c. $Q = \dfrac{2\pi f_0 L}{R_s}$ (2-10)

$ = \dfrac{6.28 \times 7950 \times 2 \times 10^{-3}}{5} = \textbf{19.98}$

d. $V_R = I_o \times R_s = 3 \times 5 = \mathbf{15\ V}$

e. $V_C = V_L = QE_T$ (2-8)

    $= 19.98 \times 15 = \mathbf{299.7\ V}$

Example 2-2

Repeat Ex. 2-1 with $L = 4$ mH and $C = 0.1\ \mu$F.

Solution

a. $f_o = \dfrac{1}{2\pi\sqrt{LC}}$

    $= \dfrac{1}{2\pi\sqrt{4 \times 10^{-3} \times 0.1 \times 10^{-6}}} = \mathbf{7950\ Hz}$

b. $I_o = E_T / R_s$

    $= 15/5 = \mathbf{3\ A}$

c. $Q = \dfrac{2\pi f_o L}{R_s} = \dfrac{6.28 \times 7950 \times 4 \times 10^{-3}}{5} = \mathbf{40}$

d. $V_R = I \times R_s = 3 \times 5 = \mathbf{15\ V}$

e. $V_C = V_L = QE_T = 40 \times 15 = \mathbf{600\ V}$

Example 2-2 retained the $L \times C$ product of Ex. 2-1. This resulted in the identical f_0 but an increased L/C ratio, Q and v_c and v_L.

A series-resonance circuit may be used in either of two ways, to pass a signal or reject a signal if the signal is at resonant frequency. This is shown in Fig. 2-5.

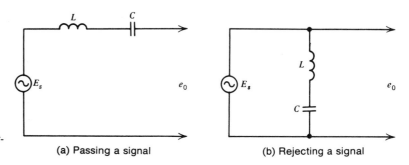

Figure 2-5 Uses of a series-resonant circuit.

(a) Passing a signal   (b) Rejecting a signal

2-5
Parallel
Resonance
The parallel-resonant circuit consists of an inductance (L) and a capacitor (C) in parallel. The resistive component of the inductor is shown as a separate resistor in series with the inductor. Refer to Fig. 2-6.

There is much similarity in the theory and formulas of the series- and parallel-resonant circuits. The parallel-resonant circuit is widely used in RF systems and serves many functions. It may be designed for operation for any RF frequency between 50 kHz and 1 GHz. The parallel-resonant circuit is commonly called a *tank* circuit, for reasons that will become apparent.

The formulas that pertain to the tank circuit are:

$$f_0 = \frac{1}{2\pi\sqrt{LC}} \qquad \text{hertz (Hz)} \tag{2-1}$$

$$X_L = 2\pi f L \qquad \text{ohms } (\Omega) \tag{2-2a}$$

$$X_C = \frac{1}{2\pi f C} \qquad \text{ohms } (\Omega) \tag{2-2b}$$

$$X_{L_0} = X_{C_0} \qquad \text{ohms } (\Omega) \tag{2-3}$$

$$Q = \frac{X_{L_0}}{R} \tag{2-7}$$

Note the Eq. (2-1) for a tank circuit with a low Q ($Q < 10$) should be modified for resonance at somewhat lower frequencies:

$$f_0 = \frac{1}{2\pi\sqrt{LC}} \times \sqrt{1 - \frac{CR^2}{L}} \tag{2-13}$$

This condition will not concern us, because we will be involved with high Q circuits ($Q \gg 10$). The total impedance that the tank circuit presents to the source voltage at resonance is given by Eq. (2-14).

$$Z_0 = \frac{L}{CR} = QX_L = Q^2 R = \frac{X_L^2}{R} = \frac{X_L X_C}{R} \tag{2-14}$$

The resonant impedance Z_0 is a *maximum* at f_0. The current drawn from the source voltage is a *minimum* at f_0, or

$$I_T = E_T / Z_0 \tag{2-15}$$

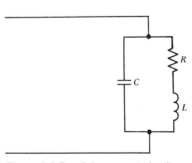

Figure 2-6 Parallel-resonant circuit.

The current *circulating* in the tank circuit is the source current multiplied by the Q, or

$$I_L = I_C = QI_T \tag{2-16}$$

The significance of these equations is that a tank circuit will act as a high impedance circuit at resonance with a high current flowing through the coil. This results in strong magnetic fields that can be magnetically coupled to another coil or tank. A plot of tank impedance versus frequency is shown in Fig. 2-7.

The current flowing in the L and C branches of the "tank" are practically equal and 180° out of phase with each other. We thus have a circulating or tank current that is almost independent of source current. The current drawn from the source is small and the L-C tank acts as a high impedance load with tank impedance related to Q.

Here, as was true for series resonance, the resistance of L branch determines Q. Theoretically it is possible to break into the tank and insert a fixed resistance in either the L or C branch. This would lower the tank Q, lower the tank impedance, draw more current from the source voltage and thus load the source. In practice, the additional resistance is contributed by a circuit placed in parallel with the tank. This paralleled circuit may be a component (L, C, R, diode, etc.) or the next amplifier stage. The net result is to *load* the tank, which in turn loads the source and draws more current. It is entirely possible to have an extremely high Q tank that may feed into a very low input resistance amplifier and kill the Q of the tank, that is, reduce the Q considerably.

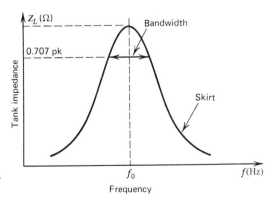

Figure 2-7 Tank circuit impedance vs. frequency.

Since the gain of an amplifier is determined in part by the collector or plate load, it is desirable to have a high impedance load for the frequency of interest. Certainly high Q will result in high impedance and high gain. But as was the case with series resonance, a high Q will result in a sharp narrow curve that may be too narrow to accommodate the band of frequencies to be amplified. Also feeding or coupling a high Q tank to a low impedance amplifier or other type of low impedance load is an experience in futility.

Once again the phase angle of the tank is zero (resistive) at resonance. However, off resonant frequency the phase angle relationships are opposite to series resonance. *Below* resonance, the L branch is the low impedance and determines the *lagging* current drawn from the source. Above resonance, X_C is smaller and results in *leading* current.

For a simple parallel-resonant tank circuit the bandwidth, resonant frequency, and Q are related as they are in the series resonant circuit.

$$Q = f_0/BW \tag{2-11}$$

A comparison of the required Q using a simple tank circuit for use with AM, FM, and TV is indicated in Ex. 2-3.

Example 2-3.

Calculate the required Q for each of the following communication systems:

a. AM broadcast ($f_0 = 1$ MHz), ± 10 kHz bandwidth
b. FM broadcast ($f_0 = 100$ MHz), ± 100 kHz bandwidth
c. TV broadcast ($f_0 = 60$ MHz), 6 MHz bandwidth

Solution

a. For AM the required $BW = \pm 10$ kHz

$$Q = \frac{f_0}{BW} = \frac{1000 \text{ kHz}}{20 \text{ kHz}} \tag{2-11}$$

$$= \textbf{50} \text{ (reasonable value)}$$

b. For FM the required $BW = \pm 100$ kHz

$$Q = \frac{100 \text{ MHz}}{0.2 \text{ MHz}} = \textbf{500} \text{ (high)}$$

c. For TV the required $BW = 6$ MHz

$$Q = \frac{60 \text{ MHz}}{6 \text{ MHz}}$$

$\quad = 10$ (low value, results in low amplifier gain)

Example 2-4

A parallel circuit has a capacitor of 250 pF in one branch and an inductance of 40 μH plus a resistance of 4 Ω in the second branch. The line voltage is 50 V. Find:

a. f_0 **d.** I_C
b. Z_0 **e.** I_L
c. I_T

Solution

a. $f_0 = \dfrac{1}{2\pi\sqrt{LC}} = \dfrac{0.159}{\sqrt{40 \times 10^{-6} \times 250 \times 10^{-12}}}$ (2-1)

$\quad = \dfrac{0.159}{100 \times 10^{-9}} = \mathbf{1.59 \text{ MHz}}$

b. $Z_0 = \dfrac{L}{RC} = \dfrac{40 \times 10^{-6}}{4 \times 250 \times 10^{-12}} = \mathbf{40 \text{ k}\Omega}$

c. $I_T = E_T / Z_0 = \dfrac{50}{40 \times 10^3} = \mathbf{1.25 \text{ mA}}$

d. and **e.**

$$Q = \frac{X_L}{R} = \frac{2\pi f_0 L}{R} = \frac{2\pi \times 1.59 \times 10^6 \times 40 \times 10^{-6}}{4} = \frac{400}{4} \quad (2\text{-}7)$$

$\quad = \mathbf{100}$

Q rise in current, $I_C = I_L = Q \times I_T$ (2-16)

$$= 100 \times 1.25 \text{ mA} = \mathbf{125 \text{ mA}}$$

Note: I_L can also be calculated by the E_T / X_L relationship:

$$I_L = \frac{E_T}{X_L} = \frac{50 \text{ V}}{400 \ \Omega} = \mathbf{125 \text{ mA}}$$

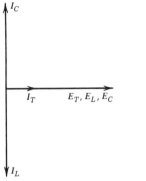

Figure 2-8 Voltage and current relationship in an ideal tank circuit.

The Z_0 is maximum and the circulating current is maximum at parallel resonance. Assuming that the maximum tank impedance results in minimum loading of the source voltage E_T at f_0, $E_L = E_C = E_T$ is maximum.

The voltage and current relationship of an ideal tank circuit is shown in Fig. 2-8.

In practice the resistive component of the coil results in a slight tilt of I_L whereby the angle between I_L and E_L becomes a little less than 90°. The amount of tilt is determined by Q and relates to the current drawn from the source (I_T). The high Q of a RF circuit makes the tilt negligible.

The tank circuit has many applications. These will be explored in the balance of this chapter and in Ch. 3.

2-6 Types of Coupling There are various methods of coupling used for RF circuits. The most common is magnetic coupling, that is, to have one tank magnetically coupled to a second tank (Fig. 2-9a). Also widely used is a single tank coupled by capacitor to the next stage (Fig. 2-9b). A more specialized form of coupling is link coupled, in which tanks are magnetically coupled to untuned coils (Fig. 2-9c). There are various other methods of coupling. We will only consider the basics of the more commonly used circuits.

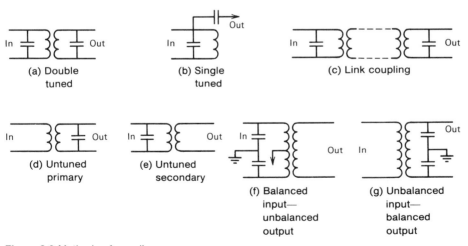

(a) Double tuned

(b) Single tuned

(c) Link coupling

(d) Untuned primary

(e) Untuned secondary

(f) Balanced input—unbalanced output

(g) Unbalanced input—balanced output

Figure 2-9 Methods of coupling.

2-6.1　The fundamentals of magnetic coupling are also the basics of
Magnetic　*link coupling* and *double-tuned tank coupling*. Therefore it is
Coupling　advisable to refresh our memories on the theory.

An ac voltage applied to the primary of a transformer causes the flow of ac primary current. This changing current sets up a magnetic field that expands and collapses with the primary current. The primary field creates flux linkages in the secondary winding that results in a secondary winding voltage. The primary and secondary windings are said to have *mutual coupling*.

$$M = k\sqrt{L_1 L_2} \qquad (2\text{-}17)$$

where: M is the mutual inductance in henries (H)

L_1 and L_2 are the self-inductance of primary and secondary in henries (H)

k is the degree of coupling expressed as a decimal fraction

If *all* the magnetic lines of the primary link with the secondary, k becomes unity. Any lesser amount of coupling results in a coefficient of coupling k less than unity.

Example 2-5
Given two coils $L_1 = 50$ mH and $L_2 = 100$ mH coupled with a coefficient of coupling $= 0.6$. Calculate the mutual inductance.

Solution

$$M = k\sqrt{L_1 L_2}$$

$$= 0.6\sqrt{50 \times 100} = 0.6 \times 70.71$$

$$= \mathbf{42.43 \ mH} \qquad (2\text{-}17)$$

In practice, RF transformers are wound with the primary and secondary windings on the same tubular form, side by side, with a powdered iron tube core. The powdered iron results in better coupling than air core, at the same time reducing the iron eddy current losses that would result from the use of laminated cores such as are used at low frequencies.

If we vary the location of the core in the coil relative to the two windings, we vary the coupling and mutual inductance. This is the usual procedure followed in aligning a receiver.

Developing a secondary voltage serves no purpose unless the voltage is applied to an electronic device. If the device is a high impedance component such as the grid of a vacuum-tube amplifier or the gate of a field effect transistor (FET), the current drawn from the secondary winding is negligibly small. The loading of the secondary is then said to be light and the loading effect on the primary winding is negligible, that is, it acts as if the secondary is open-circuited. The effect on the primary of drawing appreciable secondary current is called *reflected impedance*. This results from the fact that secondary current sets up its own magnetic field that acts as a bucking or counter field to the original primary magnetic field. The net effect at the primary is a reduced magnetic field that is equivalent to a coil with smaller self-inductance. Since it is the self-inductance, that has been opposing the flow of primary current, the final effect is an increase in primary current. This is equivalent to a *reduction* in *primary impedance*. Therefore the secondary load determines the impedance seen by the source voltage feeding the primary.

Mathematically this effect is expressed by Eq. (2-18).

$$Z_p' = Z_p - \frac{(\omega M)^2}{Z_s} \qquad \text{ohms } (\Omega) \qquad (2\text{-}18)$$

where: Z_p' is the primary impedance with a secondary load, ohms (Ω)

M is the mutual inductance, henries (H)

Z_s is the impedance of the secondary circuit, ohms (Ω)

$\omega = 2\pi f$ radians/second

Example 2-6

Given a transformer with an input impedance of 500 Ω, a mutual inductance of 40 μH, a secondary circuit load of 2 kΩ, and an operating frequency of 3 MHz. Calculate the loaded primary impedance.

Solution

$$Z_p' = Z_p - \frac{(\omega M)^2}{Z_s} \qquad (2\text{-}18)$$

$$= 500 - \frac{(2\pi \times 3 \times 10^6 \times 40 \times 10^{-6})^2}{2 \times 10^3}$$

$$= 500 - \frac{(754)^2}{2 \times 10^3} = 500 - \frac{568.5 \times 10^3}{2 \times 10^3}$$

$$= 500 - 284.2 = \textbf{215.8 } \Omega$$

2-7
Practical
Coupling
Considerations

The most widely used RF coupling is the double-tuned circuit, Fig. 2-9a. Both primary and secondary sections are tuned tanks and the coupling is magnetic.

The single-tuned circuit (Fig. 2-9b) is also widely used. This circuit couples to the load (next amplifier stage, antenna etc.) with a capacitor. In addition to the economic advantage of saving a tank circuit, the degree of coupling is readily controlled by the value of the coupling capacitor. This in turn minimizes the loading on the source. This method is frequently used in RF oscillators.

Another variation on tank coupling is to have one tank and one untuned coil. This may be tuned primary and untuned secondary (Fig. 2-9e) or vice versa (Fig. 2-9d). Specific advantages of impedance matching may result from these couplings.

The *link* coupling is a combination of tank and untuned coil (Fig. 2-9c). This type of coupling is used to transport a signal over a distance. One example is from a broadcast studio to a roof antenna. In this case the untuned link is low impedance and less susceptible to noise pickup. Two examples of balanced/unbalanced coupling is shown in Figs. 2-9f and 2-9g. The balanced line has both leads isolated from ground.

The double-tuned circuit, Fig. 2-9a, introduces the additional parameter of coefficient of coupling. A circuit designed for light coupling results in light loading and a high Q tank. However, the energy coupled to the secondary is small and the output is low. This condition is called *undercoupling* and results in a high Q type of narrow curve (Fig. 2-10a).

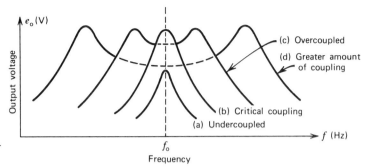

Figure 2-10 Effect of coupling on frequency response curve.

If the coupling is increased so that the reflected load impedance is equal to the primary impedance, the condition is called *critical coupling*. The output is a maximum, but the reflected load has resulted in a lower Q and a broader curve (Fig. 2-10b).

A further increase in coupling results in *overcoupling* (Fig. 2-10c). This is evidenced by a peak either side of f_0 with a valley at f_0. As the coupling increases, the peaks occur further from f_0 and the amplitude at f_0 decreases. This is a standard method of extending the bandwidth, but care must be exercised to keep the depth of the valley at f_0 within acceptable limits (Fig. 2-10d).

Improper coupling can negate an otherwise perfect circuit design. The maximum efficiency, maximum power transfer, and minimum distortion all depend on proper coupling. One or all of these symptoms may be the result of improper coupling.

Another feature of the double-tuned tank results from the type of loading. If the secondary load is resistive, the reflected load is *resistive* and the primary source of voltage (amplifier, oscillator, etc.) sees a resistive load (Fig. 2-11a). If the secondary is loaded by a capacitive circuit (Fig. 2-11b), it is reflected to the primary as its *conjugate* (an inductance). An inductive secondary load (Fig. 2-11c) is reflected to the primary as a capacitance.

Another form of coupling commonly used with transistor amplifiers is a form of autotransformer. The turns-ratio determines voltage, and the square of the turns-ratio determines impedance transfer. Transistors, more so than vacuum tubes, are dependent on impedance match for optimum power trans-

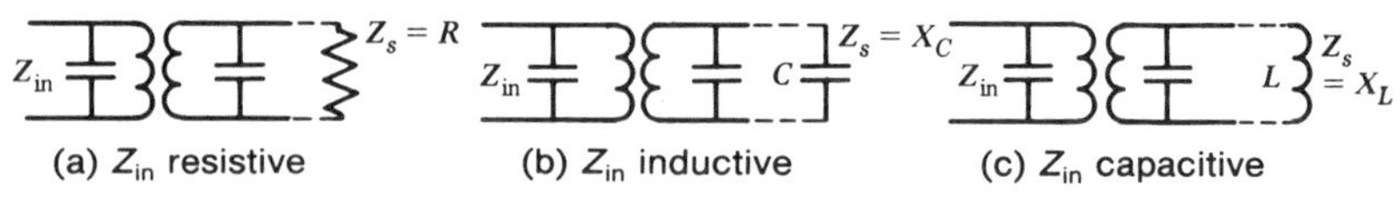

Figure 2-11 Loading effects on a double-tuned circuit.

(a) Z_{in} resistive   (b) Z_{in} inductive   (c) Z_{in} capacitive

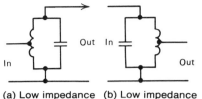

(a) Low impedance source (b) Low impedance load

Figure 2-12 Impedance matching with a tapped tank.

fer. The side facing the tap is matching a low impedance. Figure 2-12a shows a low impedance on the input to the tank circuit, and a high impedance on the output side. These conditions are reversed in Fig. 2-12b.

The effect of a parallel load can be readily calculated by determining the effective impedance of the tank circuit in parallel with a shunt resistor.

Example 2-7

Given a tank circuit consisting of $L = 120$ μH, $C = 80$ pF, and $R_s = 10$ Ω. Calculate the effective Q for a shunting resistor (R_L) of

a. 1 MΩ
b. 50 kΩ

Solution

$$Z_0 = \frac{L}{CR} = \frac{120 \times 10^{-6}}{80 \times 10^{-12} \times 10} = 1.5 \times 10^5 \; \Omega$$

$$X_L = \sqrt{R_s Z_0} = \sqrt{10 \times 1.5 \times 10^5} = 1.225 \; k\Omega$$

$$Q = \frac{Z_o}{X_L} = \frac{1.5 \times 10^5}{1.225 \times 10^3} = 122.4$$

a. For $R_L = 10^6$

$$Z_e = Z_o \| R_L = \frac{1.5 \times 10^5 \times 10^6}{(0.15 + 1) \times 10^6} = \frac{0.15 \times 10^{12}}{1.15 \times 10^6}$$

$$= 130.4 \; k\Omega$$

$$Q_e = \frac{Z_e}{X_L} = \frac{130.4 \times 10^3}{1.225 \times 10^3} = 106.4$$

b. For $R_L = 50$ kΩ

$$z_e = \frac{1.5 \times 10^5 \times 50 \times 10^3}{(150 + 50) \times 10^3} = \frac{75 \times 10^8}{2 \times 10^5} = 37.5 \; k\Omega$$

$$Q_e = \frac{37.5 \times 10^3}{1.225 \times 10^3} = 30.61$$

Note: A 50 kΩ shunt drastically reduces the impedance and Q. This would result in lower gain but increased bandwidth. If a tank circuit is connected directly to the input of a common emitter amplifier, the 1000 Ω input resistance would have a devastating effect.

2-8 There are methods of matching impedances at RF frequencies **Impedance** using L and C networks in various configurations.
Matching Networks

2-8.1 The first network to be considered is the L configuration **The** L network (Fig. 2-13).
Configuration The significant equations for both the L and C input versions **Network** are

$$Q_s = X_L / R_L \qquad (2\text{-}19)$$

where: Q_s is *circuit Q* not Q of the coil
R_L is the sum of load and coil resistance

$$R_i = (Q_s^2 + 1)R_L \qquad \text{ohms } (\Omega) \qquad (2\text{-}20)$$

where: R_i is the input resistance, ohms (Ω), which is the value of Z_i

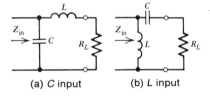

(a) C input   (b) L input

Figure 2-13 Impedance matching with an L configuration network.

$$C = \frac{1}{2\pi f Q_s R_L} \qquad \text{farads (F)} \qquad (2\text{-}21)$$

where: C is the required capacitor for a given coil Q, farads (F)

Example 2-8
A coil used in an L network to increase the impedance of a 70 Ω load at 900 kHz has an $L = 200 \ \mu H$ and a $Q = 120$ at 900 kHz. Calculate the:
a. Circuit operating Q_s.
b. Input resistance.
c. Value of capacitance.

Solution

a. $R_s = \dfrac{2\pi f L}{Q} = \dfrac{6.28 \times 900 \times 10^3 \times 200 \times 10^{-6}}{120}$

$\qquad = \textbf{9.420 } \boldsymbol{\Omega}$

$R_L = 70 + 9.420 = \textbf{79.42 } \boldsymbol{\Omega}$

$Q_s = \dfrac{X_L}{R_L} = \dfrac{2\pi \times 900 \times 10^3 \times 200 \times 10^{-6}}{79.42}$ \hfill (2-19)

$\qquad = \textbf{14.24}$

b. $R_i = (Q_s^2 + 1) \times R_L = [(14.24)^2 + 1]79.42$ \hfill (2-20)

$\qquad = 203.8 \times 79.42$

$\qquad = \textbf{16.18 k}\boldsymbol{\Omega}$

c. $C = \dfrac{1}{2\pi f Q_s R_L}$ \hfill (2-21)

$\qquad = \dfrac{1}{2\pi \times 900 \times 10^3 \times 14.24 \times 79.42}$

$\qquad = \textbf{156.4 pF}$

Example 2-9

Given an L network with an input impedance of 3000 Ω and an output impedance of 150 Ω. Calculate the operating circuit Q_s.

Solution

$$R_i = (Q_s^2 + 1) R_2 \qquad \text{ohms } (\Omega) \hfill (2-20)$$

$$Q_s = \sqrt{\dfrac{R_i}{R_2} - 1} = \sqrt{\dfrac{3000}{150} - 1}$$

$$= \textbf{4.359}$$

2-8.2
The π
Configuration
Network
The π matching network is more complex than the L network but offers specific advantages in impedance matching and harmonic rejection. In designing the components, we break down the π into two L sections. This is shown in Fig. 2-14.

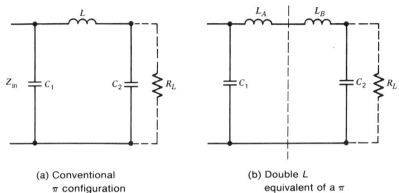

Figure 2-14 Impedance matching with a π configuration network.

(a) Conventional π configuration

(b) Double L equivalent of a π

The coil is divided into two parts L_A and L_B for design purposes, but together add up to L. The design equations are:

$$X_{L_B} = \frac{(R_L)^2 X_{C_2}}{R_L^2 + (X_{C_2})^2} \quad \text{ohms } (\Omega) \qquad (2\text{-}22)$$

where: X_{L_B} is the inductive reactance of the L_B portion of the coil

X_{C_2} is the impedance of C_2

R_L is the load resistance

$$Q_s = \frac{R_i}{X_{C_1}} = \frac{R_i}{X_{L_A}} \qquad (2\text{-}23)$$

where: Q_s is the operating Q of the π network

X_{L_A} is the impedance of the L_A portion of the coil

X_{C_1} is the impedance of C_1

The input resistance R_i relates to the output circuit as indicated by Eq. (2-24), if Q_s is greater than 10.

$$R_i = \frac{R_L X_{C_2}^2 Q_s^2}{R_L^2 + X_{C_2}^2} \quad \text{ohms } (\Omega) \qquad (2\text{-}24)$$

Unwinding Eq. (2-24) results in Eq. (2-25).

$$X_{C_2} = R_L \sqrt{\frac{R_i}{R_L Q_s^2 - R_i}} \quad \text{ohms } (\Omega) \qquad (2\text{-}25)$$

Example 2-10

Given a π network operating at 10 MHz with an operating Q of 50. It is to match the 4000 Ω output impedance of an amplifier to a 80 Ω transmission line.

Solution

$$X_{C_1} = X_{L_A} = \frac{R_i}{Q_s} \tag{2-23}$$

$$= \frac{4000}{50} = \mathbf{80\ \Omega}$$

$$C_1 = \frac{1}{2\pi f X_{C_1}} = \frac{1}{2\pi \times 10 \times 10^6 \times 80} = \mathbf{198.9\ pF}$$

$$L_A = \frac{X_{L_A}}{2\pi f} = \frac{80}{2\pi \times 10^7} = \mathbf{1.273\ \mu H}$$

$$X_{C_2} = R_L \sqrt{\frac{R_i}{R_L Q_s^2 - R_i}} \tag{2-25}$$

$$= 80\sqrt{\frac{4000}{80(50)^2 - 4000}} = 80\sqrt{\frac{4000}{196,000}}$$

$$= 80\sqrt{2.041 \times 10^{-2}} = 80 \times 1.429 \times 10^{-1}$$

$$= \mathbf{11.43\ \Omega}$$

$$C_2 = \frac{1}{2\pi f X_{C_2}} = \frac{1}{2\pi \times 10^7 \times 11.43} = \mathbf{1392\ pF}$$

$$X_{L_B} = \frac{R_L^2 X_{C_2}}{R_L^2 + X_{C_2}^2} \tag{2-22}$$

$$= \frac{(80)^2 \times 11.43}{(80)^2 + (11.43)^2} = \frac{73152}{6530.6}$$

$$= \mathbf{11.20\ \Omega}$$

$$L_B = \frac{X_{L_B}}{2\pi f} = \frac{11.20}{2\pi \times 10^7} = \mathbf{0.1783\ \mu H}$$

$$L = L_A + L_B = \mathbf{1.451\ \mu H}$$

Example 2-11

A 70 Ω load is to be matched to a 30 Ω source for a 5 MHz operating frequency and an operating Q of 15, using a π impedance matching network. Calculate C_1, C_2, and L.

Solution

$$X_{C_1} = X_{L_A} = \frac{R_i}{Q_s} = \frac{30}{15} = 2\Omega$$

$$C_1 = \frac{1}{2\pi f X_{C_1}} = \frac{1}{2\pi \times 5 \times 10^6 \times 2} = 0.01592\ \mu F$$

$$L_A = \frac{X_{L_A}}{2\pi f} = \frac{2}{2\pi \times 5 \times 10^6} = 0.06366\ \mu H$$

$$X_{C_2} = R_L \sqrt{\frac{R_i}{R_L Q^2 - R_i}} = 70\sqrt{\frac{30}{70(15)^2 - 30}}$$

$$= 70\sqrt{\frac{30}{15720}} = 70 \times 4.369 \times 10^{-2}$$

$$= 3.058\ \Omega$$

$$C_2 = \frac{1}{2\pi f X_{C_2}} = \frac{1}{2\pi \times 5 \times 10^6 \times 3.058} = 0.0104\ \mu F$$

$$X_{L_B} = \frac{(R_L)^2 X_{C_2}}{R_L^2 + (X_{C_2})^2} = \frac{(70)^2 \times 3.058}{(70)^2 + (3.058)^2} = \frac{14984}{4909.4}$$

$$= 3.052\ \Omega$$

$$L_B = \frac{X_{L_B}}{2\pi f} = \frac{3.052}{5 \times 10^6} = 0.6104\ \mu H$$

$$L = L_A + L_B = 0.06366 + 0.6104 = 0.6741\ \mu H$$

Note: the relatively large capacitors and tiny inductance for a low Q, low impedance match.

2-8.3 The T Configuration Network Another commonly used impedance matching configuration is the T network. For design purposes this also is divided into two L networks as shown in Fig. 2-15, with $C = C_A + C_B$

C_B is designed to operate with L_2 and R_2. C_A becomes part of the input R_i, L_1 circuit. The resistance seen at the divided center is designated R_{11}. The design formulas are as follows:

$$R_{11} = (Q_2^2 + 1)R_L \qquad \text{ohms } (\Omega) \qquad (2\text{-}26)$$

where: R_{11} is the resistance seen at the center of the network, ohms (Ω)

Q_2 is the Q of the output coil, L_2.

$$Q_2 = X_{L_2}/R_L \qquad\qquad (2\text{-}27)$$

$$C_B = \frac{1}{2\pi f Q_2 R_L} \qquad \text{farads (F)} \qquad (2\text{-}28)$$

$$X_{L_1} = \frac{R_{11}^2 X_{C_A}}{R_{11}^2 + X_{C_A}^2} \qquad \text{ohms } (\Omega) \qquad (2\text{-}29)$$

$$R_i = \frac{R_{11} X_{C_A}^2}{R_{11}^2 + X_{C_A}^2} \qquad \text{ohms } (\Omega) \qquad (2\text{-}30)$$

$$X_{C_A} = \sqrt{\frac{R_i R_{11}^2}{R_{11} - R_i}} \qquad \text{ohms } (\Omega) \qquad (2\text{-}31)$$

$$Q_1 = X_{L_1}/R_{11} \qquad\qquad (2\text{-}32)$$

where: Q_1 is the Q of L_1

$$Q_1 = \frac{X_{L_1}}{(Q_2^2 + 1)R_L} \qquad (2\text{-}33)$$

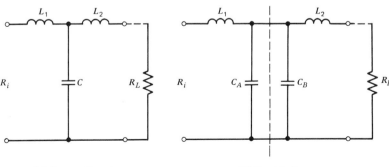

(a) Conventional T configuration

(b) Double L equivalent of a T

Figure 2-15 Impedance matching with a T configuration network.

Example 2-12

Given a T configuration impedance matching network. The input impedance is 5 kΩ, and the output circuit is a 75 Ω transmission line. The system is operating at 5 MHz, and the Q of the output coil, Q_2 is 40. Calculate L_1, L_2, and C.

Solution

$$X_{L_2} = Q_2 R_L = 40 \times 75 = \mathbf{3000\ \Omega} \tag{2-27}$$

$$L_2 = \frac{X_{L_2}}{2\pi f} = \frac{3000}{2\pi \times 5 \times 10^6} = \mathbf{95.49\ \mu H}$$

$$R_{11} = (Q_2^2 + 1)R_L = \left[(40)^2 + 1\right]75 = \mathbf{120.1\ k\Omega} \tag{2-26}$$

$$C_B = \frac{1}{2\pi f Q_2 R_L} = \frac{1}{2\pi \times 5 \times 10^6 \times 40 \times 75} \tag{2-28}$$

$$= \mathbf{10.61\ pF}$$

$$X_{C_A} = \sqrt{\frac{R_i R_{11}^2}{R_{11} - R_i}} = \sqrt{\frac{5000 \times (120.1 \times 10^3)^2}{(120.1 - 5) \times 10^3}} \tag{2-31}$$

$$= \sqrt{\frac{72.12 \times 10^{12}}{115.1 \times 10^3}} = \sqrt{626.6 \times 10^6} = \mathbf{25.03\ k\Omega}$$

$$C_A = \frac{1}{2\pi f X_{C_A}} = \frac{1}{2\pi \times 5 \times 10^6 \times 25.03 \times 10^3}$$

$$= \mathbf{1.272\ pF}$$

$$X_{L_1} = \frac{R_{11}^2 X_{C_A}}{R_{11}^2 + X_{C_A}^2} \tag{2-29}$$

$$= \frac{(120.1 \times 10^3)^2 \times 25.03 \times 10^3}{(120.1 \times 10^3)^2 + (25.03 \times 10^3)^2}$$

$$= \frac{361033 \times 10^9}{(14424 + 626.5) \times 10^6} = \frac{361033 \times 10^9}{15050.5 \times 10^6}$$

$$= \mathbf{23.99 \times 10^3\ \Omega} \tag{2-29}$$

$$L_1 = \frac{X_{L_1}}{2\pi f} = \frac{23.99 \times 10^3}{2\pi \times 5 \times 10^6} = \mathbf{763.6\ \mu H}$$

$$C = C_A + C_B = 1.272 + 10.62 = \mathbf{11.88\ pF}$$

An important application of L, π, and T networks is to satisfy the unique requirements of input and output impedances.

**2-9
Filters**
It is also possible to design L-C elements in L, T, or π configurations to shape that band of frequencies to be accepted or rejected. When used for this purpose, the networks are called *filters*.

**2-10
Low-Pass
Filters**
The filter most familiar to the student is the π configuration used as a power supply filter. The goal for this application is to pass dc (the lowest possible frequency) and to reject the 60 Hz line frequency and its harmonics.

The π, T, or L configurations of Fig. 2-16 result in the low-pass frequency response shown in Fig. 2-16d.

The series L element discourages the high frequencies from passing through and acts as a series choke. The shunt capacitors provide a low impedance path for the high frequencies. Figure 2-16a is called a choke input circuit. It can also be used to configure a T network (Fig. 2-16c) by placing half of the choke on either side of the capacitor. The *cutoff* frequency (f_c), also called the *corner* frequency, relates to the frequency at which the output has dropped 3 dB.

The input impedance presented by this L-C type of filter is related to the L/C ratio and is called *characteristic* or *iterative* or *surge* impedance. Terminating the filter in a resistance equal to the characteristic impedance makes the system appear as

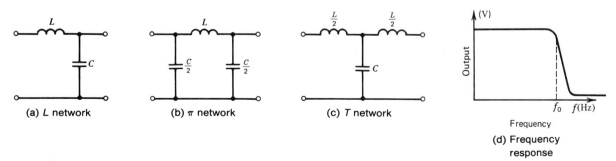

(a) *L* network   (b) *π* network   (c) *T* network   (d) Frequency response

Figure 2-16 Low-pass filters and frequency response.

though the L and C sections are repeated ad infinitum, thus making the system infinitely long. This concept will be explored further (Ch. 8) under transmission line theory.

2-10.1
Constant k
Filters
If the product of the filter shunt impedance (Z_2) and the filter series impedance (Z_1) is constant at all frequencies, the filter is called a *constant k* filter.

2-10.2
m Derived
Filter
The constant k filter characteristics can be improved by adding an element to the section that provides infinite attenuation at a frequency designated (f_∞). This improved filter is called m *derived* filter (Fig. 2-17).

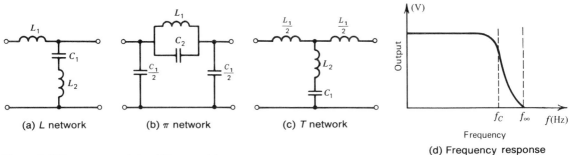

(a) L network   (b) π network   (c) T network   (d) Frequency response

Figure 2-17 Low-pass m derived filters and frequency response.

2-11
High-Pass
Filters
In a similar manner it is possible to set up the L and C elements to pass the high frequencies and attenuate the low frequencies. This is called a *high-pass* filter. The general configurations of the high-pass filter L, T, and π networks, and the frequency response are shown in Fig. 2-18. These filters can also be designed as constant k filters.

The m derived high-pass filter and frequency response is shown in Fig. 2-19.

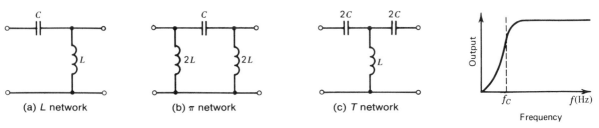

(a) L network   (b) π network   (c) T network   (d) Frequency response

Figure 2-18 High-pass filters and frequency response.

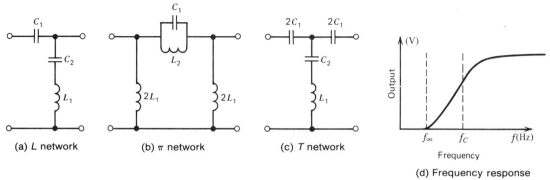

(a) *L* network   (b) *π* network   (c) *T* network

(d) Frequency response

Figure 2-19 High-pass *m* derived filters and frequency response.

2-12
Bandpass
Filters It is also possible to configure *L* and *C* elements to accept a range or band of frequencies. This network is called a *bandpass filter*. The general configurations of the bandpass *L*, *T*, and *π* networks, and the frequency response are shown in Fig. 2-20.

The bandpass filter can be designed as an *m* derived filter. In that case *two* additional infinite attenuation frequencies (f_{∞_1} and f_{∞_2}) are introduced. The networks become more elaborate and the design equations more complex.

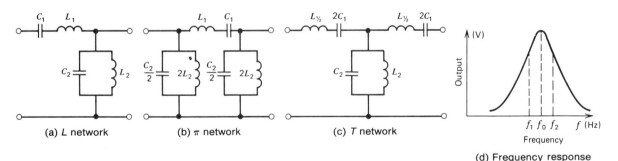

(a) *L* network   (b) *π* network   (c) *T* network

(d) Frequency response

Figure 2-20 Bandpass filters and frequency response.

2-13
Bandstop
(Band-Reject)
Filters The final filter type to be considered is the *bandstop* (band-reject, band-eliminate) filter. This filter will pass all frequencies except those in a prescribed band of frequencies. The general configuration of the bandstop *L*, *T*, and *π* networks, and the frequency response are shown in Fig. 2-21.

The bandstop filter also lends itself to *m* derived filter design. Here again the two frequencies at infinite attenuation would be involved with greater complexity of configuration and equation.

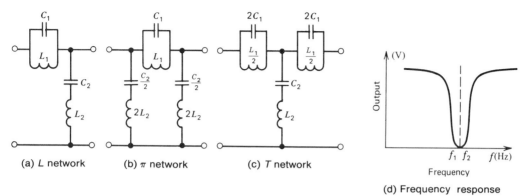

(a) L network (b) π network (c) T network

(d) Frequency response

Figure 2-21 Bandstop filters and frequency response.

In ordering a filter, in addition to the frequency and impedance requirements, you would also specify attenuation in the pass region and reject region, ripple on each attenuation, sharpness of skirts, packaging, terminals, weight, and cost.

The design equations and design criteria for the constant k and the m derived filters are included in appendix A.

2-14
Summary
RF circuits are designed with series- and parallel-resonant circuits. These circuits offer a low or high impedance at specified frequencies. They are very frequency sensitive. The frequency response is related to the Q of the circuit.

There are many methods of coupling one RF circuit to another. These include double-tuned, single-tuned, and link coupling circuits.

L and C elements can be designed to provide an impedance match between two RF circuits. L and C elements can be configured as RF filters providing low-pass, high-pass, bandpass, or bandstop frequency response. These can be accomplished as either a constant k or m derived filter.

Now return to the objectives and self-evaluation questions at the beginning of this chapter and see how well you can answer them. If you cannot answer certain questions, place a check next to them and review appropriate parts of the text. Then answer the questions and solve the problems below.

2-15
Questions
Q2-1 Compare the important parameters of series- vs. parallel-resonant circuits.

Q2-2 Define the phase angle at resonance and either side of resonance for both series- and parallel-resonant circuits.

Q2-3 a. Which form of resonant circuit (series or parallel) is more commonly used?
b. How is it used?
c. Why is it used?

Q2-4 Explain the theory of inducing a voltage in the secondary winding of a transformer by applying voltage to the primary.

Q2-5 Indicate the type of impedance (L, C, or R) seen at the input to a double tuned circuit if the output load is:
a. Resistive.
b. Inductive.
c. Capacitive.

Q2-6 What are the advantages of coupling the output of a tank through a capacitor?

Q2-7 Describe and draw the frequency response of a double tuned circuit that is:
a. Undercoupled.
b. Critically coupled.
c. Overcoupled.

Q2-8 Describe and draw the frequency response characteristics of:
a. Constant k low-pass filter.
b. m derived low-pass filter.

Q2-9 Describe and draw the high-pass frequency response characteristic of:
a. Constant k filter.
b. m derived filter.

Q2-10 Describe and draw the bandpass filter response characteristic of:
a. Constant k filter.
b. m derived filter.

Q2-11 Draw the constant k and m derived filters for the low-pass π network.

Q2-12 Draw the constant k and m derived filters for the high-pass T network.

2-16
Problems

P2-1 Given a coil with an inductance of 10 mH and a 2 Ω resistance, a 0.05 μF capacitor, and a source voltage of 10 V. These components are connected as a series-resonant circuit. At the resonant frequency, calculate:
a. f_0 d. V_R
b. I_0 e. Q rise in voltage
c. Q across C and L.

P2-2 Citizens band communications operate in the 27 MHz region. Assuming a bandwidth of ± 10 kHz, determine the required Q.

P2-3 A 100 μH inductance includes 8 Ω of resistance. This is connected in parallel with a 680 pF capacitor. The source voltage is 10 V. Calculate

a. f_0 d. I_C
b. Z_0 e. I_L
c. I_T

P2-4 If the mutual coupling is 40 mH for two adjacent coils, $L_1 = 30$ mH and $L_2 = 80$ mH, calculate the coefficient of coupling.

P2-5 Determine the primary impedance of a transformer under load for the following conditions: unloaded primary impedance = 2 kΩ, the mutual inductance = 100 μH, the load = 10 kΩ and the operating frequencys = 5 MHz.

P2-6 Given a parallel-resonant circuit with $L = 200$ μH, $C = 120$ pF, and series resistance = 5Ω. The tank is feeding a Darlington amplifier with an input impedance of 100 kΩ. Calculate the effective Q of the tank under load.

P2-7 An L network configuration is used for impedance match. The operating frequency is 1.2 MHz and the load is 100 Ω. The coil inductance is 150 μH and has a Q of 200. Calculate:

a. The circuit operating Q_s.
b. Input resistance.
c. Capacitance.

P2-8 An amplifier with an output impedance of 5 kΩ is impedance matched to a 200 Ω load with an L network configuration. Calculate the operating circuit Q.

P2-9 An amplifier output of 3 kΩ is to be matched to a 300 Ω antenna. The system is operating at 5 MHz and a π network is to be used. Design the π network.

P2-10 Given a T network to match the 50 Ω output of an emitter follower to a 100 Ω transmission line. The system is operating at 10 MHz with an operating Q of 20. Calculate the capacitance values C_1 and C_2, and the inductance L.

P2-11 The input impedance of a π network impedance matching circuit is 2 kΩ. The output feeds a 150 Ω antenna. The operating frequency is 8 MHz. The output coil has a $Q_2 = 60$. Calculate the value of the series coils L_1 and L_2, and the shunt capacitance C.

Chapter 3

RF Amplifiers

**3-1
Objectives** To learn:

1. The basics of the RF amplifier.
2. Weak signal RF amplifiers.
3. Methods of increasing RF bandwidth.
4. Requirement for neutralization.
5. Series- and shunt-fed amplifiers.
6. Various methods of biasing.
7. Classes of operation.
8. Frequency multipliers.
9. RF power amplifiers.
10. Troubleshooting RF amplifiers.

**3-2
Self-Evaluation
Questions** Test your prior knowledge of the information in this chapter by answering the following questions. Watch for the answers to these questions as you read the chapter. Your final evaluation of whether you understand the material is measured by your ability to answer these questions. When you have completed the chapter, return to this section and answer the questions again.

1. Define five functions of an RF amplifier.
2. What are the advantages of using a tuned tank as the output circuit rather than a resistor load?
3. Define *stagger tuning*.
4. Describe the *overcoupling* method of increasing bandwidth.
5. Define *neutralization*.
6. What are the desirable characteristics of an RF amplifier that is used as the input stage of a receiver?
7. What is the function of metal shields placed around tuned tanks?
8. Define class C operation.
9. Describe how bias is developed in *grid leak* bias.
10. What are the advantages of *push-pull* operation of the RF amplifier?
11. Describe the operation of *cross-neutralization*.
12. What is one use of a *push-push* RF amplifier?

**3-3
Basic RF
Amplifier
Functions** RF amplifiers may be designed to operate at any frequency from 50 kHz to 500 MHz. The amplifier may be used as the input stage of a receiver. In this mode of operation its primary function is to work with a very weak voltage signal picked up by the antenna, and amplify the signal while contributing a minimum of internally generated noise. RF amplifiers may be designed to function as the output stage of a transmitter, handling kilowatts or megawatts of signal power. It may function as a series of intermediate cascaded stages gradually building up the signal level. It may function as a mixer stage in which two signals at different frequencies are combined. It may be designed as a frequency multiplier where the output frequency is double or triple or quadruple the frequency at the input. The RF amplifier may be designed to have a narrow bandwidth of a few hertz or a wide bandwidth of 6 MHz. There are many other specialized functions for the RF amplifier, some of which will be discussed in this chapter; others will be covered in subsequent chapters.

**3-4
RF voltage
(Weak Signal)
Amplifiers** The heart of all RF amplification is the tuned or resonant circuit (usually a parallel tank circuit rather than series resonant, but both are used). The gain or amplification of an amplifier is related to the load seen by its output. Here is a listing of voltage gain of the commonly used amplifiers.

$$\textbf{Pentode:} \quad A_v = g_m R_L \qquad (3\text{-}1)$$

where: g_m = mutual transconductance in siemens (S)
R_L = ac resistance presented to output of amplifier, as a load, ohms (Ω)

$$\textbf{Triode:} \quad A_v = \mu \frac{R_L}{R_L + r_p} \qquad (3\text{-}2)$$

where: μ = amplification factor
r_p = plate resistance (internal), ohms (Ω)

$$\textbf{FET:} \quad A_v = g_{fs} R_L \qquad (3\text{-}3)$$

where: g_{fs} = forward transconductance or transconductance in siemens (S)

$$\text{\textbf{Transistor} (bipolar):} \qquad A_v = h_f \frac{R_L}{R_i} \qquad (3\text{-}4)$$

where: h_f = forward current transistor ratio (h_{fe}, h_{fc} or h_{fb} depending on configuration)

R_i = input impedance

Example 3-1

A pentode RF amplifier has a transconductance of 9000 μS and a load of 10 kΩ. Calculate the voltage gain, A_v.

Solution

$$A_v = g_m R_L$$
$$= 9000 \times 10^{-6} S \times 10 \times 10^3 \Omega = \textbf{90} \qquad (3\text{-}1)$$

Example 3-2

A triode RF amplifier has an amplification factor of 80, an internal plate resistance of 8 kΩ, and a load of 15 kΩ. Calculate the voltage gain.

Solution

$$A_v = \mu \frac{R_L}{R_L + R_p}$$
$$= 80 \frac{15\ k\Omega}{15\ k\Omega + 8\ k\Omega} = \textbf{52.17} \qquad (3\text{-}2)$$

Example 3-3

A transistor RF amplifier has a forward current gain of 60, an input resistance of 1 kΩ, and a load of 2 kΩ. Calculate the voltage gain.

Solution

$$A_v = h_f \frac{R_L}{R_i}$$
$$= 60 \frac{2\ k\Omega}{1\ k\Omega} = \textbf{120} \qquad (3\text{-}4)$$

The load resistance, R_L of RF amplifiers, is normally an LC tank. If the tank is not shunted by a load, the R_L is a very high impedance $(=L/CR=QX_L$, etc.). If the tank is coupled to a FET or vacuum tube, the loading is minimal, usually a high value resistor. In contrast to this condition, coupling a tank to a transistor with an input impedance of 1 kΩ results in excessive loading and minimal gain.

Example 3-4
Given a transistor with an $h_f=150$, a load that consists of a tank with $L=400$ μH and 10 Ω, and $C=200$ pF. The input resistance is 3 kΩ. Calculate the voltage gain:
a. As an isolated stage.
b. Feeding an identical amplifier.

Solution
a. Impedance of tank

$$Z_L = L/CR = \frac{400\times10^{-6}}{200\times10^{-12}\times10} = \textbf{200 k}\boldsymbol{\Omega} \tag{3-14}$$

$$A_v = h_f\frac{Z_L}{R_i} = 150\frac{200\text{ k}\Omega}{3\text{ k}\Omega} = \textbf{10,000} \tag{3-14}$$

b. Feeding a second stage places a 3 kΩ load across the tank resulting in an equivalent load:

$$Z_L' = Z_L \| R_i = 200 \text{ k}\Omega \| 3 \text{ k}\Omega = \textbf{2.956 k}\boldsymbol{\Omega}$$

The gain is reduced to:

$$A_v' = h_f\frac{Z_L'}{R_{in}} = 150\frac{2.956\ k\Omega}{3\ k\Omega} = \textbf{147.8}$$

**3-5
Calculations for
RF Voltage
Amplifiers**

The proper approach to the problem of a low impedance shunt of a high impedance tank is to create an impedance match by tapping the coil of the tank. This technique can be exercised for the coil receiving the output of the amplifier, the coil feeding the input to the amplifier, or both. This method will be demonstrated by various examples.

Example 3-5

Given a FET RF amplifier with $g_{fs} = 5000$ μS, $r_d = 200$ kΩ, $C_{shunt} = 8$ pF, tank components $L = 100$ μH and 4Ω, and $C = 400$ pF. The gate resistor of the next stage is 80 kΩ. Calculate:

a. gain.

b. Equivalent Q

Solution

a. Refer to Fig. 3-1.

The impedance of tank is

$$Z_0 = L/CR = \frac{100 \times 10^{-6}}{400 \times 10^{-12} \times 4} = \mathbf{62.5 \ k\Omega}$$

discarding the capacitive reactance of the shunt capacitance as being negligibly large along with the input impedance of the next FET stage, the equivalent tank impedance becomes

$$Z_e = Z_0 \| R_g = 62.5 \text{ k}\Omega \| 80 \text{ k}\Omega = \mathbf{35.09 \ k\Omega}$$

$$A_v = g_{fs} Z_e = 5000 \times 10^{-6} \times 35.09 \times 10^3 = \mathbf{175.5}$$

b. $f_0 = \dfrac{1}{2\pi\sqrt{LC}} = \dfrac{1}{2\pi\sqrt{100 \times 10^{-6} \times 400 \times 10^{-12}}}$ (2-1)

$$= \frac{1}{2\pi \times 2 \times 10^{-7}} = \mathbf{795.8 \ kHz}$$

$$X_L = 2\pi FL = 2\pi \times 795.8 \times 10^3 \times 100 \times 10^{-6} = \mathbf{500 \ \Omega} \quad\quad \text{(2-2a)}$$

$$Q_e = \frac{Z_e}{X_L} = \frac{35.09 \times 10^3}{500} = \mathbf{70.18}$$

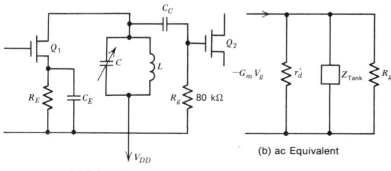

(a) Schematic

(b) ac Equivalent

Figure 3-1 Diagram for Example 3-5.

Example 3-6

Given two identical cascaded transistor RF amplifiers, Q_1 and Q_2. The transistor parameters are: output impedance, $R_o = 200$ kΩ, $h_f = 80$ and input resistance, $R_i = 200$ Ω. The tank components are $L = 200$ μH and 5 Ω, $C = 300$ pF. The coil is tapped for the second stage at a point 30% from the bottom. The input signal to $Q_1 = 100$ μV. Calculate:

a. Equivalent load impedance (primary side).
b. Signal applied to input of Q_2.
c. Equivalent Q of coupling network (primary side).

Solution

a. Refer to Fig. 3-2. The input resistance of Q_2 stage ($R_{i2} = R_i \| R_B$) is reflected to the primary side as the square of the turns ratio:

$$R'_{i2} = R_{i2}(1/n)^2 = 200 \times (1/0.3)^2$$

$$= 2.222 \text{ k}\Omega$$

$$Z_o = L/CR = \frac{200 \times 10^{-6}}{300 \times 10^{-12} \times 5} = 133.3 \text{ k}\Omega \qquad (2\text{-}14)$$

The equivalent load impedance is:

$$Z_r = Z_o \| R'_{i2} \| R_0$$

$$= 133.3 \times 10^3 \| 2.222 \times 10^3 \| 200 \times 10^3$$

$$= 2.162 \text{ k}\Omega$$

b. Gain on the primary side:

$$A_v = h_f \frac{Z_e}{R_{i_1}} = 80 \times \frac{2162}{200} = 864.8$$

Signal across tank:

$$V_t = A_v \times V_i$$

$$= 864.8 \times 100 \times 10^{-6} = 86.48 \text{ mV}$$

Tank voltage stepped down by turns ratio

$$V_{i_2} = V_t \times \frac{1}{n} = 86.48 \times 0.3$$

$$= 25.95 \text{ mV}$$

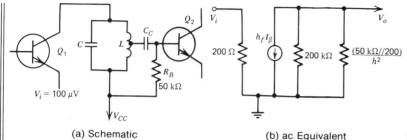

(a) Schematic   (b) ac Equivalent   **Figure 3-2** Diagram for Example 3-6.

c. $\quad f_0 = \dfrac{1}{2\pi\sqrt{LC}} = \dfrac{1}{2\pi\sqrt{200\times10^{-6}\times300\times10^{-12}}}$

$\quad\quad = \dfrac{1}{2\pi\times244.9\times10^{-9}} = \mathbf{649.7\ kHz}$

$X_L = 2\pi f_0 L = 2\pi\times649.7\times10^3\times200\times10^{-6} = \mathbf{816.5\ \Omega}$

Equivalent Q of the coupling network

$Q_e = \dfrac{Z_e}{X_L} = \dfrac{2162}{816.5} = \mathbf{2.648}$

The antenna leading to the input stage of a receiver is a low impedance device coupled directly to a low impedance untuned primary (Fig. 3-3).

Example 3-7

Given the FET RF amplifier of Fig. 3-3; $L_1 = 4$ mH, $L_2 = 400$ μH, and 5 Ω, $k = 0.05$, $C_1 = 300$ pF, $L_3 = 6$ mH, $g_{fs} = 9000$ μS, and $V_i = 80$ μV.
Calculate:
a. Voltage at input to Q_1.
b. Voltage at output of Q_1.
c. Gain from antenna to L_3.

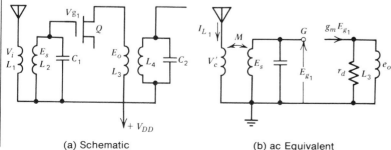

(a) Schematic   (b) ac Equivalent   **Figure 3-3** Diagram for Example 3-7.

Solution

a. $f_0 = \dfrac{1}{2\pi\sqrt{L_2 C_1}} = \dfrac{1}{2\pi\sqrt{400\times 10^{-6}\times 300\times 10^{-12}}}$

$\quad = \dfrac{1}{2\pi\times 3.464\times 10^{-7}} = \textbf{459.5 kHz}$

$\omega = 2\pi f_0 = 2\pi\times 459.5\times 10^3 = \textbf{2.887}\times\textbf{10}^\textbf{6}\textbf{ rad/s}$

$X_{L_1} = \omega L_1 = 2.887\times 10^6\times 4\times 10^{-3} = \textbf{11.55 k}\boldsymbol{\Omega}$

Neglecting resistance of L_1:

$I_{L_1} = \dfrac{E_{L_1}}{X_{L_1}} = \dfrac{80\times 10^{-6}}{11.55\times 10^3} = \textbf{6.926}\times\textbf{10}^{-\textbf{9}}\textbf{A}$

Mutual inductance between L_1 and L_2:

$M = k\sqrt{L_1 L_2} = 0.05\sqrt{4\times 10^{-3}\times 400\times 10^{-6}}$ \hfill (2-17)

$\quad = 0.05\times 12.65\times 10^{-4} = \textbf{63.25 }\boldsymbol{\mu}\textbf{H}$

Induced voltage in L_2

$E_s = \omega M I_{L_1} = 2.887\times 10^6\times 63.25\times 10^{-6}\times 6.926\times 10^{-9}$

$\quad = \textbf{1.265 }\boldsymbol{\mu}\textbf{V}$

$X_{L_2} = \omega L_2 = 2.887\times 10^6\times 400\times 10^{-6} = \textbf{1155 }\boldsymbol{\Omega}$

Q of tank circuit $L_2 C_1$:

$Q = \dfrac{X_{L_2}}{R} = \dfrac{1155}{5} = \textbf{231}$ \hfill (2-7)

Voltage at gate of Q_1:

$E_{g_1} = Q E_s = 231\times 1.265\times 10^{-6} = \textbf{292.2 }\boldsymbol{\mu}\textbf{V}$

b. Output current of Q_1:

$I_d = g_{fs} E_{g1} = 9000\times 10^{-6}\times 292.2\times 10^{-6}$

$\quad = \textbf{2.630 }\boldsymbol{\mu}\textbf{A}$

$X_{L_3} = \omega L_3 = 2.887\times 10^6\times 6\times 10^{-3}$

$\quad = \textbf{17.32 k}\boldsymbol{\Omega}$

Output voltage across L_3:

$$E_o = I_d X_{L_3} = 2.630 \times 10^{-6} \times 17.32 \times 10^3$$

$$= \textbf{45.55 mV}$$

c. Gain from antenna to L_3:

$$A_v = \frac{E_o}{V_i} = \frac{45.55 \times 10^{-3}}{80 \times 10^{-6}} = \textbf{569.4}$$

Cascaded RF amplifiers are treated in a repetitive fashion. This is illustrated in Example 3-8.

Example 3-8
Given cascaded FET RF amplifiers (Fig. 3-4), where $L_3 = L_4 = 500\ \mu H$ and 5 Ω, $C_3 = C_4 = 400$ pF, $k = 0.02$, $g_{fs} = 8000\ \mu S$. The input at gate of Q_2, $E_{i_2} = 150\ \mu V$. Calculate:
a. Q of primary, L_3.
b. Voltage at gate of Q_3.
c. Voltage gain from gate of Q_2 to gate of Q_3.

Solution
a. Q of primary:

$$f_0 = \frac{1}{2\pi\sqrt{L_3 C_4}} = \frac{1}{2\pi\sqrt{500 \times 10^{-6} \times 400 \times 10^{-12}}}$$

$$= \frac{1}{2\pi \times 4.472 \times 10^{-7}} = \textbf{355.9 kHz}$$

$$\omega = 2\pi f_0 = 2\pi \times 355.9 \times 10^3 = \textbf{2.236} \times \textbf{10}^6\ \textbf{rad/s}$$

$$X_{L_3} = \omega L_3 = 2.236 \times 10^6 \times 500 \times 10^{-6} = \textbf{1118}\ \Omega$$

$$M = k\sqrt{L_3 L_4} = 0.02\sqrt{500 \times 10^{-6} \times 500 \times 10^{-6}}$$

$$= \textbf{10}\ \mu\textbf{H}$$

$$R_r = \frac{(\omega M)^2}{R_s} = \frac{(2.236 \times 10^6 \times 10 \times 10^{-6})^2}{5}$$

$$= \frac{500}{5} = \textbf{100}\ \Omega$$

$$Q_p = \frac{X_{L_3}}{R_p + R_r} = \frac{1118}{5 + 100} = \textbf{10.65}$$

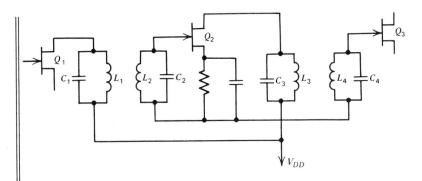

Figure 3-4 Schematic diagram for Example 3-8.

b. Voltage at gate of Q_3:

$$I_d = g_{fs}E_i = 8000 \times 10^{-6} \times 150 \times 10^{-6} = \mathbf{1.2\ \mu A}$$

$$I_{L_3} = Q_p I_d = 10.65 \times 1.2 \times 10^{-6} = \mathbf{12.78\ \mu A}$$

Induced secondary voltage:

$$E_s = \omega M I_{L_3} = 2.236 \times 10^6 \times 10 \times 10^{-6} \times 12.78 \times 10^{-6}$$
$$= \mathbf{285.8\ \mu V}$$

$$Q_s = \frac{X_{L_4}}{R_s} = \frac{1118}{5} = \mathbf{223.6}$$

$$E_{i_3} = Q_s E_s = 223.6 \times 285.8 \times 10^{-6} = \mathbf{63.91\ mV}$$

c. $\text{Gain} = \dfrac{E_{i_3}}{E_{i_2}} = \dfrac{63.91 \times 10^{-3}}{150 \times 10^{-6}} = \mathbf{426.1}$

3-6
RF
Amplifier
Bandwidth

The bandwidth for a single tank stage is defined as $BW = f_0/Q_e$ where Q_e is the loaded tank equivalent Q. If additional gain is required prior to feeding an output antenna or link or display, cascaded stages are used. The gain is increased but the skirts become sharper and the bandwidth narrows.

$$BW_n = BW_1 \sqrt{2^{1/n} - 1} \qquad (3\text{-}5)$$

where BW_n is the bandwidth for n cascaded stages
BW_1 is the bandwidth for any identical stage

Example 3-9
The bandwidth of a RF amplifier is 200 kHz. Determine the overall bandwidth if three identical stages are cascaded.

Solution

$$BW_n = BW_1 \sqrt{(2)^{1/n} - 1}$$

$$= 200 \text{ kHz} \sqrt{(2)^{1/3} - 1}$$

$$= 200 \text{ kHz} \sqrt{1.26 - 1}$$

$$= 200 \text{ kHz} \times 0.5099 = \textbf{102 kHz} \qquad (3\text{-}5)$$

Example 3-10
The required overall bandwidth of two identical RF amplifier stages cascaded is 4 MHz. Specify the bandwidth of each amplifier.

Solution

$$BW_1 = \frac{BW_n}{\sqrt{(2)^{1/n} - 1}} = \frac{4 \text{ MHz}}{\sqrt{2^{1/2} - 1}}$$

$$= \frac{4 \text{ MHz}}{\sqrt{1.414 - 1}} = \frac{4 \text{ MHz}}{\sqrt{0.4142}}$$

$$= \frac{4 \text{ MHz}}{0.6436} = \textbf{6.215 MHz}$$

There are obvious limitations in cascading RF stages. If the BW of a single stage is suitable, the BW_n is too narrow. Theoretically the BW_1 can be designed to be excessively wide so that the narrowed BW_n is still sufficiently wide. This in turn requires a *low Q*. The low Q results in a low impedance load and a low gain.

The preferred method of cascading RF stages is *stagger tuning* shown in Fig. 3-5a. Each stage is tuned to a different frequency resulting in an overall frequency response that is wide and flat.

Another method of increasing bandwidth is the combination of an overcoupled stage with a critically coupled stage shown in Fig. 3-5b. This is a more difficult adjustment. Regardless of the

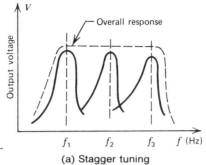 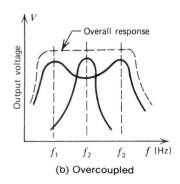

(a) Stagger tuning (b) Overcoupled

Figure 3-5 Methods of increasing bandwidth.

method, the objective is a frequency response that is reasonably flat over the desired bandpass with sharp skirts at lower and upper frequency limits.

3-7
Neutralization
of RF
Amplifiers

In the early days of radio, the triode vacuum tube was the basic RF amplifier. As the frequency range was extended deeper into the RF region, its use was limited by a tendency to oscillate. This oscillation resulted from positive feedback via the plate to grid interelectrode capacitance. This limitation prompted development of the tetrode and pentode, thus reducing the plate to grid capacitance. This in turn enabled the use of the tube at higher RF frequencies.

Transistors, FETs, and even triodes can be used at extended RF frequencies if they are *neutralized*. This process consists of taking some of the output and feeding it back to the input in such a way as to *cancel* the *positive* feedback that causes oscillation. Figure 3-6 shows some examples of *neutralization*.

Hazeltine neutralization (Fig. 3-6a) shows V_{CC} applied to a tap on the tank. Since V_{CC} is at RF ground, this places the tap at RF ground. This in turn makes the opposite ends of the tank 180° out of phase with each other. The signal at the top of the tank is the collector output that is leaking back through the base-collector junction capacitance C_{bc} and causing oscillation. The signal picked up at the bottom of the tank is opposite in phase and tends to cancel the leakage signal. The variable neutralizing capacitor C_n is adjusted to control the amount of feedback signal. Too little feedback will *not* prevent oscillation. Too much feedback unnecessarily cancels the legitimate input signal and lowers stage gain.

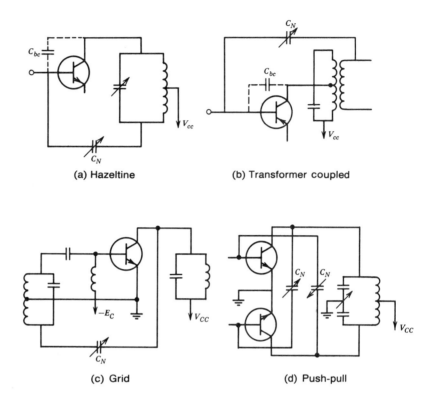

Figure 3-6 Neutralized RF amplifiers.

(a) Hazeltine   (b) Transformer coupled

(c) Grid   (d) Push-pull

Transformer coupled neutralization (Fig. 3-6b) accomplishes neutralization by means of transformer theory. The secondary winding provides a signal that is 180° out of phase with the collector output. This secondary voltage is fed back as a bucking or neutralizing voltage.

Grid neutralization (Fig. 3-6c) accomplishes neutralization by placing a ground tap on the grid tank. This makes either end of the tank out of phase with the other end. Placing some of the plate signal on the *bottom* of the grid tank results in the cancellation of the signal that *leaked* to the *top* of the tank through the interjunction capacitance.

Push-pull neutralization (Fig. 3-6d) also called *cross neutralization* is readily accomplished because the signals at the two collectors are out of phase with each other. The signal fed back to the *alternate* grid is out of phase with the leaked signal.

Neutralization is not always required. It depends on a number of conditions, such as actual RF frequency, circuit design, mechanical layout, shielding methods, impedance levels, etc.

3-8
Series- and
Shunt-Fed
RF Amplifiers
The amplifiers represented by Figs. 3-1 to 3-4 are examples of *series feed*. This means that the dc current path from collector to V_{CC} is also the path for the generation of RF. The alternative is *shunt feed*, where the dc current is blocked away from the RF tank. Both types are shown in Fig. 3-7.

The first circuit (Fig. 3-7a) has the dc collector current flowing through L and the RF signal is developed in the L-C_2 tank. The second circuit (Fig. 3-7b) shows the collector dc current path through the RF choke (RFC). The output RF signal is developed in the L-C_3 tank. The coupling capacitor C_2 connects the tank to the collector for the RF signal while blocking V_{CC} from shorting to ground through RFC and L. The RFC is a low resistance for dc but a high impedance at RF. This places V_{CC} directly on the collector with a negligible dc voltage drop across RFC. However, because RFC is a high RF impedance, its shunting effect on the tank is negligible. All these effects can be summed up with the oversimplified statement that the RFC is a zero resistance for dc and an open circuit for RF. Note that C_1 is serving as a bypass capacitor that puts the bottom of the tank or the RFC at RF ground, effectively putting the tank/RFC across the transistor output.

A similar analysis is made for the input circuit (Fig. 3-7c). The dc path from gate to $(-E_C)$ gate bias power supply is through the RF tank; therefore this is a series-fed circuit. The shunt-fed circuit (Fig. 3-7d) uses the RFC as a shorted dc path and open-circuit RF component. Note that C_2 serves as RF bypass capacitor.

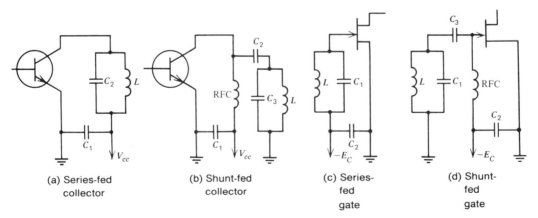

(a) Series-fed collector

(b) Shunt-fed collector

(c) Series-fed gate

(d) Shunt-fed gate

Figure 3-7 Series- and shunt-fed RF amplifiers.

Shunt-fed RF circuits offer specific advantages. In high power, high voltage transmitters, it is desirable not to have the voltage on a tank that must be handled for adjustment. In receivers, the ganged capacitor normally has one set of plates tied to the housing of the capacitor. In series-fed circuits, the dc appears at both sides of the capacitor and the capacitor must be isolated from ground. A shunt-fed circuit permits the housing to be fastened to the receiver case.

3-9 Grid-Leak Bias The $(-E_C)$ power supply of Figs. 3-7c and 3-7d provides a *fixed bias* for the RF amplifier. This may provide the sole bias for the stage or be used in conjunction with *source/emitter bias*. A third method of biasing a RF amplifier is *grid-leak* bias (Fig. 3-8).

Note that there is neither fixed nor emitter bias used. In fact, with *no* RF signal present there is *no* bias created. The incoming signal is coupled to the gate through C_3. As the RF signal goes positive it drives the gate positive. The positive gate draws current from the FET. These electrons accumulate on the gate side of C_3. As the RF signal returns to zero value, C_3 discharges. The accumulated electrons *leak* through R_g to ground. This creates a *grid-leak* voltage across R_g with the gate end negative.

In this way a bias is created for the gate. In addition the value of the bias voltage varies directly with the strength of the RF signal. The time constant R_g-C_3 is on the order of 10 periods of RF. A time constant that is too short would cause the bias to follow each cycle of RF instead of remaining a constant dc voltage. A time constant that is too long would prevent the bias from reducing its value as the RF became weaker. This would result in improper bias for the reduced RF amplitude.

The most serious limitation of grid-leak bias is the fact that with *no RF drive* (incoming RF), *no bias* is generated. If the RF amplifier is a high power stage, *excessive* dc current would flow and burn out the amplifier. A multistage system starts with a weak RF signal and amplifies it to a level appropriate for grid-leak bias. A malfunction in any early amplifier stage results in the loss of grid-leak bias and excessive plate current flow.

A precaution that is commonly taken with grid-leak bias stages is to combine it with fixed bias or emitter bias. This avoids total loss of bias with a loss of RF drive.

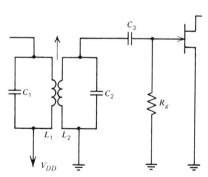

Figure 3-8 Grid-leak bias.

3-10
Classes of
Operation
The student is introduced to amplifier theory by considering the operation of an audio amplifier. Except for the push-pull circuit, the audio amplifier is *always* operated *class A*. This class of operation includes a full cycle (360°) of plate (drain) current flow (Fig. 3-9a). Because dc power (V_p, I_p) is provided for the full cycle, the plate efficiency is low, approximately 25%. Plate efficiency is readily calculated by Eq. (3-6).

$$\eta = \frac{P_o}{P_{dc}} \times 100 = \frac{V_p I_p}{V_{Pdc} I_{Pdc}} \times 100 \qquad (3\text{-}6)$$

where: η (eta) = plate efficiency in percent
P_0 = ac plate power output, watts (W)
P_i = P_{dc} = dc plate power provided, watts (W)
V_p = plate voltage (rms), volts (V)
I_p = plate current (rms), amperes (A)
V_{Pdc} = plate voltage, dc, volts (V)
I_{Pdc} = plate current, dc, amperes (A)

Example 3-11
A triode RF amplifier is provided with a dc plate voltage of 120 V and a dc plate current of 10 mA. The output signal is a rms voltage of 20 V and rms current of 15 mA. Calculate the plate efficiency.

Solution

$$P_i = P_{dc} = V_{Pdc} I_{Pdc} = 120 \times 10 \times 10^{-3} = 1.2 \text{ W}$$

$$P_o = P_{ac} = V_p I_p = 20 \times 15 \times 10^{-3} = 0.3 \text{ W}$$

$$\eta = \frac{P_o}{P_i} = \frac{0.3}{1.2} \times 100 = \textbf{25\%} \qquad (3\text{-}6)$$

The power dissipated in the tube is the difference in dc power input and ac power output ($P_{Diss} = P_i - P_o$). Push-pull circuits are commonly operated *class B* (Fig. 3-9b). Plate current flows for 180°. This mode of operation results in 50 to 60% efficiency. Theoretically a maximum efficiency of 78.5% is possible.

RF amplifiers are usually operated *class C* (Fig. 3-9c). Note that plate current flows for less than 180°. This mode of operation is acceptable for RF amplifiers because of the *flywheel*

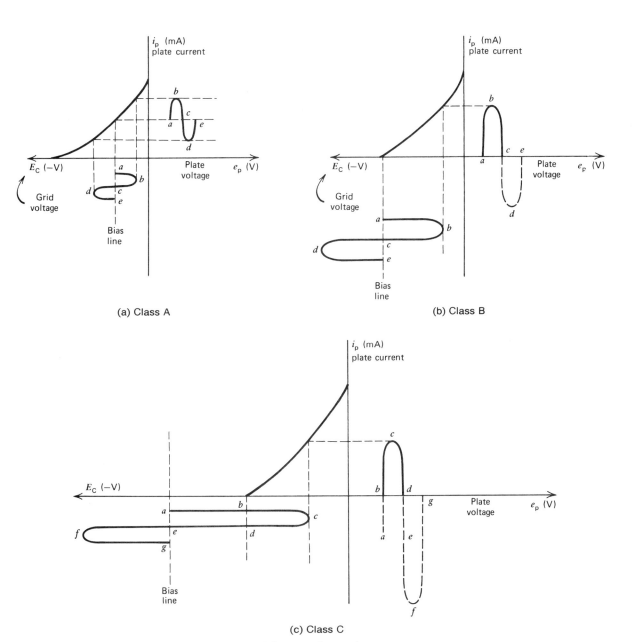

(a) Class A

(b) Class B

(c) Class C

Figure 3-9 Classes of operation.

effect of the RF tank. This refers to the ability of a tank to accept a pulse of energy and convert it to a magnetic field in the coil. As the magnetic field collapses, electron flow reverses and creates a dielectric field in the capacitor. This process repeats at a rate determined by the tank frequency. The output of the amplifier is the pure sine wave, which is characteristic of tank circuits.

The class C amplifier can operate with 75 to 90% efficiency. In general, efficiency varies inversely with plate current flow. However, if the current flow is decreased below 120° of the full cycle, the input energy is decreased, resulting in less output power. In addition a small conduction angle is equivalent to a pulse rich in harmonics, resulting in less energy at the fundamental frequency.

Another common application of RF amplifiers is in the use of grid-leak bias. This requires that the input or *drive* signal cause the grid (gate) to go positive and draw grid current. This in turn requires the driver stage to deliver power to the RF amplifier. This dissipated grid power is given by:

$$P_g = 0.9 E_{gm} I_g \qquad \text{watts (W)} \qquad (3\text{-}7)$$

where: P_g power dissipated in grid, watts (W)
E_{gm} = peak driving voltage
I_g = dc grid current

The angle of current flow obviously determines the ac power output. The designers of RF amplifiers utilize curves relating the conduction angle to the ratio of ac and dc plate currents.

3-11 Frequency Multipliers Another use for RF amplifiers is frequency multiplication. Amplifiers operating in the nonlinear portion of the characteristic curve will generate harmonics. Operating as a *frequency multiplier* it is possible to have an output frequency that is a multiple of the input frequency. Doublers and triplers are in common use, and occasionally a quadrupler will be found in equipment. The harmonic component of the incoming signal decreases rapidly with the order of the harmonic. Therefore the output of a tripler will be less than a doubler. Transmitters commonly use multipliers because the basic frequency source, which is an oscillator, will operate more stably at a low

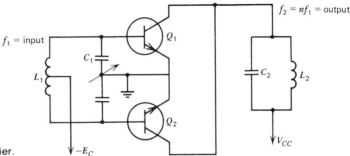

Figure 3-10 Push-push frequency multiplier.

frequency or simply cannot oscillate at the required high frequency. Since the output signal is at a different frequency than the input, there is no possibility of leaking back as positive feedback and causing oscillation. Therefore there is no requirement for neutralization in a frequency multiplier.

One method of increasing the output of a frequency multiplier is to operate the stage as a push-push amplifier (Fig. 3-10).

Note that the bases are connected for push-pull input but that the collectors are in parallel. The collector tank is tuned to the multiple of the input frequency. If required, frequency multipliers are cascaded. A doubler feeding a quadrupler results in a multiple frequency of 8.

3-12
RF Power
Amplifiers
The RF power amplifier may be identical schematically to the weak signal RF voltage amplifier. The major difference is in the power being handled by the power amplifier. The power amplifier may be a transistor, triode, or beam power (tetrode) tube. It may require no cooling or, at the other extreme, it may be designed into a water-cooled jacket. It may be an oversize transistor or larger than a man. The power rating may be a few watts or many megawatts.

FETs have low-power ratings and cannot be used for high-power applications. Transistors have limited power ratings but are used extensively in mobile communications such as walkie-talkies, citizen band, taxicabs, police cars, etc. All transmitters with power outputs in the kW or MW range are designed with vacuum tubes. If the signal to be amplified is a single (*carrier*) frequency, the RF amplifier is always operated class C. Once a carrier has been combined (*modulated*) with the intelligence (audio, video, etc.), the stage must be operated as a class A or class B linear (Doherty) amplifier.

Grid-leak bias is commonly used for the low-power stages and a combination of grid-leak and fixed bias for high-power RF amplifiers. The input (driving) signal provides the power dissipated in the grid circuit as the grid is driven positive and draws grid current.

The plate power supply provides dc voltage ($B+$) that can accommodate the wide signal swings in the plate circuit, without permitting the minimum plate voltage to swing below the maximum grid voltage. This statement is simply a recognition of the (180°) phase shift in an amplifier. As the grid is driven positive, the plate swings negative. In addition the plate circuit provides an appropriate tank frequency, an impedance match between the vacuum tube output impedance and the input impedance of the next stage (or antenna, transmission line, etc.). The plate circuit also provides a tank load with a Q that is appropriate for the required bandwidth.

These requirements can be summarized with illustrative examples.

Example 3-12
Given an RF amplifier. The tank circuit parameters are: $X_L = 1500$ Ω, the coil resistance $= 12$ Ω, the load reflects back an additional 8 Ω (R_r).
Calculate:
a. The value of Q without load.
b. The value of Q with load.
c. The efficiency of the output circuit under load conditions.

Solution
a. The unloaded $Q = Q_1$

$$Q_1 = \frac{X_L}{R} = \frac{1500}{12} = 125$$

b. The loaded $Q = Q_2$

$$Q_2 = \frac{X_L}{R + R_r} = \frac{1500}{12 + 8} = 75$$

c. The useful portion of the output energy is dissipated across R_r. The tank efficiency is:

$$\eta = \frac{R_r}{R + R_r} \times 100 = \frac{8}{12 + 8} \times 100 = 40\%$$

Note: An increase in reflected resistance (heavy loading) would improve efficiency but would lower Q and widen selectivity.

The output power and grid driving signal can be related to the tank components. This is demonstrated by the following example.

Example 3-13
A high-power RF amplifier is operating under the following conditions: dc plate voltage $(E_b) = 2500$ V, dc grid voltage $(E_c) = -150$ V, peak RF grid voltage $(E_{gm}) = 350$ V, power output $(P_o) = 800$ W, an operating frequency of 20 MHz, and a loaded $Q = 12$. Calculate L and C of the tank.

Solution
The maximum positive value of the grid is the bias voltage added to the positive swing of the driving signal.

$$E_{c(max)} = E_{gm} + E_c = 350 - 150 = \textbf{200 V}$$

The minimum allowable plate voltage is the maximum positive grid voltage:

$$E_{b(min)} = E_{c(max)} = 200 \text{ V}$$

The peak value of the plate output voltage thus becomes

$$E_{pm} = E_b - E_{b(min)} = 2500 - 200 = \textbf{2300 V}$$

Relating the peak voltage swing to output power results in the impedance of the output circuit:

$$Z_0 = \frac{E_{pm}^2}{2P_0} = \frac{(2300)^2}{2 \times 800} = \textbf{3306 } \Omega$$

This value of Z_0 defines X_L

$$X_L = \frac{Z_0}{Q} = \frac{3306}{12} = \textbf{275.5 } \Omega$$

$$L = \frac{X_L}{2\pi f} = \frac{275.5}{2\pi \times 20 \times 10^6} = \textbf{2.192 } \mu\textbf{H}$$

$$C = \frac{1}{2\pi f X_C} = \frac{1}{2\pi f X_L} = \frac{1}{2\pi \times 20 \times 10^6 \times 275.5}$$

$$= \textbf{28.89 pF}$$

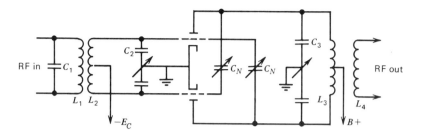

Figure 3-11 Push-pull RF amplifiers.

High-power RF amplifiers are frequently designed as a push-pull stage. The usual advantages of this circuit result for RF operation in increased gain, suppressed harmonics, increased output impedance, and higher efficiency. The disadvantage is the requirement for additional driving power and special (split-stator) tank capacitors (Fig. 3-11).

The heater is shown as a cathode; in practice, it would more likely be a filament heater with a special (balanced) filament transformer providing power. The input and output are shown as split-stator tanks that permit the rotor sections to be at ground. Cross neutralization is indicated. The input and output coils (L_2 and L_3) are at center-tap ground by virtue of the power supplies ($-E_c$ and $B+$). A truly high-power stage is fed by a push-pull driver stage to build up the driver power. The output coupling (L_4) can be any one of a wide choice of coupling networks, depending on the circumstances of the load.

3-13
Analytic
Troubleshooting

A common difficulty for the student is relating the function of a component to the result of shorting out or opening the component. This analysis should be done with a view to the effect in the immediate circuit and the effect on the output signal of a system. This is the first chapter to include complete amplifiers, which permits this analytic approach. It will also be utilized in succeeding chapters where the systems are more complex.

Figure 3-12 is the input RF stage of a receiver. Its function is to receive a weak signal from the antenna and amplify it. The stage must have the capability of tuning through the frequency range of the receiver. It must have an adequate bandwidth. But on the other hand, its bandwidth should be sufficiently narrow to reject undesired adjacent signals. The amplifier should have a

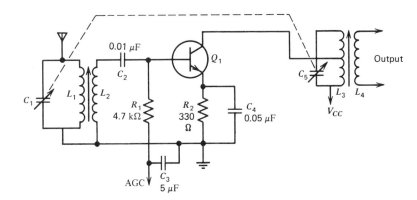

Figure 3-12 Tuned RF amplifier.

low noise figure since it is dealing with a weak signal. The functions of the individual components are:

1. C_1 and C_5 are variable capacitors that are part of tuned tanks and are rotated or tuned at the same time. They constitute a ganged capacitor that is rotated as you tune a receiver, tuning the tanks to the same frequency at all times.

2. C_1 and L_1 constitute a high impedance tank that is transformer coupled to a low impedance secondary L_2. The impedance of L_2 matches the low input impedance of transistor Q_1. Shorting L_1 shorts the input and results in no output. Shorting C_1 has the same effect as shorting L_1. Opening either L_1 or C_1 opens the tank and offers an untuned tank for the antenna. This results in no input and no output. A shorted L_2 shorts the input to Q_1 and no output results. An open L_2 effectively kills the input to Q_1 and results in no output.

3. C_2, R_1, and C_3 are required because AGC is being applied to this stage. The function of AGC will be discussed in the receiver chapter. Suffice it to say that the AGC line is a slowly varying dc voltage. C_2 serves the double function of isolating AGC from L_2 and ground, as well as coupling the L_2 signal to the base of Q_1. Note the 0.01 μF value of C_2. At RF frequencies, X_C is considered a negligibly low impedance, practically a short circuit.

R_1 has the function of providing a dc path to the base for AGC. If R_1 is made too small it will short out the signal appearing at L_2. If R_1 is made too large it would attenuate the AGC signal. The 4.7kΩ value used for R_1 is four to six times greater than the input impedance of Q_1. As a result its shunting effect on the L_2 signal is acceptable.

A shorted C_2 shorts AGC to ground through L_2. This upsets the bias and results in no output. An open C_2 opens the signal path and results in no output. A shorted R_1 places the AGC line directly on the base. Because the AGC line is an RF short (through C_3), the input signal is shorted with a resulting no output. An open R_1 removes AGC bias and results in no output.

4. C_3 has a large value of 5 μF because it is serving as a filter for low frequency audio signals that may be on the AGC line. It will also filter out any RF that appears at the bottom of R_1 and keep it off the AGC line. C_3 shorted: removes AGC bias and results in no output. C_3 open: results in improper filtering of the AGC line. This can result in extraneous modulation of the base or even oscillation.

5. R_2 and C_4 constitute the emitter bias for the stage. R_2 is required for long term and temperature stabilization. R_2 is selected on the basis of current specifications and recommended bias. The C_4 value of 0.05 μF should result in an X_c equal to approximately $0.1R_2$ at the RF frequency. C_4 effectively places the emitter at RF ground. Another view of the R_2-C_4 function is to consider the unit as a time constant. C_4 maintains the voltage across R_2 constant despite the RF variation of emitter current.

R_2 shorted: upsets the bias; no output results. R_2 open: opens the path for emitter current; no output results. C_2 shorted: upsets the bias; no output results. C_2 open: leaves the emitter resistor unbypassed. This results in a current form of negative feedback, a drastic decrease of voltage gain, and a low output signal.

6. C_5 and L_3 constitute a tuned tank for the output circuit. The transistor output impedance is matched to the tank by means of the tap. V_{CC} is applied to the collector through the lower portion of L_3. The entire L_3 is used as an RF tank, but only a portion handles power supply current. L_4 is a smaller winding than L_3. It is designed to match the input impedance of the next stage.

L_3 shorted: shorts the tank. This presents a zero impedance as a collector load that kills the voltage gain; no output results. C_5 shorted: has the same effect as a shorted L_3. L_3

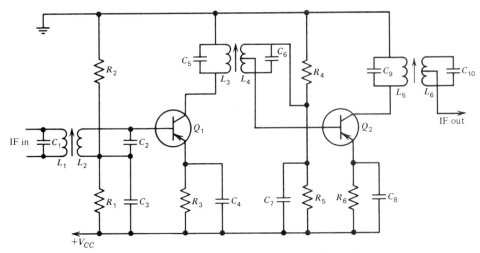

Figure 3-13 Cascaded IF amplifier.

open: opens the collector current path; no output results. C_5 open: converts a high impedance tank to a low impedance coil. This kills the gain; no output results.

The next circuit (Fig. 3-13) to be analyzed is a cascaded IF amplifier.

This circuit is tuned to a fixed (IF) frequency. Most of the components functions are identical to those of (Fig. 3-12). The significant variation relates to the method of base biasing. R_2 and R_1 perform a voltage divider function as does R_4 and R_5. C_3 and C_7 function as RF bypass capacitors. These capacitors effectively remove the biasing resistors from RF consideration.

1. C_1-L_1 are the input tank circuit. Either one shorted: shorts the input signal; no output results. Either component open: opens the tank; no output results.
2. C_2-L_2 are the base input tank. The same analysis applies as C_1-L_1.
3. R_2, R_1, and C_3 create Q_1 base bias. R_2 open: places V_{CC} voltage on Q_1 base, upsets the bias; no output results. R_2 short: puts Q_1 base bias at zero volts; no output results. R_1 open: removes bias voltage from base; no output results. R_1 short; places V_{CC} voltage on Q_1 base; no output results.
4. In order to appreciate the contribution of C_3, refer to Fig. 3-14.

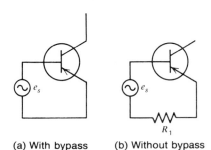

(a) With bypass   (b) Without bypass

Figure 3-14 Effect of RF bypass capacitor.

In normal operation (Fig. 3-14a) C_3 places the bottom of tank L_2-C_2 at RF ground. The top of the tank is directly at the base. C_4 places the emitter at RF ground. Thus the tank signal (e_s) is applied between base and emitter. If C_3 is open (Fig. 3-14b), the tank signal is divided between R_1 and the transistor input resistance. A very weak signal output results. C_3 short: places V_{CC} voltage on base; no output results.

5. R_3-C_4. Emitter bias components, function is similar to R_2-C_4 of Fig. 3-12.
6. C_5-L_3. Collector tank, function is similar to C_5-L_3 of Fig. 3-12.
7. L_4-C_6. Q_2 base tank, function is similar to L_2-C_2 tank, tapped for impedance match.
8. R_4, R_5, and C_7. Q_2 base bias, function is identical to R_1, R_2, and C_3.
9. R_6-C_8. Q_2 emitter bias, function is identical to R_3-C_4.
10. L_5-C_9. Q_2 tank, function is identical to C_5-L_3.
11. L_6-C_{10}. Output tank is tapped for impedance match. Either component shorted: shorts the signal; no output results. Either component open: the tank is open; no output results.

If neutralization is required for Fig. 3-13, it could be made available from the secondary windings. There are high frequency transistors currently available with very low junction capacitances. This makes it possible to operate transistors at high frequencies without neutralization. Recent developments in communications have transistor amplifiers operating in the 4 to 5 GHz range.

RF and IF coils are normally fabricated within a metal shield. This confines the magnetic field to the coil itself and isolates the coil from stray magnetic fields. The vacuum tube used as a high frequency amplifier may also be placed in a tube shield. This is common practice for tubes used in the tuner section of the TV receiver.

3-14 Summary RF amplifiers have many functions. They amplify extremely weak signals. They can produce output power in megawatts. It can function as a tunable amplifier or a fixed frequency cascaded amplifier. RF amplifiers may require neutralization and be series or shunt fed. It may function as a frequency multiplier. RF amplifiers may be analyzed for troubleshooting.

Now return to the objectives and self-evaluation questions at the beginning of this chapter and see how well you can answer them. If you cannot answer certain questions, place a check next to each of them and review appropriate parts of the text. Then answer the questions and solve the problems below.

3-15
Questions

Q3-1 If you were writing the specifications of an RF amplifier, which parameters would be included?

Q3-2 What is the disadvantage of coupling the output tank of one stage directly to the input of the next transistor stage?

Q3-3 What are the common methods of coupling between two transistor RF amplifiers?

Q3-4 What is the common cause of oscillation in an RF amplifier?

Q3-5 Sketch two methods of neutralizing an RF amplifier, and explain how they function.

Q3-6 What problem may arise if the signal coupled through the neutralizing capacitor is:
a. Too weak?
b. Too strong?

Q3-7 Referring to Fig. 3-12 indicate the specific effect of these malfunctions:
a. C_1 shorted.
b. L_2 open.
c. R_2 shorted.
d. C_4 open.
e. C_5 open
f. L_4 shorted.
g. R_1 shorted.

Q3-8 Referring to Fig. 3-13 indicate the specific effect of these malfunctions:
a. L_2 shorted.
b. R_2 open.
c. C_3 open.
d. C_3 shorted.
e. C_5 shorted.
f. C_6 open.
g. C_7 open.
h. L_5 open.
i. C_8 shorted.

Q3-9 Distinguish between *series* and *shunt feed* and sketch circuits for each.

Q3-10 What advantages derive from shunt feed?

Q3-11 List some methods of cooling an RF power amplifier.

Q3-12 Why does class C operation of an RF amplifier result in undistorted output?

Q3-13 What advantage results from class C operation of an RF amplifier?

Q3-14 What is the potential harm resulting from the use of grid leak bias? How can it be minimized?

Q3-15 Referring to Fig. 3-7d, what is the function of the:
a. RFC?
b. C_2?
c. C_3?

Q3-16 What advantage is there in using a series feed for an RF amplifier?

Q3-17 Describe the operation of *Hazeltine* neutralization.

Q3-18 Describe the operation of *grid* neutralization.

Q3-19 Why are frequency *multipliers* necessary?

Q3-20 Compare the RF amplifier to the frequency multiplier with respect to:
a. Schematic.
b. Efficiency.
c. Output power

Q3-21 Describe the major difference between a *push-push* RF amplifier and a push-pull RF amplifier.

Q3-22 Under what conditions would you substitute a *Doherty* amplifier for a class C RF amplifier?

3-16 **P3-1** Given the following data for a pentode RF amplifier: $g_m = 9000$ μS, $L = 100$ μH, $C = 500$ pF; the resistance of the coil is 100 Ω. Calculate the voltage gain.

Problems

P3-2 Given the following data for a triode RF amplifier: $\mu = 100$, $Q = 30$, $R = 20$ Ω, $r_p = 6000$ Ω. Calculate the voltage gain.

P3-3 Given the following data for a FET RF amplifier: $g_{FS} = 6000$ μS $X_L = 200$ Ω, resistance of coil is 10 Ω. Calculate the voltage gain.

P3-4 Given the following data for a transistor RF amplifier: $h_f = 60$, $R_i = 1000$ Ω, $L = 50$ μH, and $C = 2000$ pF; the resistance of the coil is 30 Ω. Calculate the voltage gain.

P3-5 If the required overall bandwidth of two cascaded RF amplifiers is 4 MHz, what is the bandwidth of each stage?

P3-6 If the bandwidth of each RF amplifier is 800 kHz, what is the bandwidth of three such stages cascaded?

P3-7 A RF transistor amplifier has an $h_f = 100$. The load tank components are $L = 300$ μH and 8 Ω, $C = 400$ pF. The input resistance is 1500 Ω. Calculate the voltage gain:
a. As an isolated stage.
b. Feeding an identical amplifier.

P3-8 An FET RF amplifier has: $g_{FS}=8000\ \mu S$, $r_d=100\ k\Omega$, $C_{shunt}=4$ pF. The tank components are: $L=200\ \mu H$ and $10\ \Omega$, $C=300$ pF. The gate resistor of the next stage is $10\ k\Omega$. Calculate:
a. Gain.
b. Equivalent Q.

P3-9 Two cascaded transistor RF amplifiers have: output impedance $=100\ k\Omega$, input resistance $=500\ \Omega$, tank components of $L=400$ μH and $10\ \Omega$, $C=500$ pF. The coil is tapped for the second stage at a point $\frac{1}{3}$ from the bottom. The input signal to $Q_1=200$ μV. Calculate:
a. Equivalent load impedance of the primary side.
b. Signal applied to input of second stage.
c. Equivalent Q of coupling network of the primary side.

P3-10 For the FET RF amplifier of Fig. 3-3, $V_i=100\ \mu V$. The tank components are: $L_1=10$ mH, $L_2=800\ \mu H$ and $8\ \Omega$, $k=0.02$, $C_1=500$ pF, $L_3=4$ mH, $g_{FS}=4000\ \mu S$. Calculate the voltages:
a. At input of Q_1.
b. Output of Q_1.

P3-11 For the cascaded FET RF amplifiers of Fig. 3-4, $L_3=L_4=800$ μH and $8\ \Omega$, $C_3=C_4=600$ pF, $k=0.05$, $gFS=5000\ \mu S$. The input at the gate of Q_2, $E_{i_2}=10\ \mu V$. Calculate
a. The Q of primary.
b. Voltage at gate of Q_3.
c. Voltage gain from gate of Q_2 to gate of Q_3.

P3-12 A triode RF amplifier is provided a dc plate voltage of 250 V and dc plate current of 15 mA. The output signal is a rms voltage of 25 V and rms current of 20 mA. Calculate the plate efficiency.

P3-13 The tank circuit of a triode RF amplifier has an $X_L=1200\ \Omega$, and a coil resistance $=8\ \Omega$. The load reflects back an additional $10\ \Omega$. Calculate:
a. The value of Q without load.
b. The value of Q with load.
c. The efficiency of the output circuit under load conditions.

P3-14 A triode RF amplifier is operating at 15 MHz under the following conditions: dc plate voltage $=2000$ V, dc grid voltage $=-120$ V, peak RF grid voltage $=280$ V, power output $=1.2$ kW, and a loaded $Q=15$. Calculate the tank L and C.

Chapter 4

RF
Oscillators

4-1
Objectives To learn:

1. The basic requirements for oscillation.
2. Phase shift oscillator.
3. Negative resistance oscillators.
4. Armstrong oscillators.
5. Hartley oscillators.
6. Colpitts oscillators.
7. Crystal oscillators.
8. Parasitic oscillations.

4-2
Self-Evaluation
Questions
Test your prior knowledge of the information in this chapter by answering the following questions. Watch for the answers to these questions as you read the chapter. Your final evaluation of whether you understand the material is measured by your ability to answer these questions. When you have completed the chapter, return to this section and answer the questions again.

1. Define the general requirements for an amplifier to function as an oscillator.
2. List five waveshapes available from oscillators.
3. List five pieces of equipment or systems that use RF oscillators.
4. List seven parameters that may be included in the specifications of an oscillator.
5. Describe the operation of an *Armstrong* oscillator.
6. What is the basic distinction between the *Hartley* and *Armstrong* oscillators?
7. Does the *Colpitts* have any advantage over the *Hartley* oscillator? Any disadvantage?
8. How would you check an oscillator for proper operation?
9. What is *parasitic* oscillation?
10. Why is the crystal oscillator commonly used for broadcast transmitters?
11. Define *piezoelectric* effect.

12. What kind of impedance does a parallel-resonant mode crystal present to a circuit?

13. Which parameters would you specify in ordering a crystal?

14. What is the significance of the thickness of the crystal slab?

4-3 Introduction to Oscillators An oscillator is an electronic device that provides an output signal with nothing more provided as an input except a dc power supply. The output signal must be repetitious, usually of a fixed frequency and a particular waveshape. The output waveshape may be sinusoidal, pulse, square wave, sawtooth, triangular, or several other shapes. Readers who had a digital course have some familiarity with the family of multivibrator oscillators (astable, monostable, etc.) that produce square waves. Other oscillators are low frequency or audio oscillators such as the Wien Bridge sinusoidal oscillator.

This introduction is limited to RF oscillators providing a sinusoidal output. The RF sinusoidal oscillator is used for most modern receivers, certainly all PM, FM, and TV receivers. It is used at the broadcasting station as part of the transmitter. It is used in radar systems, microwave ovens, diathermy machines, etc. There are a multitude of RF oscillator circuits and many variations of each. We will consider the most commonly used types and analyze their operation as transistor, FET, and vacuum tube circuits.

4-4 General Requirements The basic requirements for any oscillator is to encourage an amplified signal that produces self-sustaining oscillations. Of course just having a sustained signal is not the entire purpose of a design. Some of the significant parameters that may be specified for the design of an RF oscillator are the following: frequency, output voltage, output power, deviation of frequency with change in load, temperature, and power supply voltage. Purity of output waveshape may be of interest, in the sense that the percentage of harmonics is specified.

Many junior engineers or technicians have designed an RF amplifier and to their consternation produced an oscillator! This means that at least one form of RF oscillator is schematically identical to an RF amplifier. The feedback for the oscillator can be accomplished in any one of several ways. It may be coupled through the interelectrode/interjunction capacitance. An output coil may be magnetically coupled to an input coil. The circuit tank coil may be tapped to provide a portion for the input circuit. Likewise the circuit tank capacitor may be tapped with a portion of the capacitance in the input circuit. It is also possible to insert an entire magnetic link between output and input circuits. Various coupling methods will be investigated in the course of our discussion.

4-5
Feedback
Requirements
An oscillator functions on the basis of feedback. The possibility of *inadvertent* feedback was considered in Sec. 3-7. The standard approach to a discussion of feedback theory is the one used in the study of fundamentals of an amplifier. Refer to Fig. 4-1.

$$A_{v_f} = \frac{A_v}{1 - BA_v} \qquad (4\text{-}1)$$

where: A_{v_f} is the voltage gain with feedback
A_v is the voltage gain without feedback (open loop condition)
B is the feedback factor, a decimal fraction

As studied in a fundamental amplifier course, the B factor is a negative term that causes a reduction of the open loop output. This condition is termed *inverse* feedback or *negative* feedback.

If the B factor is *positive*, the gain is greater than the open loop gain A_v. This condition is but *one* of the *two* requirements needed by an amplifier to function as an oscillator. The second requirement is a *sufficient* amount of positive feedback to overcome the losses in the stage.

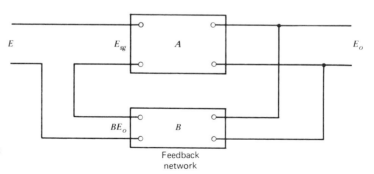

Figure 4-1 Block diagram of a feedback amplifier.

The *Barkhausen criterion* for oscillation specifies a feedback product of BA_v equal to unity and the feedback phase angle equal to zero or some whole number multiple of 2π.

There are many RF oscillators that can be discussed. The subject can readily constitute an entire text. There are several variations of each type of oscillator. There will be no attempt to cover *all* the variations of any type of oscillator included in this chapter.

4-6
Phase
Shift
Oscillator

The *phase shift* oscillator accomplishes the phase shift by means of an appropriate grouping of frequency sensitive RC networks. Refer to Fig. 4-2.

Each RC pair results in a 60° phase shift for a total of 180°. The FET provides the conventional amplifier an additional 180° phase shift. Analysis of the circuit results in the following equations.

$$f_0 = \frac{1}{2\pi\sqrt{6}\ RC} \qquad \text{Hertz (Hz)} \qquad (4\text{-}2)$$

The amplifier gain must be sufficient to compensate the attenuation in each of the three RC sections. Each section loses $1/3$ of the signal level. Therefore the *minimum* gain required of the active element is $3\times3\times3$ or 27. The distortion in output signal will be minimized by keeping the stage gain as close to unity as possible. Even this design results in 5 to 10% distortion of the output signal. The phase shift oscillator can be varied in

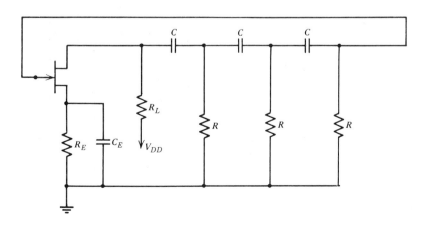

Figure 4-2 Phase shift oscillator.

frequency by varying the three resistors simultaneously. This in turn affects the load on the amplifier and the gain. The net result is to place severe restrictions on the permissible frequency variation. In practice the phase shift oscillator is designed for a fixed frequency and can be used up to a frequency of 500 kHz.

Example 4-1

Given the phase shift oscillator of Fig. 4-2 with $R = 25$ kΩ and $C = 0.001$ μF. Calculate the frequency of oscillation, f_0.

Solution

$$f_0 = \frac{1}{2\pi\sqrt{6}\ RC} \quad \text{Hz}$$

$$= \frac{1}{2\pi\sqrt{6}\ \times 25 \times 10^3 \times 0.001 \times 10^{-6}}$$

$$= \frac{1}{0.3848 \times 10^{-3}} = \textbf{2599 Hz} \tag{4-2}$$

**4-7
Negative
Resistance
Oscillator** Any component that demonstrates an *increase* in current as the applied voltage *decreases* is a *negative resistance* device. The original negative resistance device is the tetrode vacuum-tube amplifier. Its characteristic curves include a negative resistance portion that is a result of *secondary* emission. More recently some solid state devices, such as the *tunnel diode* and *unijunction transistor*, were developed and these devices also demonstrate the negative resistance characteristic. Theoretically, oscillation can be sustained in a tank circuit by shunting it with a negative resistance device.

The unijunction transistor is a single junction device but nevertheless is considered to be a three element unit. It is more commonly used as a pulse or timing oscillator, but can be used as an RF oscillator. The emitter volt-ampere characteristic curves are shown in Fig. 4-3a. The portion A-B is a normal resistance segment. Section B-C is a negative resistance segment. As long as the unit is biased for operation in the B-C region, it can provide the necessary energy for oscillation. Refer to Fig. 4-3.

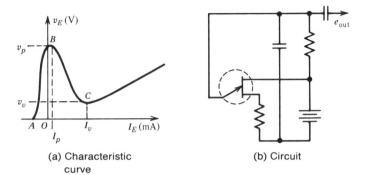

(a) Characteristic
curve

(b) Circuit

Figure 4-3 Unijunction oscillator.

The designations V_p, V_v, I_p, and I_v indicate the valley and peak voltages and currents. A typical unijunction oscillator circuit is shown in Fig. 4-3b.

4-8
Armstrong
Oscillator
The *Armstrong* oscillator is not one of the preferred receiver types, but the operation is readily understood. It is a good first choice of *tunable* oscillator for discussion. Refer to Fig. 4-4.

The Armstrong oscillator operates on the principle of electromagnetic feedback. Referring to Fig. 4-4a, note M_1 coupling the plate signal to the grid input circuit. The output (e_0) is also electromagnetically coupled by M_2, but this is not a necessary requirement for the oscillator. The output could have been capacitive coupled.

For the actual operation of the oscillator, it is well to review some basic theory. At the instant of turning on the unit, there is a surge of plate current. The waveform of this surge of current represents all frequencies, which are generated in the plate coil L_1. These frequencies are all passed to L_2. The only frequency that the grid tank (L_2-C_1) is receptive to is its resonant frequency. For all other frequencies the grid tank is a low impedance circuit.

The resonant frequency tank signal is applied to the grid, driving it positive and drawing grid current to the plate of C_2. This current will discharge through R and create a negative grid voltage for bias. Here again we have grid-leak bias. The R-C_2 time constant must be appropriate for the period of the resonant frequency. The circuit would function with a properly designed

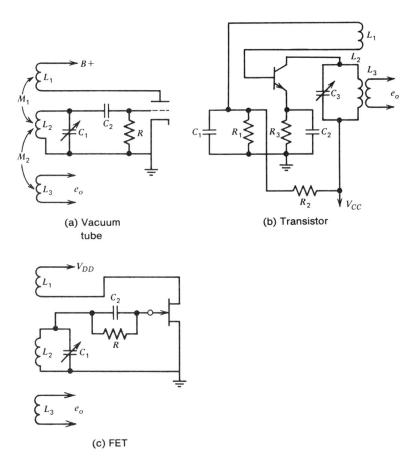

(a) Vacuum
tube

(b) Transistor

(c) FET

Figure 4-4 Armstrong oscillators.

fixed bias, either cathode bias or $(-E_c)$. However, there is some advantage to grid-leak bias. It is self-adjusting with signal strength. Since signal strength varies inversely with loading, the bias will adjust as well.

Thus, all the requirements of an oscillator are present. There is feedback from plate to grid of the proper (positive) phase. The amount of feedback, determined by M_1, is a small portion of the output. This small quantity of feedback signal is amplified back to the level of the output signal. The frequency is determined by the L-C of the tank.

Figure 4-4b shows an Armstrong oscillator using a transistor. The tuned circuit is the output rather than the input. The stage uses emitter bias. The base is conventionally biased with voltage divider R_1 and R_2. C_1 places the bottom of L_1 at ground. This places the entire L_1 signal across the base-emitter junction.

Figure 4-4c shows an Armstrong FET oscillator. The R-C_2 elements constitute a grid-leak bias. In this circuit the dc bias current is in series with the RF tank signal. This is a form of series-fed bias, which contrasts with the shunt-fed bias of Fig. 4-4a.

4-9 Hartley Oscillator The Hartley oscillator is a commonly used circuit, particularly for the lower RF frequency ranges. The coil of the L-C tank is tapped.

A portion of the coil is in the output circuit and the balance in the input circuit. This oscillator is tunable over a wider frequency range than the Armstrong.

The frequency is determined by the entire coil $(L_1 + L_2)$ and the tank capacitor. The tap on the coil is placed so as to divide the coil in the same ratio as the stage gain without feedback.

The frequency of oscillation is the standard resonant frequency equation:

$$f = \frac{1}{2\pi\sqrt{(L_1 + L_2)C}} \tag{4-3}$$

The needed minimum amplification factor for the various amplifying devices is indicated by the following formulas.

$$\text{Transistor:} \qquad h_f \geqslant \Delta^h \frac{L_1}{L_2} \tag{4-4}$$

$$\text{FET:} \qquad g_{FS} \geqslant \frac{L_1}{r_d L_2} \tag{4-5}$$

$$\text{Vacuum tube:} \qquad \mu \geqslant \frac{L_1}{L_2}$$

where $\Delta^h = h_i h_o - h_r h_f$

Figure 4-5a shows a *Hartley oscillator* with the portion of the coil that represents the output circuit (L_1) in series with the emitter. The emitter and collector current are the same, and signal can be generated in either element. Since the dc current and RF signal are both in series with the emitter, this circuit is series fed. The R_1-C_2 components establish the grid-leak bias. An emitter input presents a lower impedance than a collector

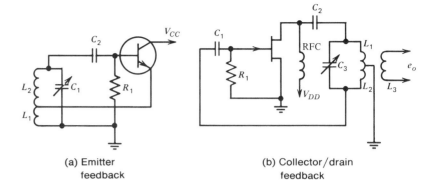

(a) Emitter
feedback

(b) Collector/drain
feedback

Figure 4-5 Hartley oscillators.

output. Impedance match is less of a problem and greater stability results.

Figure 4-5b shows a Hartley oscillator with the output portion of the tank coil in the drain side of an FET. The dc current is provided through the parallel RFC thus making the unit shunt fed. C_2 is a low reactance coupling capacitor that isolates V_{DD} from ground and couples RF from the drain element. The output is coupled inductively but other methods (RC) could be used. There are many variations of the Hartley oscillator, but the circuit is readily identified by the tapped coil.

Example 4-2
Given the Hartley oscillator of Fig. 4-5a. $C = 100$ pF, $L_1 = 300$ μH, $L_2 = 10$ μH, $h_{oe} = 100$ μS, $h_{ie} = 1$ kΩ, $h_{re} \cong 0$. Determine the operating frequency and the required minimum transistor h_f.

Solution

$$f_0 = \frac{1}{2\pi\sqrt{(L_1 + L_2)C}} = \frac{1}{2\pi\sqrt{(300 + 10)10^{-6} \times 100 \times 10^{-12}}}$$

$$= \frac{1}{2\pi \times 1.761 \times 10^{-7}} = \textbf{903.9 kHz} \qquad (4\text{-}3)$$

$$\Delta^h = h_i h_o - h_r h_f \approx h_i h_o$$

$$= 1 \times 10^3 \times 100 \times 10^{-6} = \textbf{0.1}$$

Required minimum h_f, Eq. (4-2)

$$h_f \geqslant \Delta^h \frac{L_1}{L_2} = 0.1 \times \frac{300}{10} = 3$$

Example 4-3

Given the Hartley oscillator of Fig. 4-5b. $L_1 = 1$ mH, $L_2 = 25$ μH, $C = 2000$ pF, $r_d \approx 10$ kΩ. Calculate the circuit frequency of oscillation and the required minimum FET transconductance.

Solution

$$f_0 = \frac{1}{2\pi\sqrt{(L_1 + L_2)C}}$$

$$= \frac{0.1592}{\sqrt{(1 + 0.025)10^{-3} \times 2000 \times 10^{-12}}}$$

$$= \frac{0.1592}{1.432 \times 10^{-6}} = 111.2 \text{ kHz} \qquad (4\text{-}3)$$

Required minimum g_{FS}

$$g_{FS} = \frac{L_1}{r_d L_2} = \frac{1 \times (10)^{-3}}{10 \times 10^3 \times 25 \times 10^{-6}} = 4000 \text{ } \mu\text{S} \qquad (4\text{-}5)$$

4-10
Colpitts
Oscillator

The *Colpitts* oscillator is also widely used as a *tunable* source of frequency. Along with the Hartley oscillator, both are the most common oscillator circuits used for a variable frequency signal. The Colpitts circuit is seen in many configurations but is readily recognized by the *tapped capacitor* in the *tank* circuit. In the Colpitts circuit, the interelectrode/interjunction capacitance can be incorporated as part of the tapped capacitance. This feature enables the operation of the Colpitts oscillator at ultra-high frequencies (UHF), such as TV channels 14 to 83 (470 to 890 MHz).

Figure 4-6a shows a Colpitts oscillator using a FET. The series capacitors C_1 and C_2 constitute the C of the tank. Recall that $C = C_1 C_2 / (C_1 + C_2)$ for series capacitors. If this C is too small for the design frequency, a third capacitor can be used across the *entire coil* to make up the difference. C_2 provides the feedback energy. Here, again, the C_1/C_2 ratio must be smaller than the voltage gain without feedback. The frequency is determined by C_1 and C_2 in series (see Eq. 4-7).

$$g_{FS} \geqslant \frac{C_2}{r_d C_1} \qquad (4\text{-}6)$$

$$f_0 = \frac{1}{2\pi\sqrt{LC_{eq}}} \qquad (4\text{-}7)$$

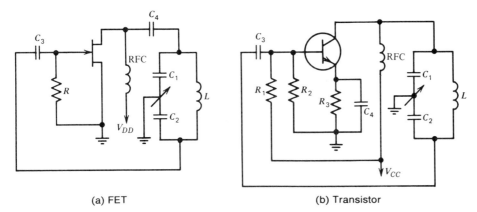

(a) FET   (b) Transistor

Figure 4-6 Colpitts oscillators.

where:

$$C_{eq} = \frac{C_1 \times C_2}{C_1 + C_2}$$

The unit is shunt fed and uses grid-leak bias.

Figure 4-6b is a transistor Colpitts design. The RFC is not capacitive coupled, since C_1, C_2, and C_3 effectively isolate V_{CC} from ground. Emitter bias is used, with R_1 and R_2 maintaining the base at proper dc voltage. For UHF applications, common base configuration is a popular design. The output may be coupled magnetically or capacitively. The applicable equation for minimum required h_{fe} of a transistor is

$$h_{fe} = \Delta^h \frac{C_1}{C_2} \tag{4-8}$$

Example 4-4

For the Colpitts oscillator circuit of Fig. 4-6a determine the frequency of oscillation and the required minimum value of FET g_{FS}. $C_1 = 300$ pF, $C_2 = 1500$ pF, $L = 40$ μH, $r_d = 50$ kΩ.

Solution

$$g_{FS} \geqslant \frac{C_2}{r_d C_1} = \frac{1500 \times 10^{-12}}{50 \times 10^3 \times 300 \times 10^{-12}} = 100 \ \mu S \tag{4-6}$$

$$C_{eq} = \frac{C_1 C_2}{C_1 + C_2} = \frac{300 \times 10^{-12} \times 1500 \times 10^{-12}}{(300 + 1500) \times 10^{-12}} = 250 \ pF$$

$$f_0 = \frac{1}{2\pi\sqrt{LC_{eq}}} = \frac{0.1592}{\sqrt{40\times10^{-6}\times250\times10^{-12}}}$$

$$= \frac{0.1592}{10^{-7}} = 1.592 \text{ MHz} \tag{4-7}$$

Example 4-5

For the Colpitts oscillator circuit of Fig. 4-6b determine the frequency of oscillation and the required minimum value of transistor h_f. $C_1 = 100$ pF, $C_2 = 500$ pF, $L = 10$ μH, $h_i = 3000$ Ω, $h_o = 500$ μS, $h_f = 60$, and $h_r = 0$.

Solution

$$\Delta^h = h_i h_o - h_f h_r$$

$$= 3000 \times 500 \times 10^{-6} - 60 \times 0$$

$$= 1500 \times 10^{-3} = 1.5$$

Required minimum h_f:

$$h_f = \Delta^h \frac{C_2}{C_1} = 1.5 \times \frac{500\times10^{-12}}{100\times10^{-12}} = 7.5 \tag{4-8}$$

$$C_{eq} = \frac{C_1 C_2}{C_1 + C_2} = \frac{(100\times10^{-12})(500\times10^{-12})}{(100+500)\times10^{-12}} = 83.33 \text{ pF}$$

$$f_0 = \frac{1}{2\pi\sqrt{LC_{eq}}} = \frac{0.1592}{\sqrt{10\times10^{-6}\times83.33\times10^{-12}}}$$

$$= \frac{0.1592}{28.87\times10^{-9}} = 5.514 \text{ MHz} \tag{4-7}$$

**4-11
Clapp
Oscillator** The *Clapp* oscillator is a variation of the Colpitts oscillator. The distinguishing feature of the Clapp oscillator is the series resonating capacitor, C_4 (Fig. 4-7).

The series capacitor improves the frequency stability of the oscillator. The frequency of oscillation is calculated by assuming the equivalent capacitance to be C_2, C_3, and C_4 in series.

Example 4-6

For the Clapp oscillator of Fig. 4-7, the component values are: $C_2 = C_4 = 500$ pF, $C_3 = 1000$ pF, $L = 800$ μH. Calculate the resonant frequency, f_0.

Solution

$$C_{eq} = \frac{1}{\dfrac{1}{C_2} + \dfrac{1}{C_4} + \dfrac{1}{C_3}} = \frac{1}{\dfrac{1}{500} + \dfrac{1}{1000} + \dfrac{1}{500}} = 200 \text{ pF}$$

$$f_0 = \frac{1}{2\pi\sqrt{LC}}$$

$$= \frac{1}{2\pi\sqrt{800 \times 10^{-6} \times 200 \times 10^{-12}}}$$

$$= \frac{1}{2\pi \times 4 \times 10^{-7}} = 397.9 \text{ kHz} \qquad (2\text{-}1)$$

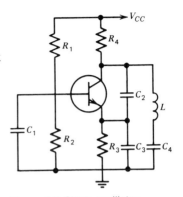

Figure 4-7 Clapp oscillator.

4-12 Tuned-Input, Tuned-Output Oscillator This circuit is identical to the conventional double-tuned RF amplifier circuit. As an RF amplifier it usually requires a neutralizing capacitor connected between output tank and input tank to prevent oscillation. The *absence* of the neutralizing capacitor (Fig. 4-8) results in oscillation. The feedback path is the interjunction capacitance of the FET.

The vacuum-tube equivalent of this circuit is called the *tuned-plate*, *tuned-grid* oscillator, and this name is often applied to non vacuum-tube equivalents. The circuit of Fig. 4-8 therefore is the *tuned-gate*, *tuned-drain* oscillator. The transistor equivalent circuit is the *tuned-base*, *tuned-collector* oscillator. In practice, for optimum oscillation the output tank is tuned to a frequency that is slightly *lower* then the frequency of the *input* tank.

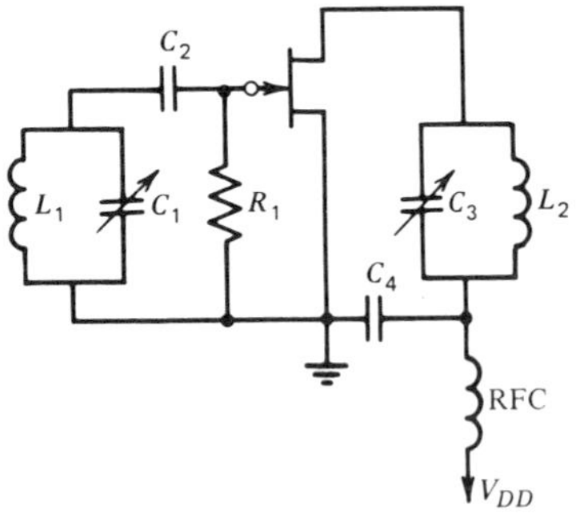

Figure 4-8 Tuned-input, tuned-output oscillator.

4-13 Electron-Coupled Oscillator The *electron-coupled* oscillator uses the screen grid (functioning as a positive biased plate), control grid, and cathode as the oscillator elements (Fig. 4-9a).

The oscillator action modulates the electron stream that continues to the plate and plate circuit. The electron-coupled oscil-

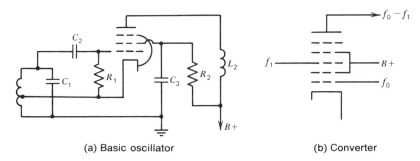

Figure 4-9 Electron-coupled oscillator.   (a) Basic oscillator   (b) Converter

lator circuit is commonly used with a five grid (pentagrid) vacuum-tube amplifier (Fig. 4-9b) as a *converter*. In this application a signal (f_1) is applied to one of the two control grids. The oscillator signal (f_0) is created at and applied to the other control grid. Both signals modulate the electron stream. The output signal at the plate is the sum or difference of the two signals, $f_0 + f_1$, or $f_0 - f_1$ depending on the frequency of the plate tank.

4-14 Parasitic Oscillations *Parasitic oscillations* occur at frequencies other than the desired design frequency. Parasitic oscillation may occur at frequencies above (multiplier) or below (subharmonic) the design frequency. There are various approaches to prevent parasitic oscillations. One obvious method is to lower the gain of the unit by lowering the Q of the tank. This is easily done using a shunting *suppression resistor*. Appropriate insertion of RF chokes will also minimize parasitic oscillations. Detuning a tank slightly also may be effective.

Frequently an oscillator may function properly for a long period before developing parasitic oscillations. Many parameters in the design of an oscillator will change with time. These include the hybrid parameters of the transistor, the internal resistance and amplification factor of the vacuum tube, as well as the R, L, and C values of discrete components.

These problems can be minimized by including stabilization in the design of the oscillator, temperature control of the environment, temperature compensating components and, of course, *light loading* of the oscillator stage.

4-15
Frequency
Range of an
Oscillator

A *tunable* oscillator must be tunable over a specified frequency range. An AM broadcast receiver has an approximate receiving frequency range of 0.5 to 1.5 MHz. This is a $3:1$ frequency ratio. Since frequency is determined by the square root of the tunable element ($f = 1/2\pi\sqrt{LC}$), the variable L or C must have a range factor of $(3)^2$ or 9. In practice the ganged variable air capacitor, used as the tunable element for AM receivers, has an approximate capacitance range of 30 to 300 pF, or $10:1$ ratio.

FM broadcast range is 88 to 108 MHz; this is a $1.227:1$ frequency ratio. The required capacitance range factor of the tunable capacitor is $(1.227)^2$ or only 1.506. Assuming a tuning capacitor minimum capacitance of 100 pF, the required maximum capacitance is 150.6 pF.

The VHF-TV broadcast frequency range (54 to 216 MHz) is usually done with a fixed (nontunable) capacitor for each of the 13 channels. UHF-TV broadcast frequency range (470 to 980 MHz) is approximately $2:1$ frequency ratio, requiring a capacitance range factor of 4.

It is also possible to have the tunable tank consist of a fixed capacitor and a variable inductance. The same ratios apply for the required inductance range. Variation of L is accomplished by inserting a powdered iron movable core into the coil. Automobile radios are occasionally designed with a variable inductance tuning element because it is less subject to vibration.

A broadcast receiver that is to cover a broad range of frequencies would be designed with several discrete bands of frequency with no band covering a frequency range greater than $3:1$ ratio.

4-16
Piezoelectric
Effect

RF oscillators using L-C elements for the tuned circuit are subject to frequency drift. Even if the bulky tunable (L or C) element is replaced with a fixed value component, there is some frequency drift. This may result from variations in the temperature of the environment, power supply voltage variations, humidity, or simply variation of the values and parameters of the components with time (aging).

Federal Communications Commission (FCC) regulations on the frequency stability of the carrier frequency assigned to a broadcast station are very stringent. It is impossible for any of the L-C oscillators discussed to stay within the narrow frequency range assigned to a broadcast station by FCC.

Some crystalline materials such as quartz crystal have an unusual characteristic. If a thin slice of the material is cut from the natural (hexagonal-shaped) molecular structure, and a voltage applied across the facing surfaces, the material goes into a mechanical vibration. The rate of vibration is at an *accurately defined frequency*.

This interchange of electrical to mechanical energy and back is called *piezoelectric effect*. It is analogous to the flywheel effect of the *L-C* tank with its continuous interchange of inductive magnetic and capacitive dielectric energy. The vibration or oscillation of the crystal will continue as long as the natural energy losses in the crystal are compensated for on a regular or repetitive basis by the addition of electric energy.

4-17 Crystal Characteristics The electrical equivalent of a crystal is a combination of a series-resonant circuit and a parallel-resonant circuit. This is shown in Fig. 4-10a. The frequency response of the crystal reflects both the series- and parallel-resonance condition (Fig. 4-10c). The symbol for a crystal is shown in Fig. 4-10b.

The two resonant frequencies are close together and offer either the low impedance as a series-resonant circuit or a high impedance as a parallel-resonant circuit (Fig. 4-10c). The mode of operation, series or parallel, as well as frequency, temperature coefficient, size, type of mounting, and power rating are all specified when ordering the crystal from the manufacturer. The equivalent Q of a crystal is much higher than the Q of an *L-C* tank, 10,000 to a million compared to the 100 to 200 range for an *L-C* tank.

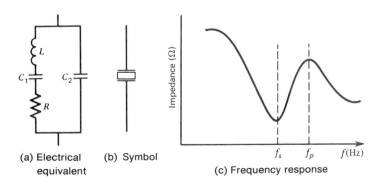

Figure 4-10 Crystal characteristics.

(a) Electrical equivalent   (b) Symbol

(c) Frequency response

The crystal in its natural state is a rough hexagonal shape. Depending on the direction or *plane of the cut* of the crystal slab, the *temperature characteristic* is determined. That is, it may be cut in the vertical, horizontal, at a bias, parallel to the sides, perpendicular to the sides, from one corner to another, etc. Each direction of cut is identified by a letter or letters, such as *X*, *Y*, *Z*, *AT*, *BT*, *CT*, etc. The temperature coefficient may be positive, negative or zero, depending on type of cut (Fig. 4-11).

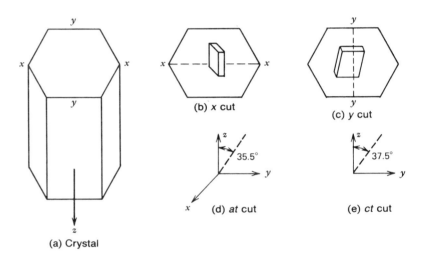

Figure 4-11 Crystal cuts.

**4-18
Crystal
Temperature
Characteristics**
Temperature coefficient of a crystal defines the change of operating frequency for each degree Celsius change of ambient temperature.

$$\Delta f = TC \times f \times \Delta T \qquad \text{Hertz (Hz)} \qquad (4\text{-}7)$$

where: Δf is the change in crystal operating frequency, Hertz (Hz)

TC is the crystal temperature coefficient, parts per million per degree Celsius (ppm/°C)

f = frequency, in megahertz (MHz)

ΔT is the change in ambient temperature, degrees Celsius (°C)

The significance of this equation is readily demonstrated by example.

Example 4-7

A quartz crystal has a temperature coefficient rating of 2 ppm/°C. Calculate the frequency drift if the crystal oscillator is operating at 46 MHz and the ambient temperature rises from 25 to 60°C.

Solution

$$\Delta f = TC \times f \times \Delta T \qquad (4\text{-}7)$$

$$\Delta f = 2 \times 46 \times (60 - 25) = \textbf{3220 Hz}$$

Note: The frequency *increases* because the temperature coefficient is *positive* and the temperature *increased*.

Example 4-8

A CT cut quartz crystal has a negative temperature coefficient of 1.5 ppm/°C. The crystal oscillator is operating at 75 MHz. The ambient temperature drops 35°C. Calculate the frequency drift.

Solution

$$\Delta f = TC \times f \times \Delta T$$

$$= (-1.5) \times 75 \times (-35)$$

$$= \textbf{3938 Hz increase} \qquad (4\text{-}7)$$

The temperature coefficient is not constant over a wide range of temperatures but must be determined for the temperature range of interest. Some crystal cuts such as GT have a temperature coefficient of very nearly zero. Different crystal cuts are recommended for operation at different frequency ranges. In general the crystal *thickness* determines the frequency, but the length to width ratio is also a parameter. If the crystal slab is made too thin, it won't have sufficient mechanical strength to withstand the vibrations. The highest practical frequency that a crystal can be cut for is 30 MHz. However, the crystal can operate on harmonics of the fundamental and reach approximately 100 MHz. It is entirely feasible to increase the operating frequency of a crystal by opening the case and *carefully* removing some of the crystal body with a fine file. But once you have made the frequency *too* high, the crystal is useless.

4-19
Crystal
Oscillator
Circuits
A number of RF crystal oscillator schematics will be shown, and comment made where appropriate. Here again there are many circuit variations. Many of the *L-C* tank type of RF oscillators are used with a crystal substituted. There is the variation with the crystal used as a *series*-resonant element, increasing the number of possible variations using crystals.

Figure 4-12a shows a crystal oscillator with the crystal operating as a parallel-resonant element. The feedback is via the drain to gate capacitance. This circuit is equivalent to the tuned plate-tuned grid oscillator. The bias is a combination of source (emitter) bias and grid (gate) leak bias. There is no coupling capacitor from crystal to gate since the crystal itself is the electrical equivalent of a capacitor. The RFC is included because the value of R_1 is so small that it would seriously shunt the crystal, and lower its effective Q.

Figure 4-12b shows a parallel mode crystal oscillator with the collector side using a Colpitts schematic. The output tank is the L and C_2-C_3 in series. The feedback (C_3) is applied to the emitter leg, whose impedance is kept artificially high with the RFC. C_1 isolates the crystal from the dc bias on the base. This isolation may be advisable if the bias is a high voltage. The crystal has a limited dc voltage rating.

The crystal oscillator may be designed with the crystal performing as a series-mode resonant circuit.

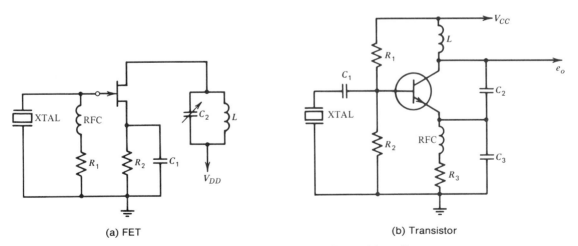

(a) FET   (b) Transistor

Figure 4-12 Crystal (parallel-mode) oscillators.

The crystal is placed in the feedback path and offers a low impedance only to the oscillator frequency. Figure 4-13a shows a transistor crystal oscillator. The feedback is inserted at the emitter. C_2 is adjusted for amount of feedback. R_1 and R_2 set the base voltage. C_1 places base at RF ground, making the stage a common base configuration.

Figure 4-13b shows an FET oscillator using series-resonance feedback. The crystal and R result in grid-leak bias. C isolates the crystal from V_{DD}. The stage may also include source bias, which results in a combination of fixed and grid leak bias.

Crystal oscillator circuits may be designed to operate with any one of a large number of crystals. Each crystal shifts the frequency of oscillation to a different fixed frequency. The crystal is simply plugged into a crystal socket.

A *crystal oven* can be used for applications that require a greater frequency stability than can be accomplished with the normal change of ambient temperature according to time of day and season of year. The oven is heated electrically to a higher ambient temperature and contains a thermostatic control that can maintain the temperature within a fraction of one degree. Once the crystal frequency is established at the elevated oven temperature, the output frequency is established at the elevated oven temperature, the output frequency is maintained constant unless subjected to an ambient temperature higher than the oven temperature.

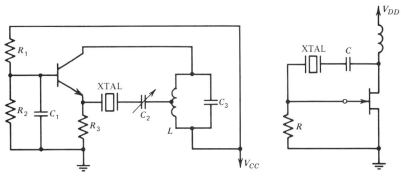

Figure 4-13 Crystal (series-mode) oscillators.

(a) Transistor

(b) FET

4-20
Summary

The basic requirements for oscillation are a signal feedback from output to input, of proper phase, and sufficient amplitude. Some oscillators use R-C elements for phasing. Tunable oscillators generally function with L-C elements. Almost any type of amplifying device (i.e., an op amp) can be used as an oscillator, but care must be exercised to avoid parasitic oscillation. *Fixed* frequency oscillators use *crystals* as the frequency controlling element.

Now return to the objectives and self-evaluation questions at the beginning of this chapter and see how well you can answer them. If you cannot answer certain questions, place a check next to each of them and review appropriate parts of the text. Then answer the questions and solve the problems below.

4-21
Questions

Q4-1 Referring to Fig. 4-4b indicate the effect on the operation of the oscillator of the following malfunctions:
  a. C_1 open.
  b. R_3 shorted.
  c. C_3 shorted.
  d. L_3 open.
  e. L_1 open.
  f. C_2 open.

Q4-2 Compare Figs. 4-4a and 4-4c and note the differences.

Q4-3 Compare Figs. 4-4b and 4-4c and note the differences.

Q4-4 Describe the operation of the Hartley oscillator.

Q4-5 Compare the circuits of Figs. 4-5a and 4-5b with respect to simplicity and stability.

Q4-6 Referring to Fig. 4-5b indicate the effect on the operation of the following malfunctions:
  a. Open C_1.
  b. Shorted C_1.
  c. Open RFC.
  d. Shorted RFC.
  e. Shorted L_1.
  f. Open L_3.
  g. Open R_1.
  h. Shorted C_2.

Q4-7 Referring to Fig. 4-6a, describe the operation of a Colpitts oscillator.

Q4-8 Referring to Fig. 4-6b, indicate the effect on the operation of the following malfunctions:
  a. Shorted C_1.

b. Open R_3.

c. Shorted C_3.

d. Open RFC.

e. Open C_2.

f. Shorted RFC.

Q4-9 Referring to Figs. 4-6a and 4-6b, what are the significant differences? Why is a plate/collector coupling capacitor required in one design but not in the other?

Q4-10 List five other types of RF oscillators.

Q4-11 What is the basic advantage of a crystal oscillator over the tunable oscillators?

Q4-12 What is the electrical equivalent circuit of a quartz crystal?

Q4-13 What is the significance of the plane in which the crystal slab is cut out of the raw crystal?

Q4-14 What is the limitation on the highest frequency of operation of a crystal?

Q4-15 Referring to Figs. 4-12a and 4-12b compare:

a. The types of oscillators.

b. The feedback method.

c. The bias.

d. The function of RFC.

e. Lack of gate coupling capacitor compared to function of base coupling capacitor.

Q4-16 Referring to Fig. 4-12b indicate the effect on the operation for the following malfunctions:

a. Open R_1.

b. Shorted L.

c. Open C_2.

d. Shorted RFC.

e. Open R_3.

f. Shorted C_1.

Q4-17 What is the basic distinction between the units of Fig. 4-12 and Fig. 4-13?

Q4-18 Compare Figs. 4-13a and 4-13b as to method of feedback.

Q4-19 Referring to Fig. 4-13a indicate the effect on the operation of the following malfunctions:

a. Open crystal.

b. Shorted C_1.

c. Open L.

d. Shorted C_2.

e. Open R_3.

f. Shorted R_1.

Q4-20 Describe the function and operation of a crystal oven.

**4-22
Problems**

P4-1 Referring to the Hartley oscillator, Fig. 4-5a, determine the frequency of oscillation and minimum h_f required for the stage: $L_1 = 400$ mH, $L_2 = 10$ mH, $C = 100$ pF, $h_o = 500$ μS, $h_i = 2$ kΩ, and $h_r \approx 0$.

P4-2 Referring to the Colpitts oscillator, Fig. 4-6a, given $C_1 = 280$ pF, $C_2 = 1000$ pF, $L = 50$ μH, and $r_d = 20$ kΩ, determine the frequency of oscillation and the minimum value of g_{FS}.

P4-3 Given a crystal temperature coefficient characteristic of 3 parts per million per °C, and an oscillator frequency of 50 MHz, determine the drift in crystal frequency if the room temperature rises 45 °C.

P4-4 Referring to the phase shift oscillator, Fig. 4-2, given $R = 15$ kΩ and $C = 300$ pF, calculate the frequency of oscillation.

P4-5 Referring to the Clapp oscillator, Fig. 4-7, given $C_2 = C_4 = 200$ pF, $C_3 = 400$ pF, $L = 200$ μH, calculate the resonant frequency.

P4-6 A short-wave receiver frequency range is 30 to 120 MHz. The minimum capacitance of the tuning capacitor is 60 pF. Calculate the maximum capacitance.

P4-7 Referring to the Hartley oscillator, Fig. 4-5b, determine the frequency of oscillation and minimum g_{FS} required for the stage: $L_1 = 600$ μH, $L_2 = 15$ μH, $C = 300$ pF, $r_d = 25$ kΩ.

P4-8 Referring to the Colpitts oscillator, Fig. 4-6b, determine the frequency of oscillation and minimum value of h_f: $C_1 = 1000$ pF, $C_2 = 6000$ pF, $L = 500$ μH, $h_o = 900$ μS, $h_i = 1200$ Ω, and $h_r \approx 0$.

Chapter 5

Amplitude Modulation

5-1
Objectives
To learn:

1. The basics of amplitude modulation (AM).
2. The frequency components of an AM wave.
3. The calculation of index of modulation.
4. The power components of an AM wave.
5. Methods of modulating an RF signal.
6. The basics of pulse modulation.

5-2
Self-Evaluation
Questions
Test your prior knowledge of the information in this chapter by answering these questions as you read the chapter. Your final evaluation of whether you understand the material is measured by your ability to answer these questions. When you have completed the chapter, return to this section and answer the questions again.

1. Why are carrier frequencies necessary?
2. Define a carrier frequency.
3. Distinguish between the oscillator frequency and the carrier frequency at the transmitter.
4. Can an unmodulated carrier convey intelligence? Explain.
5. What are the characteristics of AM?
6. Distinguish between high-level and low-level modulation.
7. What is the function of the buffer in the AM transmitter?
8. What is the function of an RF driver?
9. Which is the modulator stage?
10. What are the advantages and disadvantages of high-level and low-level modulation?
11. Define the "envelope" of the AM waveform.
12. What is the output of an AM broadcast station during a pause in a speech?
13. Why does FCC forbid overmodulation?

5-3
Introduction
to Amplitude
Modulation (AM)
Telephone communication takes the original audio signal at the transmitter and transports it through cable to the receiver *without converting* the audio to any other form. Low frequency (audio) *cannot* economically be radiated through space. The method used for transmission of audio signal *in space* is to *relocate* the audio frequencies to the RF range. The process of *mixing* the audio with the radio frequency (RF) is called *modulation*. The original (pure) RF signal is called the *carrier* signal (frequency assigned by FCC to a broadcast station). This term means that the original RF will *carry* the audio signal. The *mixed* carrier is now *modulated* (altered) by the audio signal. The audio signal is called the *modulating* signal.

5-4
Types of
Modulation
The carrier signal may be altered (modulated) in any one of several ways to reflect the presence of the modulating audio. The *amplitude* of the carrier may be varied to correspond to the audio variations. This is called *amplitude modulation* (AM). The *frequency* of the carrier may by varied, in which case it is called *frequency modulation* (FM). The carrier signal may be switched ON and OFF in alternate intervals to represent a form of Morse code. The carrier transmission may be pulsed ON in some specific sequence, in which case it is a form of *pulse* modulation.

There are also many combinations of the above-listed forms of modulation. There are also sophisticated methods of modulation involving *time sharing* or *frequency sharing*; these are called *multiplexing* methods of modulation. This chapter will concentrate only on the characteristics of *amplitude modulation* (AM) and methods of generating and transmitting an AM carrier.

5-5
ICW
Modulation
The simplest amplitude-varied carrier is a *crystal oscillator*, transmitting at a fixed frequency, in which the transmission is interrupted by opening one of the transistor legs (base, emitter, or collector). If the oscillator *ON-time* is controlled, the traditional *dot* and *dash* of the internationally recognized Morse code is generated. This type of transmission where only *pure* RF is transmitted at the output is called *continuous wave* (CW) transmission. There are many applications of this form of *interrupted CW* (*ICW*), including satellites, radio telegraphy and teletype transmissions.

5-6
AM
Waveforms

In order to represent the *original* (modulating) *audio* signal, the transmitted carrier must reflect a variation that corresponds to the *amplitude* and the *frequency* of the audio. If *either* parameter is missing, the intelligence is *incomplete*.

The results of amplitude modulation (AM) are readily seen on a cathode-ray oscilloscope (CRO) if the frequency range of the scope covers the carrier frequency. In order to simplify the discussion, assume that the modulating signal is a *pure sine* wave, rather than the actual complex waveshape of speech or music. Figure 5-1 shows a typical CRO display. Corresponding to the interval A-B, there is no modulating signal and the RF output is the carrier signal. This is seen to be a high frequency (carrier) sine wave of constant frequency, and maximum amplitude. During interval *B-C*, the modulating signal is increasing. During interval *C-D*, the audio returns to zero, and the RF returns to its original carrier peak. Interval *D-E* has the audio going negative and the carrier peaks decreasing. Interval *E-F* returns the audio to zero and the carrier peaks to normal. Interval *G-H* shows no audio and a normal unmodulated carrier.

Figure 5-1 also shows that the output of a broadcast station continues as pure carrier whenever there is a momentary pause in speech or music. The outline of the modulated carrier is called the *envelope*. To simplify the drawings, the individual RF sine waves will be deleted and the envelope of the amplitude modulated RF signal used, as shown in subsequent figures.

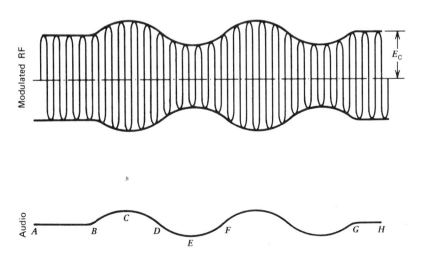

Figure 5-1 AM waveforms.

The *degree of change* of the carrier from its normal unmodulated state is a measure of the *index of modulation* or *percentage of modulation*. If the carrier amplitude corresponding to the negative peak of the audio signal approaches zero, the carrier is then said to be *overmodulated*. Various degrees of modulation are shown in Fig. 5-2, as represented by the envelope or outline of the actual RF amplitude.

Figure 5-2 shows three degrees of modulation. Interval *A-B* (Fig. 5-2a) is an example of AM modulation that is less than 100%. That is to say, the RF peak is not doubled, and at the minimum point there is still RF output. Interval *B-C* (Fig. 5-2b) is longer than interval *A-B*. This signifies a longer period and therefore a lower modulating frequency. The RF peak doubles on the positive half cycle and goes to zero at the negative peak of the audio signal. This is the waveshape for 100% AM modulation. Interval *C-D* (Fig. 5-2c) demonstrates an audio signal that has both a higher frequency and an amplitude that is *too* large. The RF peaks more than double on the positive audio peak and drops to zero when the negative audio becomes larger than the permissible level. This condition is a modulation greater than 100% and is called AM *overmodulation*. FCC regulations prohibit overmodulation operation. It may exceed permissible maximum power for the broadcast station and will generate spurious frequencies beyond the range allocated to the station.

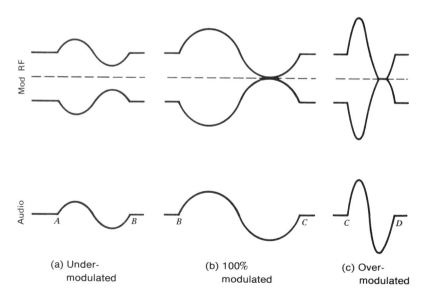

Figure 5-2 Degrees of modulation.

(a) Under-
modulated

(b) 100%
modulated

(c) Over-
modulated

5-7
Calculation
of Modulation
Index

The calculation of the modulation index (percentage of modulation) is easily shown using Fig. 5-3 and Eq. (5-1):

$$m = E_m / E_c \qquad (5\text{-}1)$$

where: m = index of modulation (no units) found from Eq. (5-2)
E_m = peak value of modulating audio signal, volts (V)
E_c = peak value of RF carrier signal, volts (V)

In general the index of modulation (m) is the ratio of the increase of the peak of the modulated RF to the peak of the unmodulated carrier.

In terms of Fig. 5-3, which is readily monitored by a CRO,

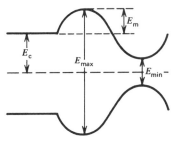

$$m = \frac{E_{max} - E_{min}}{E_{max} + E_{min}} \qquad (5\text{-}2)$$

Figure 5-3 Calculation of Index of Modulation.

The index of modulation can be expressed as a percent modulation by multiplying by 100. The term *modulation factor* or *modulation ratio* is also used for index of modulation.

Example 5-1
Given Fig. 5-3 with $E_{max} = 18$ V, $E_{min} = 6$ V, determine the following
a. Index of modulation
b. Percentage modulation

Solution

a. $m = \dfrac{E_{max} - E_{min}}{E_{max} + E_{min}} = \dfrac{18 - 6}{18 + 6} = \dfrac{12}{24} = \mathbf{0.5}$

b. Percentage modulation $= m \times 100 = 0.5 \times 100$

$$= \mathbf{50\%}$$

5-8
AM Voltage
Calculations

Since the carrier is a pure sine curve it may be expressed as

$$e_c = E_c \sin \omega_c t \qquad (5\text{-}3)$$

where: e_c = instantaneous value of carrier voltage (V)
E_c = peak value of carrier voltage (V)
$\omega_c = 2\pi f_c$ carrier frequency (radians per second)

Similarly, the modulating audio signal is

$$e_m = E_m \sin \omega_m t \qquad (5\text{-}4)$$

where: e_m = instantaneous value of modulating voltage (V)
E_m = peak value of modulating voltage (V)
ω_m = $2\pi f_m$ modulating frequency (radians per second)
When modulation takes place, the instantaneous amplitude of the modulated RF is expressed as

$$e = E_c \sin \omega_c t + m \frac{E_c}{2} \cos(\omega_c - \omega_m)t \ - \frac{mE_c}{2} \cos(\omega_c + \omega_m)t \quad (5\text{-}5)$$

Each of the three terms in Eq. (5-5) for the modulated RF is related to the carrier frequency $\omega_c(=2\pi f_c)$. The first terms is the pure carrier itself. The second term is the carrier frequency *minus* the audio frequency. The third is the carrier *plus* the audio frequency. It becomes apparent that modulating a carrier with a single frequency audio tone contributes a side frequency *above* and *below* the carrier as well as retaining the carrier. These are called the *sideband* frequencies. All three frequencies are broadcast and picked up by the AM receiver. Speech modulation would require a minimum band of frequencies of approximately 4 kHz on either side of the carrier. Music modulation requires 15 kHz on either side of the carrier. AM broadcast is not permitted so much bandwidth except for high fidelity stations. The fact remains that a truly faithful reproduction of the original sound requires a bandwidth that is twice the highest audio signal frequency.

Example 5-2
An AM broadcast station is transmitting at its assigned frequency of 880 kHz. The carrier is modulated by a 3.5 kHz sine wave. Determine the transmitted frequencies.

Solution
The three RF frequencies transmitted are the carrier, lower sideband and upper sideband.

$$\text{Carrier} = \mathbf{880} \text{ kHz}$$
$$\text{Lower sideband} = 880 - 3.5 = \mathbf{876.5} \text{ kHz}$$
$$\text{Upper sideband} = 880 + 3.5 = \mathbf{883.5} \text{ kHz}$$

Equation (5-5) also demonstrates the relative amplitudes of the carrier and each sideband. If the index of modulation is at the 100% maximum, the amplitude of each sideband signal is half the carrier. For m less than one, the sideband voltage is still smaller.

**5-9
AM Power
Calculations**
Translating the voltage relationships into power relationships, the total transmitted power is related to the carrier power (P_c) and sideband power.

$$P_t = P_c + \frac{m^2}{4} P_c + \frac{m^2}{4} P_c \qquad \text{watts (W)} \qquad (5\text{-}6)$$

where: P_t = total transmitted power, watts (W)
$\quad\quad\ P_c$ = carrier power, watts (W)
The second and third terms in Eq. (5-6) are the power of each sideband. Assuming uniform sidebands and combining the sideband power results in:

$$P_t = P_c + \frac{m^2}{2} P_c \qquad \text{watts (W)} \qquad (5\text{-}7)$$

If m is unity, the total sideband power is half of the carrier power. Actually this is true only for sine wave modulation that is not a practical means of communicating. Nevertheless we will use the equations as applicable to all broadcasting.

The intelligence is represented by the sidebands, not the carrier. In fact, the carrier frequency could be deleted from the transmission and a specially designed receiver could pick up and translate the message. This in itself would save a minimum of 66.7% of all the power transmitted. Taking this philosophy a step further, one of the two sidebands could be deleted from the transmission, since the complete intelligence is contained in *each* sideband. This practice is actually accomplished in a form of communication called *Single Sideband* (SSB). Such transmission is done with or without the carrier. It results in savings of transmitted power and required bandwidth. With carrier deleted, the system is called *Single Sideband-Suppressed Carrier* (SSB-SC).

Example 5-3
An AM broadcast station transmits 2 kW of carrier power and uses an index of modulation of 0.7. Calculate:
a. Power of each sideband.
b. Total sideband power.
c. Total transmitted power.
d. Percentage of total power in the sidebands.
e. Percentage of power that can be saved with single sideband transmission.
f. Percentage of power that can be saved with single sideband-suppressed carrier transmission.

Solution

a. Power in each sideband $= \dfrac{m^2}{4} P_c$ (5-6)

$$= \frac{(0.7)^2}{4} \times 2000 \text{ W}$$

$$= \textbf{245 W}$$

b. Total sideband power $= 2 \times 245 = \textbf{490 W}$

c. Total transmitted power, $P_t = P_c + P_{sb} = (2 + 0.49) \text{ kW} = \textbf{2.49 kW}$

d. Percentage of total power in the sidebands

$$\frac{P_{sb}}{P_t} = \frac{0.49}{2.49} \times 100 = \textbf{19.68\%}$$

e. Percentage of power that can be saved with SSB transmission

$$\text{Saving} = \frac{power\ in\ one\ sideband}{total\ power}$$

$$= \frac{0.245}{2.49} \times 100 = \textbf{9.839\%}$$

f. Percentage of power that can be saved with single sideband-suppressed carrier transmission

$$\text{Saving} = \frac{power\ in\ carrier\ plus\ one\ sideband}{total\ power}$$

$$= \frac{2.245\text{W}}{2.490\text{W}} \times 100 = \textbf{90.16\%}$$

5-10
AM Current
Calculations
The operation of a transmitter is commonly monitored by measuring the *antenna* current. Translating the power equation into its current equivalent, the result is

$$I_t = I_c\sqrt{1 + \frac{m^2}{2}} \qquad \text{amperes (A)} \qquad (5\text{-}8)$$

where: I_t is the modulated RF current, amperes (A)
I_c is the unmodulated carrier current, amperes (A)

Example 5-4
An AM broadcast station monitors the antenna current during transmission. The unmodulated carrier current is 200 A. The index of modulation is 0.6. Calculate the modulated antenna current.

Solution

$$I_t = I_c\sqrt{1 + \frac{m^2}{2}} = 200\sqrt{1 + \frac{(0.6)^2}{2}} \qquad (5\text{-}8)$$

$$= 200\sqrt{1.18} = 200 \times 1.086 = 217.3 \text{ A}$$

If more than one audio signal is involved in modulating the carrier, they are combined to form a total modulation factor that is then used in the various equations.

$$m_t = \sqrt{m_1^2 + m_2^2 + m_3^2 + \cdots} \qquad (5\text{-}9)$$

where: m_t = total modulation index
m_1, m_2, m_3 = modulation indexes of the three modulating signals
The total modulation index is required to be no greater than unity.

Example 5-5
An AM transmitter is modulated by three sources of audio with $m_1 = 0.5$, $m_2 = 0.7$, and $m_3 = 0.4$. The unmodulated carrier power is 50 kW. Calculate the modulated power output.

Solution

$$m_t = \sqrt{m_1^2 + m_2^2 + m_3^2} = \sqrt{(0.5)^2 + (0.7)^2 + (0.4)^2}$$

$$= \sqrt{0.25 + 0.49 + 0.16} = \sqrt{0.9} = \textbf{0.9487}$$

$$P_t = P_c + \frac{m^2}{2} P_c = P_c \left(1 + \frac{m^2}{2}\right) = 50 \left[1 + \frac{(0.9487)^2}{2}\right]$$

$$= 50 \left(1 + \frac{0.9}{2}\right) = 50 \times 1.45 = \textbf{72.5 kW}$$

5-11
High-Level
vs.
Low-Level
Modulation

Mixing of the carrier and the audio may take place anywhere in the transmitter, that is where the RF signal power is at its greatest or smallest level or some power level in between. These options are shown in Fig. 5-4.

There are two distinct paths in the AM transmitter: the RF path and the audio path. The mixing of the two signals is the process of modulation. The RF stage is modulated. The audio stage is the modulator. The first RF stage is a fixed frequency, crystal oscillator. Depending on the specifications for frequency stability, it may be housed in an elaborately controlled temperature oven. The buffer acts as an isolator between the oscillator and the rest of the system. This is accomplished by having the oscillator output lightly coupled to the buffer, which is an RF amplifier. The frequency multipliers may not be required for the AM broadcast stations, but other (high frequency) types of AM

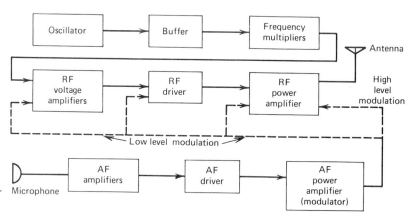

Figure 5-4 High-level vs. low-level modulation.

transmitters, such as short wave, would require them. The RF amplifiers are low-level stages cascaded, each one building up the signal level. The RF driver or excitation stage begins the conversion from voltage level to power output. The final RF stage is the power amplifier. This stage feeds the transmission line that couples to the antenna. Since the main concern is a transfer of power, impedance matching is an important consideration.

The second path is the audio signal. The signal originates electrically in a microphone. It is then passed through as many cascaded audio amplifiers as required. When dealing with high audio power the last voltage amplifier feeds an audio driver stage. The last stage is the power amplifier, which functions as the modulator. Here, too, impedance matching is important. The RF stage (to which the audio power is coupled) becomes part of the audio impedance load.

Conventional AM broadcast practice uses high-level modulation. This method has the audio output connected to the plate/collector of the RF power amplifier. The advantage of high-level modulation is that all the RF stages including the power amplifier can be designed for high efficiency class C operation. When dealing with power of more than 50 kilowatts, this is no laughing matter. The disadvantage of high-level modulation is the requirement to develop a great deal of audio power. Since audio amplifiers are normally operated as low efficiency class A stages (with the possible exception of driver and power amplifier), this method of modulation may require a great deal of audio amplification with a corresponding need for high dc power.

Low-level modulation is the method of mixing the audio and RF at any point in the transmitter prior to the plate/collector of the last stage RF (power) amplifier.

Usually low-level modulation involves the grid/base of the RF power amplifier, but it is possible, particularly for a transistorized transmitter, that both the base of the power amplifier and the collector of the (preceding) RF driver stage will be modulated by the audio. The advantage of low-level modulation is that less audio power is needed. The disadvantage is that the RF, once it is modulated, must be amplified in a linear manner. This results in less efficient operation of all the RF stages amplifying the modulated signal.

5-12 **AM** **Plate** **Modulation** Commercial *broadcasting* is one of the few groups in the electronic industry that is still restricted to vacuum-tube technology. Power outputs ranging in the hundreds of kilowatts or megawatts cannot as yet be accomplished with solid state components. The most common form of AM used in the broadcasting industry is *plate modulation*. This is a form of high-level modulation that results in maximum efficiency. Plate modulation requires variation of the plate voltage of the RF power amplifier in proportion to the modulating signal.

Figure 5-5 shows the general approach used to insert a modulating signal in series with the RF plate voltage. The change in voltage applied to the plate of the RF power amplifier varies the plate current. This in turn determines the amplitude of the RF output. In this way, the RF output is modulated by the audio.

Figure 5-5b is a type of modulator that is no longer popular. The Heising modulator is shown here because it demonstrates some of the problems basic to all forms of plate modulation. The audio choke L_1 is both the load of modulator V_2 and in series with the $B+$ line to the RF power amplifier V_1. As audio is developed across L_1, the V_1 plate voltage varies directly. R_2 lowers the dc voltage to V_1, which is necessary to obtain 100%

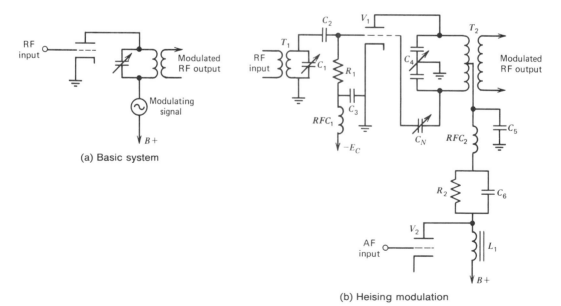

(a) Basic system

(b) Heising modulation

Figure 5-5 AM plate modulation.

modulation. Nevertheless, it is wasteful of energy and lowers overall efficiency. C_6 must be able to pass the lowest modulating frequency, so that R_2 will not act as an attenuator for the audio. C_5 has the conventional RF bypass function but, in addition, it must be selected to have a high impedance to the highest audio frequency. Note that grid-leak bias $(C_2 - R_1)$ is used in addition to fixed bias. The grid-leak bias prevents the grid from drawing excessive grid current when the signal on the plate swings the plate voltage to minimum value. Neutralization is required since V_1 is a triode. The load across V_2 is L_1 in parallel with plate output of V_1. Under these conditions it is difficult to obtain an impedance match for V_2 output.

Heising plate modulation was eventually replaced with a more straightforward form of plate modulation, (Fig. 5-6). In this circuit the Heising audio choke is replaced with a *high quality* audio transformer.

Both the RF power amplifier and the modulator stages are push-pull, and each requires a power driver stage preceding the push-pull stage. *High-power* amplifiers are designed to operate with a plate voltage of *many* kilovolts. A voltage of this magnitude *cannot* be applied to an indirectly heated cathode emitter

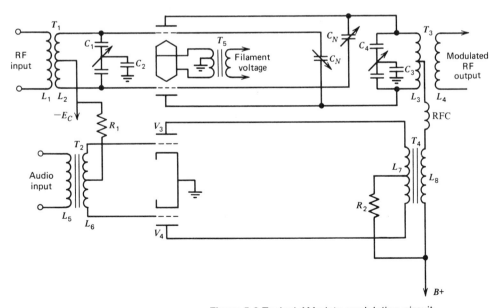

Figure 5-6 Typical AM plate modulation circuit.

without causing serious deterioration of the emitter chemical coating.

The filament emitters shown for V_1 and V_2 require a special transformer power supply. The split-stator tuning capacitors are used in both input and output tanks. Push-pull neutralization is required. The push-pull audio uses transformer coupling at both input and output. These must be high quality components to accommodate the high power and still provide fidelity throughout the frequency range of the modulator. The modulator output transformer is designed for proper impedance match, which guarantees maximum modulator output power. This design is simple compared to the Heising modulator circuit because the dc power provided to the RF power amplifier is *isolated* from the modulator primary.

5-13 AM Grid Modulation The second most common type of AM modulation is *grid modulation*. This has been defined as a form of *low-level* AM modulation. It may be well to note that in TV broadcasting, which also uses amplitude modulation, the high-level modulation is the modulation of the *grid* of the RF power amplifier, rather than the plate. Figure 5-7 shows a typical example of grid modulation.

Figure 5-7 shows a relatively low-power system, but the design is also applicable to high-power requirements. In the

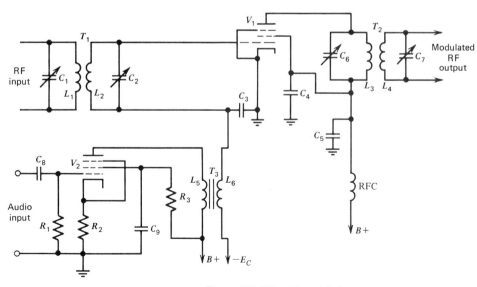

Figure 5-7 AM grid modulation.

high power systems *both* the modulator *and* the RF amplifier are push-pull stages. This circuit (Fig. 5-7) has the modulating signal in series with the $(-E_c)$ line, which biases the grid. In essence we are varying the bias on the RF amplifier in proportion to the audio. This in turn varies the RF amplification. The circuit is reasonably straightforward. Both stages use *beam-power* tubes. The modulator uses cathode bias, which is unbypassed for stabilization. Note the lack of neutralization, since the RF stage is not a triode.

It is common practice to operate the RF amplifier with *fixed* bias rather than *grid-leak* bias, and to adjust the bias for class C operation. However, the grid is *not* driven positive since this would result in distortion of the modulated envelope.

5-14 Alternate Methods of AM Modulation The modulating audio may be inserted in series with tube elements other than plate or grid. The modulation of the cathode or screen grid would result in advantages (and disadvantages) *similar* to plate modulation: A highly efficient RF stage, *but* much modulator power. The modulation of a suppressor grid would have the operating advantages of grid modulation. Figure 5-8 shows these approaches.

Of these three alternate methods of AM modulation, the suppressor grid modulation (Fig. 5-8a) is the *most* sensitive, requiring the *least* audio power. Both cathode modulation (Fig. 5-8b) and screen grid modulation (Fig. 5-8c) require *more* audio

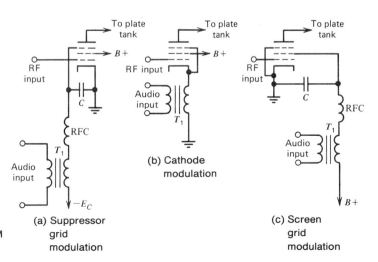

Figure 5-8 Alternate methods of AM modulation.

(a) Suppressor grid modulation

(b) Cathode modulation

(c) Screen grid modulation

power than the control grid or suppressor grid modulation. The screen grid as used in screen grid modulation must be set at a lower voltage than normal. This prevents excessive screen grid voltage and current on the positive peaks of the modulating signal.

5-15
AM Modulation
Using
Transistors

Transistors used as AM modulated systems are presently limited in power output to a few kilowatts. They are useful for mobile applications or conditions where space is severely limited. Transistors can be modulated at base, collector or emitter, with the comparable advantages (similar to respective tube circuits) accruing to each method, as discussed directly below.

5-15.1
AM
Collector
Modulation

In general the advantages of *collector* modulation are similar to those of *plate* modulation. One major distinction is the common practice of modulating the collectors of the RF power amplifier and the RF driver. This shown in Fig. 5-9.

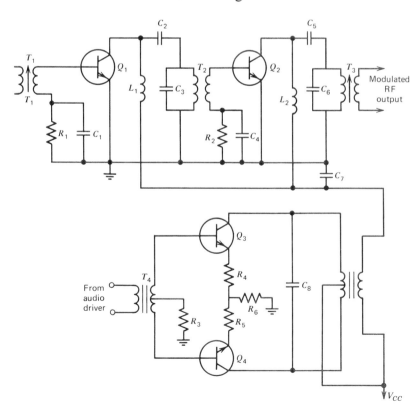

Figure 5-9 AM collector modulation.

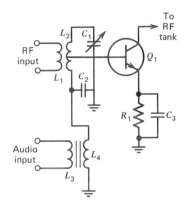

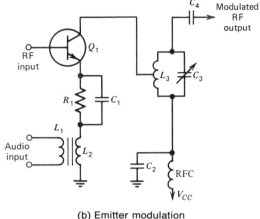

(a) Base modulation (b) Emitter modulation

Figure 5-10 AM base and emitter modulation.

The RF section is conventional, using grid leak bias and shunt feed for the collectors. The audio section uses a driver amplifier preceding a push-pull power amplifier.

5-15.2
AM Base
and Emitter
Modulation

AM *base* modulation is equivalent to *grid* modulation and is subject to the advantages and disadvantages of grid modulation. A typical schematic is shown in Fig. 5-10a.

AM emitter modulation is equivalent to cathode modulation. A typical schematic is shown in Fig. 5-10b.

5-16
Vestigial
Sideband
Modulation

Television broadcast uses a modified form of single sideband modulation. The upper sideband is transmitted in its entirety but only a *small* portion (vestige) of the lower sideband (1.25 MHz) is included (Fig. 5-11). The video portion covers 5.25 MHz and uses amplitude modulation. The sound carrier uses frequency modulation. The total bandwidth assigned to a TV channel is 6 MHz.

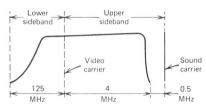

Figure 5-11 Television signal bandwidth.

5-17
Summary
Audio frequencies cannot be transmitted in their original form over distances. They are mixed with an RF signal that then becomes the *carrier* frequency. The process of mixing audio and RF is *modulation*. Amplitude modulation (AM) represents the modulating audio signal by varying the amplitude of the RF carrier in accordance with the amplitude of the audio (and at a rate in accordance with the frequency of the audio). The two basic methods of modulation are high-level and low-level modulation.

Now return to the objectives and self-evaluation questions at the beginning of this chapter and see how well you can answer them. If you cannot answer certain questions, place a check next to each of them and review appropriate parts of the text. Then answer the questions and solve the problems below.

5-18
Questions

Q5-1 Referring to Fig. 5-5b indicate the effect on the operation for the following malfunctions:
a. L_1 shorted.
b. RFC_1 open.
c. C_N shorted.
d. R_2 open.
e. C_6 open.
f. C_5 shorted.
g. C_3 open.

Q5-2 Referring to Fig. 5-6 indicate the effect on the operation the following malfunctions:
a. L_8 open.
b. L_6 shorted.
c. L_5 open.
d. L_7 shorted.
e. C_N open.
f. L_4 shorted.

Q5-3 Referring to Fig. 5-7 indicate the effect on the operation for the following malfunctions:
a. L_1 shorted.
b. C_4 open.
c. C_3 shorted.
d. L_3 open.
e. C_7 shorted.
f. R_2 open.
g. R_3 shorted.

Q5-4 Compare the relative advantage or disadvantage of these various methods of modulation:
a. Plate.

b. Screen grid.
c. Suppressor grid.
d. Grid (control).
e. Cathode.

Q5-5 Referring to Fig. 5-9 indicate the effect on the operation for the following malfunctions:
a. C_1 shorted.
b. L_2 open.
c. C_2 shorted.
d. C_3 open.
e. L_1 shorted.
f. R_6 open.

Q5-6 Referring to Fig. 5-10a indicate the effect on the operation for the following malfunctions:
a. C_2 shorted.
b. L_3 open.
c. R_1 open.
d. C_1 open.

Q5-7 Referring to Fig. 5-10b indicate the effect on the operation for the following malfunctions:
a. L_2 open.
b. C_3 shorted.
c. C_2 shorted.
d. RFC open.
e. C_4 open.

Q5-8 Define ICW modulation.

Q5-9 Explain the reasons for using vacuum-tube modulators rather than solid state modulators.

Q5-10 What is the disadvantage of Heising modulation?

Q5-11 What is the major distinction of plate modulation vs. collector modulation?

**5-19
Problems**

P5-1 Sketch relative AM waveforms resulting from these modulating audio signals. Assume no overmodulation results.
a. 5 V, 500 Hz.
b. 2 V, 1 kHz.
c. 10 V, 5 kHz.

P5-2 Assuming a modulating voltage of 8 V results in 100% modulation, sketch the relative waveforms resulting from the following:
a. 8 V, 200 Hz.
b. 4 V, 400 Hz.
c. 12 V, 600 Hz.

P5-3 Referring to Fig. 5-3, assume $E_{max} = 15$ V, $E_{min} = 5$ V. Calculate the index of modulation.

P5-4 Assuming a broadcast carrier of 880 KHz, and music modulation ranging to 8 kHz, what band of frequencies will be broadcast?

P5-5 Assuming a carrier voltage of 10 V, and a modulation factor of 0.6, what is the amplitude of the voltage on each sideband?

P5-6 Assume a carrier power of 500 W and a modulation index of 0.8 and calculate:

a. Power in each sideband.

b. Percentage of total power in each sideband.

c. Percentage of power saved with single sideband-suppressed carrier transmission.

P5-7 Assume a carrier power of 10 kW and a modulation index of unity, calculate the percentage of total power represented in the sidebands.

P5-8 The unmodulated carrier antenna current is 250 A. The modulation index is 0.8. Calculate the total antenna current with modulation.

P5-9 An AM transmitter is modulated by two audio signals with modulation indexes of 0.6 and 0.8, respectively. If the carrier power is 100 kW, calculate the total power.

Chapter 6 Frequency Modulation

6-2
Self-Evaluation
Questions

Test your prior knowledge of the information in this chapter by answering the following questions. Watch for the answers to these questions as you read the chapter. Your final evaluation of whether you understand the material is measured by your ability to answer these questions. When you have completed the chapter, return to this section and answer the questions again.

1. Define *frequency modulation* (FM).
2. Define the *modulation index* for FM.
3. How do the AM and FM broadcast sidebands compare?
4. Define *phase modulation* (PM).
5. Explain the requirement for *preemphasis* at the FM transmitter.
6. Explain the generation of FM using a capacitor microphone.
7. How is a *varactor diode* used to generate FM?
8. How is a *reactance tube modulator* used to generate FM?
9. Explain the operation of an AFC circuit.
10. What is the distinction between frequency mixing and multiplying?
11. Explain the operation of FM *stereo transmission*.

6-3
Theory of
Frequency
Modulation

Frequency modulation (FM) differs from amplitude modulation (AM) in many important respects. Instead of varying the amplitude of the peak of the RF signal in proportion to the amplitude of the modulating signal, in FM the amplitude of the peak is held *constant*.

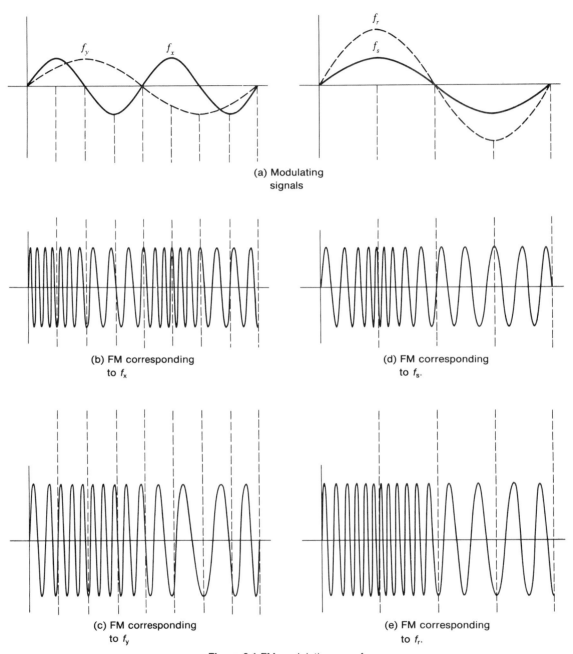

(a) Modulating
signals

(b) FM corresponding
to f_x

(d) FM corresponding
to f_s.

(c) FM corresponding
to f_y

(e) FM corresponding
to f_r.

Figure 6-1 FM modulation waveforms.

The *amplitude* of the *modulating* signal is represented by the *amount* of *frequency deviation* of the RF from the center (rest, carrier) frequency. The *frequency* of the modulating signal is represented by the *rate* of deviation of the carrier frequency (Fig. 6-1).

Comparing the results of modulating signals f_x and f_y, note that the absolute change in the frequency of the FM wave is the same. This derives from the fact that both f_x and f_y have the same maximum amplitude. However Fig. 6-1c has a *single* cyclic variation compared to the *double* cycle of Fig. 6-1b. This feature denotes the relative frequencies of f_x and f_y.

A similar comparison of the results of modulating signals f_r and f_s demonstrates a *single* cycle for both in Figs. 6-1d and 6-1e. This is valid since f_r and f_s are equal in frequency. Figure 6-1e shows a higher change in frequency than Fig. 6-1d. This results from the greater amplitude of f_r over f_s.

6-4 Mathematical Analysis of FM

The instantaneous *frequency* of the frequency modulated wave is expressed mathematically as

$$f = f_c (1 + kE_m \cos \omega_m t) \qquad \text{hertz (Hz)} \qquad (6\text{-}1)$$

where: f_c = unmodulated carrier frequency, hertz (Hz)
k = proportionality constant
ω_m = $2\pi \times f_m$ (modulating frequency), rad/s
E_m = peak voltage of modulating signal, volts (V)

The maximum change or the deviation of carrier frequency occurs when $\cos \omega_m t = \pm 1$, at which time the instantaneous frequency becomes

$$f = f_c (1 \pm kE_m) \qquad \text{hertz (Hz)} \qquad (6\text{-}2)$$

The maximum frequency deviation, delta (δ), is expressed as

$$\delta = f_c kE_m \qquad \text{hertz (Hz)} \qquad (6\text{-}3)$$

where: δ = maximum frequency deviation, hertz (Hz

Mathematically it can be shown that the instaneous *voltage* of the FM signal is

$$e = A \sin \left(\omega_c t + \frac{\delta}{f_m} \sin \omega_m t \right) \qquad \text{volts (V)} \qquad (6\text{-}4)$$

where: A = maximum voltage of carrier frequency, volts (V)
   $\omega_c = 2\pi f_c$ rad/s

The *modulation index* for FM is expressed as

$$m_f = \frac{\text{(maximum) frequency deviation}}{\text{modulating frequency}} = \frac{\delta}{f_m} \qquad (6\text{-}5)$$

where: m_f = modulation index

The basic voltage equation for FM can now be rewritten as

$$e = A \sin(\omega_c t + m_f \sin \omega_m t) \qquad (6\text{-}6)$$

It is significant that the index of modulation for FM is dependent on the ratio of two distinct and independent components. The deviation δ would be defined for any particular broadcasting system. Commercial FM stations operating in the 88 to 108 MHz range use a deviation of ± 75 kHz. The audio system of a television broadcast is FM, and operating with a maximum deviation of ± 25 kHz. Other less demanding FM systems, such as the SCA (Subsidiary Communications Authorization) and narrow bandsystems use a δ of ± 15 kHz in their transmissions.

Example 6-1

Assume an FM system has a frequency deviation of 10 kHz when the modulating signal has an amplitude of 4 V and a frequency of 2kHz. Determine the frequency deviation if the audio signal is

a. Increased to 6 V.

b. Changed to 5 kHz.

c. Increased to 10 V and a frequency of 8 kHz.

Solution

a. $\delta \approx k E_m f_c = k' E_m$ (6-3)

  $10 \text{ kHz} = k'(4 \text{ V})$

  $k' = \dfrac{10 \text{ kHz}}{4 \text{ V}} = 2.5 \text{ kHz/V}$

  Deviation at $E_m = 6$ V

  $\delta = 2.5 \dfrac{\text{kHz}}{\text{V}} \times 6 \text{ V} = 15 \text{ kHz}$

b. The frequency of the modulating signal has no bearing on the amplitude of deviation; therefore the deviation remains the original 10 kHz.

c. Ignoring the change in frequency, the deviation becomes

$$\delta = 2.5 \frac{\text{kHz}}{\text{V}} \times 10 \text{ V} = \textbf{25 kHz}$$

Example 6-2

For the values of Ex. 6-1, determine the index of modulation.

Solution

a. $m_f = \dfrac{\delta}{f_m} = \dfrac{15 \text{ kHz}}{2 \text{ kHz}} = \textbf{7.5}$ $\qquad\qquad$ (6-5)

b. $m_f = \dfrac{10 \text{ kHz}}{5 \text{ kHz}} = \textbf{2}$

c. $m_f = \dfrac{25 \text{ kHz}}{8 \text{ kHz}} = \textbf{3.125}$

Example 6-3

For an FM wave represented by the voltage equation $e = 10 \sin(8 \times 10^8 t + 7 \sin 6 \times 10^4 t)$
determine:

a. The carrier frequency.
b. The modulating frequency.
c. The modulation index.
d. The maximum deviation.
e. The power dissipated in an 8 Ω load.

Solution

a. $f_c = \dfrac{\omega_c}{2\pi} = \dfrac{8 \times 10^8}{2\pi} = \textbf{127.3 MHz}$ $\qquad\qquad$ (6-4)

b. $f_m = \dfrac{\omega_m}{2\pi} = \dfrac{6 \times 10^4}{2\pi} = \textbf{9.549 kHz}$

c. $m_f = 7$ (from given equation)

d. $\delta = m_f \times f_m = 7 \times 9.549 = \textbf{66.84 kHz}$ $\qquad\qquad$ (6-5)

e. $P = \dfrac{(E_{\text{rms}})^2}{R} = \dfrac{(10/\sqrt{2})^2}{8} = \dfrac{50}{8} = \textbf{6.25 W}$

6-5
Frequency
Components
of an FM Wave

The description of the FM wave is considerably more complex than the equivalent AM wave. The AM consisted of a constant strength carrier with the addition of an upper and lower sideband displaced from the carrier by the frequency of the modulating signal. FM, on the other hand, contains many sidebands. Each successive sideband is displaced from the next adjacent band by the frequency of the modulating signal. The number of sidebands and the *signal strength* of each sideband is determined by the *modulation index*.

Mathematically the sidebands are defined by a set of tables or curves (Fig. 6-2) called *Bessel* functions. These functions are plotted relative to the amplitude of the carrier and trace the *relative amplitude* of each sideband and carrier for different values of *modulation index*. A plot of Bessel functions is shown in Fig. 6-2.

Each of the sidebands whose amplitudes are determined by the curves in Fig. 6-2 present a waveshape in the form of a damped oscillation, which is a function of their instantaneous modulation index. The carrier signal represented by J_o actually disappears at *specific* high values of m_f. At a particular value of m_f the energy will be distributed over the many sidebands in a manner indicated by the chart.

FM also differs from AM with regard to variation in total transmitted power with modulation. AM increases total transmitted power with a modulation up to a maximum increase of

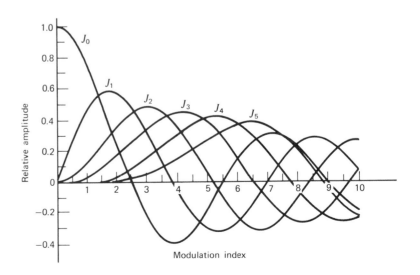

Figure 6-2 Bessel functions.

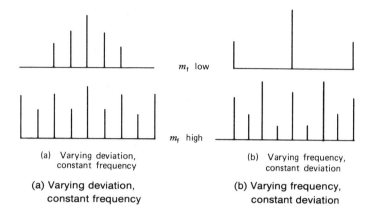

(a) Varying deviation,
constant frequency

(b) Varying frequency,
constant deviation

Figure 6-3 FM frequency spectra.

(a) Varying deviation,
constant frequency

(b) Varying frequency,
constant deviation

50%. During the process the carrier power remains constant and the 50% increase appears as sideband power. In the FM wave the total power remains constant, but the distribution of energy over the sidebands varies with modulation.

The modulation index (m_f) for FM varies directly with the deviation (δ) and inversely with the modulating frequency. The deviation (δ) varies with amplitude of modulating signal. Therefore m_f can be varied by holding the frequency constant and varying the amplitude of the audio signal. This results in sidebands that are frequency spaced the same amount but the amplitudes (and extent) of the sidebands would differ. This is shown in Fig. 6-3a. Another possibility for m_f variation is to keep the deviation constant and vary the frequency of the modulating signal. This results in sidebands that are spaced differently as shown in Fig. 6-3b. In practice, both the amplitude and frequency of the modulating signal are varying and the result is a complex FM waveshape described mathematically by Bessel functions.

The bandwidth required for an FM system can be calculated after referring to the Bessel function tables and deciding which is the highest J term to be included for a particular modulation index. A rough approximation of required sideband is the sum of deviation plus highest modulating frequency. The bandwidth then becomes this number doubled. A more specific definition of this relationship is listed in Table 6-1.

FM broadcast standards specify a maximum deviation of 75 kHz and a maximum modulating frequency of 15 kHz. This equates to an m_f of 75/15 or 5.

Table 6-1
Bandwidth Required for a FM Signal

Modulation Index (m_f)	Number of Significant Sidebands	Bandwidth	
		As Multiple of Modulating Frequency	As Multiple of Frequency Deviation
0.1	2	2	20
0.5	4	4	8
1	6	6	6
2	8	8	4
5	16	16	3.2
10	28	28	2.8

Example 6-4

Assuming FM broadcast deviation standards of ± 50 kHz and a maximum modulating frequency of 10 kHz. Determine the bandwidth.

Solution

$$m_f = \frac{\delta}{f_m} = \frac{50 \text{ kHz}}{10 \text{ kHz}} = 5 \qquad (6\text{-}5)$$

From Table 6-1, for $m_f = 5$, the required bandwidth is $3.2 \times$ frequency deviation

$$\text{BW} = 3.2\,\delta = 3.2 \times 50 \text{ kHz} = \mathbf{160 \text{ kHz}}$$

6-6 Phase Modulation
Phase Modulation (PM) and FM are forms of angle modulation. If the phase of the carrier is shifted slightly during the interval of a period, the result is a change in the frequency of the carrier. Further if this phase change corresponds to a *modulating* audio signal, the output is then a form of FM.

Mathematically the PM equation is expressed

$$e = A \sin(\omega_c t + m_p \sin \omega_m t) \qquad (6\text{-}7)$$

where: m_p is the modulation index for phase modulating.
Note that with the exception of m_p all other terms are identical to Eq. (6-6).

The modulation index of FM varies with f_m as well as audio amplitude. The modulation index of PM is proportional to audio amplitude only. For a fixed f_m, both FM and PM would vary in the same manner. In practice, since low frequencies increase the m_f for FM, but have no effect on the m_p for PM, an interesting feature develops at the receiver. PM received by an FM receiver would seem to be lacking bass.

Example 6-5

A PM transmitter is operating at a carrier of 100 MHz with a carrier voltage of 8 V. The modulating signal has an amplitude of 3 V and a frequency of 6 kHz resulting in a deviation of 60 kHz. Write the voltage equation for the following conditions.

a. Original values.
b. Audio amplitude increased to 4 V.
c. Audio frequency increased to 8 kHz.
d. Audio changed to 2 V and 3 kHz.

Solution

a. $\omega_c = 2\pi f_c = 6.283 \times 100 \times 10^6 = \mathbf{6.283 \times 10^8 \ rad/s}$

$\omega_m = 2\pi f_m = 6.283 \times 6 \times 10^3 = \mathbf{3.77 \times 10^4 \ rad/s}$

$m_p = m_f = \delta/f_m = \dfrac{60 \ kHz}{6 \ kHz} = \mathbf{10}$

$e = 8 \sin(6.283 \times 10^8 t + 10 \sin 3.77 \times 10^4 t) \ V$ \hfill (6-7)

b. For an audio voltage increased to 4 V:

$m_p = \tfrac{4}{3} \times 10 = \mathbf{13.33}$

$e = 8 \sin(6.283 \times 10^8 t + 13.33 \sin 3.77 \times 10^4 t) \ V$

c. Audio frequency variation does not change m_p.

However $\omega_m = 6.283 \times 8 \times 10^3 = \mathbf{5.027 \times 10^4 \ rad/s}$

$e = 8 \sin(6.283 \times 10^8 t + 10 \sin 5.027 \times 10^4 t) \ V$

d. An audio amplitude of 2 V changes m_p to $\tfrac{2}{3} \times 10 = 6.667$. An audio change to 3 kHz results in

$\omega_m = 6.283 \times 3 \times 10^3 = \mathbf{1.885 \times 10^4 \ rad/s}$

$e = 8 \sin 6.283 \times 10^8 t + 6.667 \sin 1.885 \times 10^4 t) \ V$

**6-7
Comparison
of AM
and FM**

1. FM transmissions are performed at high carrier frequencies (VHF). This results in a radius of reception that is approximately *line of sight* (antenna to antenna). This restriction on the area of coverage enables the FCC to assign the same frequency channel to adjacent communities. AM has a wider area of coverage but cannot be assigned to adjacent communities.

2. FM is relatively noise free. This results from the less noisy atmosphere at VHF where FM is located. Also the FM *receiver* is designed to minimize noise superimposed on the signal by atmospheric or man-made noise during transmission. Assuming a *white spectra* noise for both AM and FM, the *noise powers per unit bandwidth* is the same. Analysis proves, however, because of the *ratio* of bandwidths, the FM system shows a signal-to-noise improvement over the AM system of 19 dB.

3. Another advantage of FM systems results because of the *capture effect*. In AM systems two signals transmitted at the *same carrier* frequency are both accepted by the receiver and interfere with each other. The identical situation in a FM receiver results in the elimination of the *weaker* carrier. The stronger signal *captures* the receiver.

4. FM systems transmit a *constant* power when modulated. The only variation is a distribution of this constant power over the sidebands as defined by the Bessel functions. The transmitted power of an AM system can increase up to 50%. This feature enables the design of a more efficient FM transmitter, where all RF stages are operated class C.

5. Adjacent channel interference is less of a problem with FM systems because of the 25 kHz guard band for each station.

6. For a single frequency modulating signal, FM can have an *infinite* number of sidebands; AM is limited to one pair.

7. The carrier frequency of the FM may actually disappear at specific values of m_f called *eigen values*. (This condition is not possible for AM unless a *suppressed-carrier* mode is in use.)

8. Sidebands are always symmetrical for both AM and FM systems.

9. On the other hand the increased bandwidth and limited area of reception can be considered *disadvantages* of FM systems.

10. The circuitry of FM systems is more complex and the designs more sophisticated.

**6-8
Narrow Band
Frequency
Modulation**
Narrow Band Frequency Modulation is used for voice communications systems that do *not* require high fidelity reproduction. This would limit the bandwidth to a maximum of ± 15 kHz. *Mobile* communications used in taxicabs, trucks, police, and ambulances fall into this category. As the name implies there are few sidebands in narrow band FM and the index of modulation is usually less than unity.

The first pair of sidebands are the most significant. Their vector phase angles are of opposite sign. The resultant of this phasor sum is combined with the carrier phasor, which is at right angles. The mathematical notation of the result is the standard Eq. (6-7) for phase modulation.

The sound used for TV is frequency modulated. The bandwidth is ± 25 kHz and the quality is adequate for all but the most critical listeners.

**6-9
Preemphasis
Circuits**
The relative amplitudes of the high frequency components of the modulating signal are comparatively small. FM tends to deteriorate the quality of the higher modulating frequencies. This feature is neutralized by using *preemphasis* circuits at the transmitter. This technique artificially amplifies the higher frequency audio signals prior to modulating the carrier. By this means the deviation corresponding to the higher frequencies is increased. This in turn results in higher m_f. The net result is a reduction of noise deterioration for the high audio frequencies.

Since the high frequencies are artificially increased at the transmitter, this process must be compensated at the receiver. This is accomplished in the audio section of the FM receiver by means of a *deemphasis* circuit.

The amount of high frequency amplification or preemphasis has been standardized. In the United States, FM broadcast and TV sound transmission uses a 75 μs preemphasis. Some other countries use a different standard. A circuit that would result in the proper preemphasis is shown in Fig. 6-4a.

A 75 μs preemphasis results in a frequency response curve that has a 3 dB rise at the frequency whose time constant is 75 μs (where $f = 1/2\pi\tau = R/2\pi L$). This is shown in Fig. 6-4b.

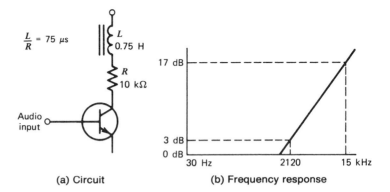

$\frac{L}{R} = 75\ \mu s$

L 0.75 H

R 10 kΩ

Audio input

17 dB

3 dB
0 dB

30 Hz   2120   15 kHz

Figure 6-4 FM preemphasis.   (a) Circuit   (b) Frequency response

---

Example 6-6

The Australian FM broadcast system requires a preemphasis circuit time constant of 50 μs. Design an appropriate preemphasis circuit.

Solution

For Fig. 6-4, assume an $R_L = 10$ kΩ
Time constant $= \tau$ (tau) $= 50$ μs

$= L/R$ seconds

$$L = \tau \times R = 50 \times 10^{-6} \times 10^4 = \mathbf{0.5\ H}$$

6-10
FM Stereo
Transmission

Most quality FM receivers include a *FM stereo* mode of operation. This is generated at the transmitter using *subcarriers*. Figure 6-5 shows a block diagram of a stereo transmitting system.

The audio is picked up by two microphones located to emphasize different (left and right) sections of the orchestra. These are labeled *left* and *right* channels. The microphone outputs are combined in two distinctly different manners. The monaural (monophonic) mixer is a straightforward mix of the two channels. This results in the sum of the channels $(L + R)$ in the frequency range 0-15 kHz.

The second channel receives a more sophisticated treatment. The output of the stereo mix is the difference of the two microphones $(L - R)$, in the frequency range 0 to 15 kHz. This is fed to the balanced modulator. Also fed to the balanced modulator is a 38 kHz carrier provided by a subcarrier generator. The balanced modulator mixes the audio and 38 kHz and

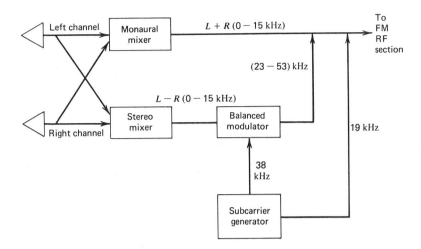

Figure 6-5 FM stereo transmitter.

creates the ± sidebands. Mixing (0-15) kHz with 38 kHz results in a lower sideband of 23 to 38 kHz and an upper sideband of 38 to 53 kHz. At the same time the original 38 kHz carrier is eliminated.

The final frequency groups modulating the FM transmitter are $(0-15)$ kHz representing the *sum* of the two channels, (23-53) kHz representing the *difference* of the two channels, and the 19 kHz signal derived from the 38 kHz subcarrier and used as a synchronizing or local oscillator at the receiver.

The above stereo system permits compatible *monophonic* reception by FM receivers that do not have stereo capability.

6-11 FM Generating Circuits The simplest approach to the generation of FM is to place a capacitor microphone across an oscillator tank (Fig. 6-6a). The total capacitance of the circuit is the sum of the microphone capacitance and the fixed capacitance of the tank. As sound is applied to the microphone, the total capacitance is varied, and the frequency of oscillation deviates accordingly. By this means the total frequency deviation reflects the amplitude of the audio, and the rate of deviation corresponds to the frequency of the audio.

A similar generation is accomplished with a coil (Fig. 6-6b) placed across the oscillator tank and its inductance varied in step with a modulating audio signal.

A variable-capacitance diode called a *varactor* (Fig.6-6c) can have its capacitance varied by changing the amount of reverse bias applied to the diode. If the reverse bias varies with audio, a method of FM generation results.

A basic method of FM generation is the use of a *reactance tube / transistor modulator*. This is a stage that can be designed to

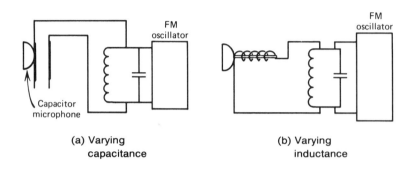

(a) Varying capacitance

(b) Varying inductance

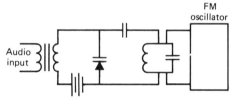

Figure 6-6 Methods of generating FM.

(c) Varactor diode

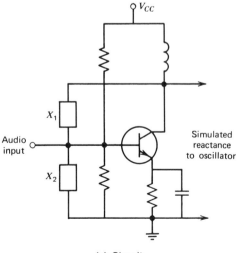

Figure 6-7 Transistor reactance modulator.

(a) Circuit

X_1	X_2	Modulator reactance
L	R	L
C	R	C
R	L	C
R	C	L

(b) Type of reactance

act as an inductance or a capacitance. The amount of L or C the circuit presents to an oscillator tank can be varied by an audio signal or a dc bias voltage that may be adjusted slightly. A typical reactance transistor modulator is shown in Fig. 6-7a. The impedance of X_1 is much greater $(X_1 > 5X_2)$ than the impedance of X_2. For the first grouping in Fig. 6-7b, the $X_1 - X_2$ branch is highly inductive. The voltage applied to the base (voltage across X_2) is lagging the output voltage. As a result, the stage appears inductive (L).

The same type of circuit is used in the FM receiver as an *automatic frequency control* (AFC) device. As such it keeps the receiver *locked* on the incoming signal.

6-12 Direct Method of FM Generation Frequency stability requires crystal control. Since the crystal oscillator cannot be frequency shifted by a modulating voltage, another method must be used (Fig. 6-8). The output frequency of the transmitter (f_s) is compared to the frequency of a highly stable reference crystal oscillator (f_x). These are combined in a mixer and the difference frequency $(f_s - f_x)$ results. The difference frequency is amplified in the IF amplifier that feeds a discriminator. The output of the discriminator is a dc correction voltage that varies with the value of the difference frequency. The dc voltage is applied to a reactance modulator. This varies the simulated L or C output that is applied across the tank of the FM oscillator. This reactance *shifts* the frequency of the FM oscillator in a direction that *minimizes* the difference frequency.

The buffer guarantees a light load for the FM oscillator, thus encouraging frequency stability. The RF amplifier and limiter result in an RF output with uniform peaks. This is necessary

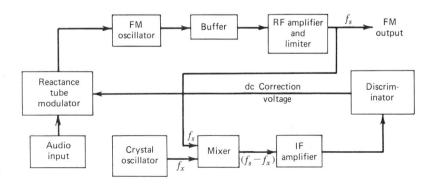

Figure 6-8 FM transmitter using AFC.

because the discriminator is sensitive to peak variations as well as frequency variations. A typical block diagram is shown in Fig. 6-8.

6-13
Indirect
Method
of FM
Generation

The indirect method of generating FM uses the Armstrong system. The advantage of this first generation method over the indirect or AFC system is the use of a crystal oscillator as the basic FM oscillator. It is a form of phase modulation (PM) and requires both frequency mixing (translation) and frequency multiplication.

The distinction between frequency mixing and frequency multiplication can be readily expressed by monitoring the sideband frequencies. Assume a carrier frequency of 10 MHz with a sideband frequency of 5 kHz. If the signal is fed through a doubler and then a tripler for a total multiplication of six, the resulting output frequency will be a carrier of 60 MHz with a sideband frequency of 30 kHz. On the other hand, if the carrier is translated to 60 MHz by mixing the 10 MHz with a 50 MHz signal, the sideband will remain the original 5 kHz.

The Armstrong system uses some circuits that have not been discussed previously. These are shown in block diagram form in Fig. 6-9.

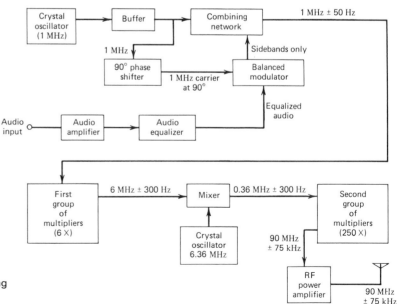

Figure 6-9 FM transmitter using Armstrong system.

The assigned oscillator frequencies and deviations are included as an illustrative set of figures that vary for each FM transmitter. The basic crystal oscillator operates at a low RF frequency (1 MHz), which results in stability and a frequency deviation of ± 50 Hz. The limitation of this system is the small amount of frequency deviation that can be accomplished at the oscillator frequency. This is multiplied 6 times, resulting in 6 MHz ± 300 Hz.

In order to transform ± 300 Hz deviation to the specified ± 75 kHz, a multiplication factor of 75/0.3 or 250 is required. This same multiplication applied to the 6 MHz frequency results in a carrier of 1500 MHz instead of the required 90 MHz. The frequency translation following the first group of multipliers results in an output of 0.36 MHz ± 300 Hz. A further multiplication of 250 results in the FCC required carrier of 90 MHz ± 75 kHz.

Referring to Fig. 6-9, it is noted that the 1 MHz oscillator signal is sent through a phase shifter and shifted 90°. The *balanced modulator* receives the phase shifted 1 MHz and the modulating equalized audio. The sidebands are created in the balanced modulator. In addition the 1 MHz RF signal is cancelled, leaving only the 90° shifted sidebands as the balanced modulator output.

The combining network accomplishes the vector addition of the sidebands and the original 1 MHz. The resulting output is FM.

The audio equalizer introduces bass boosting of the audio. This amplifies the *low* frequency end of the audio and results in FM rather than PM.

6-14 Summary

1. Frequency modulation is a method of communications in which the carrier frequency is varied in accordance with the amplitude of the modulating audio at a rate that corresponds to the frequency of the audio.
2. Phase modulation is a variation of FM.
3. Bessel tables define the characteristics of the FM sidebands.
4. FM is less susceptible to noise interference than AM.
5. FM may be wide band, narrow band, or stereo transmission.
6. FM transmitters use preemphasis circuits.

Now return to the objectives and self-evaluation questions at the beginning of this chapter and see how well you can answer them. If you cannot answer certain questions, place a check next to each of them and review appropriate parts of the text. Then answer the questions and solve the problems.

**6-15
Questions**

Q6-1 What are the FCC specifications for:
   a. Broadcast FM.
   b. Audio FM of TV transmission.
   c. Mobile FM.
Q6-2 What is the significance of Bessel functions to FM?
Q6-3 Compare change in total power transmission with modulation for AM and FM.
Q6-4 If frequency deviation is held constant and the audio frequency is increased, what effect is there on the modulation index and sidebands?
Q6-5 If the modulating frequency is held constant and the amplitude is increased, what effect is there on the modulation index and sidebands?
Q6-6 State the rule for approximating the required FM bandwidth.
Q6-7 Explain the difference in modulation index for FM and PM.
Q6-8 Define the advantage and/or disadvantage of AM vs. FM with regard to:
   a. Broadcast range.
   b. Complexity of transmitter circuitry.
   c. Efficiency of transmission.
   d. Noise free transmission.
   e. Adjacent channel interference.
   f. Bandwidth requirements.
Q6-9 What is the significance of deemphasis?
Q6-10 What is the U. S. standard for preemphasis?
Q6-11 In the FM transmitter diagram of Fig. 6-8 define the function of the following:
   a. Buffer.
   b. Limiter.
   c. Discriminator.
   d. Mixer.
Q6-12 Explain the operation of Fig. 6-8.
Q6-13 For the Armstrong system of Fig. 6-9 define the function of the following:
   a. 90° phase shifter.
   b. Balanced modulator.
   c. Audio equalizer.
   d. Combining network.
Q6-14 Explain the operation of the Armstrong system of Fig. 6-9.
Q6-15 What is the relationship of sidebands and narrow band FM?

6-16
Problems

P6-1 Assume an FM system has a frequency deviation of 15 kHz when the modulating signal has an amplitude of 5 V and a frequency of 3 kHz. Determine the deviation if the audio signal is

a. Decreased to 4 V.

b. Changed to 4 kHz.

c. Increased to 8 V and a frequency of 6 kHz.

P6-2 For the values of Problem 6-1, determine the index of modulation.

P6-3 For an FM wave represented by the voltage equation

$$e = 8\sin(6 \times 10^8 t + 5\sin 4 \times 10^4 t)$$

determine:

a. Modulating frequency.

b. Carrier frequency.

c. Modulation index.

d. Maximum deviation.

e. Power dissipated in a 6 Ω load.

P6-4 A PM transmitter is operating at a carrier of 110 MHz with a carrier voltage of 12 V. The modulating signal has an amplitude of 4 V and a frequency of 5 kHz, resulting in a deviation of 50 kHz. Write the equation for the followng conditions:

a. Original values.

b. Audio amplitude increased to 6 V.

c. Audio frequency increased to 10 kHz.

d. Audio changed to 3 V and 4 kHz.

P6-5 Determine the value of L for the preemphasis circuit (Fig. 6-4a) assuming a preemphasis time constant of 60 μs and resistance of 8 kΩ.

P6-6 Using Fig. 6-9 as a guide, design a transmitter to operate at 108 MHz with a deviation of ± 50 kHz.

P6-7 Assuming FM broadcast standards of ± 60 kHz and a maximum modulating frequency of 6 kHz, determine the required bandwidth.

P6-8 An FM wave is defined by the voltage equation

$$e = 12\sin\left(14 \times 10^8 t + 9\sin(8 \times 10^4 t)\right)$$

Determine:

a. The power dissipated in a 8 Ω load.

b. Maximum frequency deviation.

P6-9 Assuming FM broadcast standards of ± 60 kHz and a modulating frequency of 12 kHz. Deterime the bandwidth.

P6-10 Refer to Fig. 6-9. Design a FM system to operate at 100 MHz with a deviation of ± 60 kHz.

Chapter 7

**AM
and
FM
Receivers**

**7-1
Objectives**

To learn:

1. The basic components of an AM receiver.
2. The crystal headset receiver.
3. The TRF receiver.
4. The superheterodyne receiver.
5. The FM receiver.
6. The FM discriminator.

**7-2
Self-Evaluation
Questions**

Test your prior knowledge of the information in this chapter by answering the following questions. Watch for the answers to these questions as you read the chapter. Your final evaluation of whether you understand the material is measured by your ability to answer these questions. When you have completed the chapter, return to this section and answer the questions again.

1. What is the advantage of the crystal headset receiver?
2. What is one disadvantage of the TRF receiver?
3. State the advantages of the superheterodyne AM receiver.
4. Give the function of the local oscillator.
5. What frequencies are found in the mixer stage?
6. Why is the IF frequency the only signal out of the mixer?
7. Define the image frequency.
8. Define the function of AGC.
9. Define receiver tracking.
10. Define AM receiver sensitivity.
11. Define receiver selectivity.
12. Define the function of the FM discriminator.

**7-3
Introduction**

Receivers are available in many forms, applications, and prices. AM receivers are available in cigarette-package size for $1.50 and in high fidelity units for many hundreds of dollars. There are FM receivers, stereo FM receivers, and TV color and black and white receivers. There is a variety of specialized communications receivers, including multiband short-wave receivers, ship-to-shore receivers, radar receivers, satellite receivers, loran receivers, citizens band receivers, and a host of other receivers. This chapter will concentrate on the principles of AM and FM receivers.

7-4 Crystal Headset Receiver The simplest AM receiver is the *crystal headset* receiver. The unit requires no external power. Therefore it can be stored away indefinitely and used in an emergency. It can be used in lifeboats, wilderness, mountains, etc. The receiver contains an antenna, which could be made of a hundred feet of wire, a tunable section to select the desired transmitted frequency, a *detector* that extracts the audio from the modulated RF, and the headset that converts the audio signal to sound. A typical crystal headset is shown in Fig. 7-1.

The antenna intercepts all RF signals in the area and passes them to the primary coil L_1. The tank L_2C_1 is tunable. The desired RF signal is determined by the L_2C_1 tank. This signal is impressed across the series circuit, consisting of the diode D and the capacitor C_2, which make up the *AM detector*.

Assume the input signal is amplitude-modulated RF. Because the diode is connected for reception of *positive* signals, the AM-RF is *rectified* as indicated in Fig. 7-2a.

This rectified signal is *filtered* by C_2 with the results shown in Fig. 7-2b. The capacitor acts as a low impedance for RF and a high impedance for audio frequency. The coil of the headset acts in reverse. The output is a combination of audio superimposed on a dc level. This is similar to the operation of a half-wave rectifier power supply. The *dc level* of the detector output is determined by the *carrier peak amplitude*. The audio signal passes to the headset producing a fluctuating magnetic field in the speaker coil. This actuates an air-pressure cone that converts the electrical signal to sound pressure variations.

The literature on the AM crystal headset receiver often includes a notation on the *cat's whisker*, that is, a variable quartz-crystal diode. This is a reference to the technology of the 1920s. The quartz crystal diode had no permanent connection. A fine springlike wire (cat's whisker) was moved along the crystal surface until a good contact was made.

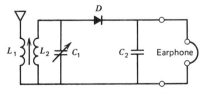

Figure 7-1 AM crystal headset receiver.

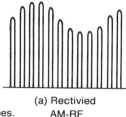

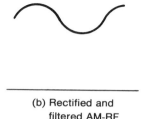

(a) Rectivied
AM-RF

(b) Rectified and
filtered AM-RF

Figure 7-2 AM detector output waveshapes.

The quality of the AM crystal headset receiver is poor in every respect. The *sensitivity* refers to the *weakest* signal that can be properly receiver. For this receiver to operate the incoming tank signal must be greater than the forward bias of the diode. *Selectivity* refers to the ability of the receiver to *reject signals adjacent* to the desired signal. For the crystal headset receiver this parameter is a poor quality because the Q of the tank is low. This is due to the long leads of the tuning capacitor plus the shunting effect on the tank circuit of drawing diode current.

The best that can be said for the AM crystal headset receiver is that beggars cannot be choosers. If a receiver is required and no battery is available to power it, the unpowered receiver of Fig. 7-1 may be the solution.

7-5 AM Tuned Radio Frequency (TRF) Receiver Historically, the early AM receiver was the *tuned radio frequency* (*TRF*) receiver. This consisted of an antenna, 2 or 3 vacuum-tube RF individually tuned amplifier stages, a detector and one or two vacuum-tube audio amplifiers ending with a loudspeaker. The receiver was powered with wet cell batteries that required frequent recharge (Fig. 7-3).

Each tuning capacitor was mechanically coupled to an indexed dial. To tune in a station the dials would be set to the identical number, representing a broadcast station. If the number was correct and each RF tank properly aligned, a signal would come through. The signal would then be optimized by further dial adjustment.

Eventually the tuning was simplified by mechanically coupling all the tuning capacitors to a *single* dial (as shown in Fig. 7-3 by the dashed lines).

The great weakness of the TRF receiver was a tendency to oscillate. This resulted from the multiple triode vacuum-tube RF amplifiers operating at the same frequency. If a small per-

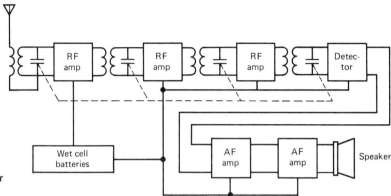

Figure 7-3 Tuned radio frequency receiver (TRF).

centage of the RF signal output at the high-level stage leaked back to the input RF stage, positive feedback and oscillation could result. This leakage might result from power supply coupling, stray capacitance coupling, radiation coupling, or coupling through any other element common to the input and output stages.

Another weakness of the TRF receiver derives from the fact that *every* tuned tank was tunable from 500 to 1600 kHz. The Q of the tank remains approximately the same through the frequency range. This results from the increase with frequency of X_L and the coil resistance due to *skin effect*. The bandwidth being related to the tuned signal (Eq. 2-11), $BW = f_0/Q$, increases as the frequency increases.

Example 7-1

Assuming that the AM TRF receiver bandwidth is an appropriate 20 kHz at the low frequency end, determine the bandwidth at the high frequency end.

Solution

$$Q = f_0/\mathrm{BW} = 550/20 = 27.5 \qquad (2\text{-}11)$$

Assuming a uniform Q, the resulting bandwidth at the high frequency end is

$$\mathrm{BW} = f_0/Q = 1600/27.5 = \textbf{58.18 kHz}$$

Note: A bandwidth of this magnitude would result in the acceptance of undesired adjacent channels. Nevertheless the TRF receiver is superior to the crystal headset receiver in sensitivity and selectivity.

**7-6
Superheterodyne
Receiver**
In 1927 the TRF receiver was superseded by the *superheterodyne* receiver usually called *superhet*. This is the basic operation of almost all modern receivers. As the unit is analyzed, it becomes apparent that both sensitivity and selectivity are improved in comparison to the TRF receiver. A block diagram of the AM superhet receiver is shown in Fig. 7-4.

The dotted lines indicate that the tuning capacitors for the RF amplifier, mixer, and local oscillator (LO) are mechanically on the same shaft. They are thus ganged together, and the capacitor is a ganged capacitor. The LO is designed to operate at a frequency that is 455 kHz higher than that of the incoming modulated RF signal to which the RF amplifier and mixer input are tuned.

The *superhet principle* is a form of *frequency translation*. For the broadcast signal illustrated in Fig. 7-4, the RF amplifier is tuned to 1000 kHz. Likewise the input to the mixer is tuned to 1000 kHz. The LO frequency is always 455 kHz higher than the incoming signal. For the selected station, the LO is oscillating at 1455 kHz.

The process of combining in the mixer the 1000 kHz modulated RF from the RF amplifier with the 1455 kHz pure RF from the LO results in the creation of all combinations of the two signals. In addition to 1000 kHz and 1455 kHz there is also present in the mixer the sum and the difference of the two signals. These are 2455 kHz and 455 kHz. Also present are harmonics of all of these. The second harmonic frequencies are 2000 kHz, 2910 kHz, 4910 kHz, and 910 kHz.

The *mixer* stage is receptive to the introduction of various signals but amplifies only one narrow band of frequencies. The

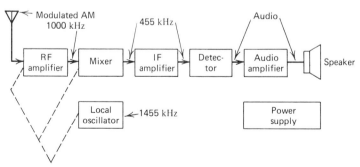

Figure 7-4 AM superheterodyne receiver.

band of frequencies to be amplified is the one that finds a high impedance load at the output of the mixer stage. Since the mixer output tank circuit is designed to be resonant at 455 kHz, this insures amplification of only frequencies close to the 455 kHz signal. All other frequencies see a low impedance tank at the mixer output. Therefore the stage offers low gain for these other frequencies.

Another interesting feature in the operation of a mixer stage is to note the effect on the sidebands of a modulated signal. Assume the same frequencies with a sideband signal at 1010 kHz. Combining this with the LO frequency of 1445 kHz results in 435 kHz. It is apparent that what had originally been an upper sideband is now a *lower* sideband of the 455 kHz carrier. This inversion of sidebands at the output of the mixer is of particular significance in TV receivers.

The next stage is the intermediate (fixed) frequency (IF) amplifier. As a fixed frequency (455 kHz) amplifier, regardless of the station to which the receiver is tuned, there is no need for ganged capacitors. The tanks are fixed, of optimum design, and shielded. The stage has high gain and can be designed as two or three stages cascaded without fear of oscillation.

The detector has a similar function to the TRF receiver detector stage except that the input signal is modulated IF instead of modulated RF.

The audio section may be one or more amplifiers as required for the loudspeaker sound level.

**7-7
RF
Amplifier** Inexpensive AM broadcast receivers are designed without the input RF amplifier. This is possible because local broadcast stations transmit a strong signal, and the receiver need not be of high quality to receive and process the signal.

The RF stage is deleted for economy. The manufacturer saves a stage and can simplify the tuning capacitor from three to two sections. In the highly competitive communications industry, such savings are significant.

High-quality receivers, however, always use an RF amplifier input stage. There are a number of advantages to this design. A comparison of the internal noise of the RF amplifier and the mixer shows considerably less noise in the RF amplifier. This

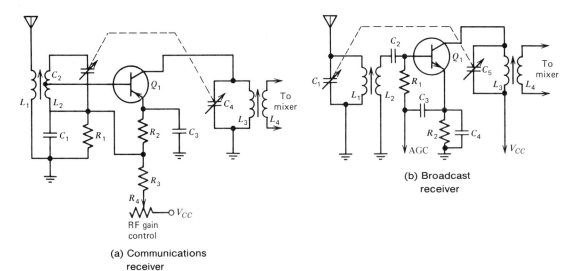

(a) Communications
receiver

(b) Broadcast
receiver

Figure 7-5 RF amplifiers.

feature is readily appreciated if note is taken of the amplitude of the oscillator output. This LO output is on the order of 1 to 5 V. Mixing this level directly with the weak broadcast signal results in a high level of noise that tends to interfere (mask) with the broadcast signal. On the other hand, if the broadcast signal has been amplified in the RF stage, there is less noise masking in the mixer.

The *sensitivity* of a receiver is a measure of the weakest signal that can be accommodated. Conventional AM receivers require an input signal that is greater than the noise developed at the input to the first stage. In the superhet receiver sensitivity is improved through the use of an RF amplifier input stage.

Two typical circuits for RF amplifiers are shown in Fig. 7-5.

Figure 7-5a shows a type of RF amplifier used in communications receivers. The incoming signal may be an extremely weak signal after traveling halfway around the world. It is imperative to set the amplifier bias (operating point) at the optimum value for best reception of the weak signal. This is done manually with a potentiometer labeled *RF Gain*. Do not confuse this adjustment with the *volume control* knob, which simply taps off a portion of the audio signal available in the audio amplifier stages.

The functions of the other components in Fig. 7-5a are similar to those discussed in Ch. 3: L_2 is tapped for impedance match, R_1-R_3 constitute a voltage divider, C_1 is an RF bypass for R_1, R_2 develops emitter bias, and C_2-C_4 are sections of a ganged capacitor.

Figure 7-5b shows a typical RF amplifier used in broadcast receivers. The incoming signal is strong and can afford a little *bucking* or reduction. The AGC line is feeding back a bias voltage that acts as a bucking voltage. This voltage is developed in the detector stage and is proportional to the strength of the carrier of the incoming signal. The significant feature of this method is that even weak input signals will be faced by a bucking voltage but the amount of bucking is less than that which a strong input signal will experience. The fact remains that AGC systems include a built-in penalty.

In summation the advantages/disadvantages of the RF amplifier are:

1. Less noise input.
2. Better image frequency rejection (Sec. 7-8).
3. Additional gain.
4. More efficient method of coupling to the antenna.
5. Some improvement in rejecting adjacent channels.
6. Isolate local oscillator from antenna.

The major disadvantage of including an RF amplifier is the additional cost.

7-8 Image Frequency Rejection One of the above-stated advantages (of including the RF amplifier stage) is *image-frequency rejection*. The image frequency (f_i) of a broadcast signal is a second broadcast signal that is separated from the desired signal by a frequency twice the IF frequency. For example, assume a desired signal at 600 kHz. The image frequency is $(600 + 2 \times 455)$ kHz = 1510 kHz. The RF amplifier would normally tune in the 600 kHz and tune out the 1510 kHz. In the absence of the RF stage, both the 600 kHz signal and the 1510 kHz signal appear at the antenna, are passed to the mixer, and then mixed with the LO signal. For a 600 kHz input the LO frequency is $(600 + 455)$ kHz = 1055 kHz. Mixing 1055 kHz with 600 kHz results in the appropriate 455 kHz IF. However, at the same time the 1055 kHz is mixing with the 1510 kHz image frequency and this difference is *also* the 455 kHz IF. The result is two distinct signals at 455 kHz and both are accepted by the IF amplifier. The listener hears two stations simultaneously.

Example 7-2

For an AM broadcast receiver determine the image frequency and the LO frequency if the desired signal is 550 kHz.

Solution

$$f_i = f_s + 2 \times \text{IF}$$
$$= (550 + 2 \times 455) \text{ kHz}$$
$$= (550 + 910) \text{ kHz}$$
$$= \textbf{1460 kHz}$$
$$\text{LO} = f_s + \text{IF}$$
$$= (550 + 455) \text{ kHz}$$
$$= \textbf{1005 kHz}$$

The degree of image-frequency rejection offered by a single tuned circuit is defined as the ratio of the gain at the desired signal frequency to the gain at the image frequency. The calculation is determined by Eq. (7-1).

$$\alpha = \sqrt{1 + Q^2 \rho^2} \tag{7-1}$$

where: α (alpha) = degree of image frequency rejection

$$\rho \text{ (rho)} = \frac{f_i}{f_s} - \frac{f_s}{f_i} \tag{7-2}$$

where: f_i = image frequency, hertz (Hz)
f_s = desired signal, hertz (Hz)

Example 7-3

Given an AM superhet receiver, determine the image frequency rejection if the Q of the input tank is 125 and the receiver is tuned to 1200 kHz.

Solution

$$f_i = f_s + 2 \times IF = 1200 + 2 \times 455 = 2110 \text{ kHz}$$

$$\rho = \frac{f_i}{f_s} - \frac{f_s}{f_i} \qquad (7\text{-}2)$$

$$= \frac{2110}{1200} - \frac{1200}{2110} = 1.758 - 0.5687 = \mathbf{1.19}$$

$$\alpha = \sqrt{1 + Q^2 \rho^2} \qquad (7\text{-}1)$$

$$= \sqrt{1 + (125)^2 (1.19)^2}$$

$$= \sqrt{1 + 22130}$$

$$= \mathbf{148.8}$$

7-9 Mixers

7-9 Mixers The *mixing* of two signals of different frequencies within an amplifier requires operation in the nonlinear portion of the characteristic curves. This is accomplished in the mixer stage by using a high voltage (1 to 5 V) oscillator signal to *sweep* the operating point through the entire characteristic curve. Superimposed on the LO signal is the weak AM-RF signal. The net result is operation in the nonlinear portion of the characteristic curves.

The mixer accepts the signals from the RF stage, and LO and amplifies the difference signal that is passed to the succeeding stage, the IF amplifier. The converter contains the LO as an integral part of the stage, rather than a separate stage. Therefore the only external signal received is the RF. There may or may not be an RF stage in either case.

In the days of vacuum-tube technology, tubes with multiple grids were commonly used for the mixer or converter. These included pentodes, pentagrids, and multiple-function tubes such as duo-triode or triode-hexode tubes.

As noted earlier, mixers are notoriously noisy. In addition, there is much less gain than would normally accrue to a single frequency amplifier. Bear in mind that two frequencies are being mixed and a resulting weak difference frequency is then amplified.

The most commonly used local oscillator circuits are the Hartley, Colpitts, and variations of each. The Hartley oscillator is used at low RF and the Colpitts at UHF with a poorly defined division of frequency between them. The Armstrong circuit is occasionally found at low RF. In vacuum-tube technology the electron coupled oscillator (ECO) was a common technique. Some typical circuits are shown in Fig. 7-6.

Figure 7-6a shows both the mixer (Q_1) and the local oscillator (Q_2). The LO is an Armstrong oscillator, tuned by the C_7-L_5 tank. Feedback is accomplished through L_6-C_4. Base bias is the result of the R_3-R_4 voltage divider. V_{cc} decoupling is done with the R_6-C_6 decoupling network. L_7 is the LO output signal. This signal is inserted in the mixer by means of the emitter leg of Q_1. The collector network is decoupled by R_2-C_3. The Q_1 collector output is impedance matched by the tap on L_3.

Figure 7-6b shows only the mixer with the two signals to be mixed applied to the gates G_1 and G_2. This stage is the equivalent of a multigrid vacuum tube. This improves the isolation

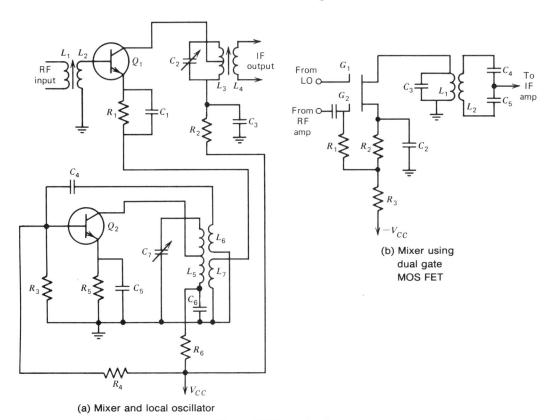

(a) Mixer and local oscillator

(b) Mixer using dual gate MOS FET

Figure 7-6 Mixer circuits.

between the RF input and the LO circuit.

Recent integrated circuit (IC) technology has resulted in high frequency components that are the equivalent of individual transistors coupled together through a third transistor. This technique provides complete isolation and will eventually be the standard for the industry.

7-10
Converters

In vacuum-tube technology, it was common practice to design the LO as an integral part of the mixer, using a pentagrid (five grids) tube. The identical function can be accomplished with a transistor. When the mixing and oscillation functions are combined the circuit is called a *converter*. Figure 7-7 is a typical converter circuit.

The collector configuration contains two distinct circuits. The tank C_5-L_6 is tuned to the IF frequency. This results in the usual amplification of the IF. Also in the collector network is L_4. Physically, L_4 is mounted on a coil form alongside L_5 and L_3. The oscillator frequency signal is not affected by the IF tank in the collector circuit, because it is an off-resonance frequency. Therefore the oscillator signal is passed to L_4. It is then coupled to the L_5-C_4 tank that is tuned to oscillator frequency. This oscillator signal is then reinserted into the amplifier by means of L_3.

This method of using a collector for two frequencies is common in AM-FM receivers. In this case two tanks, AM at 455

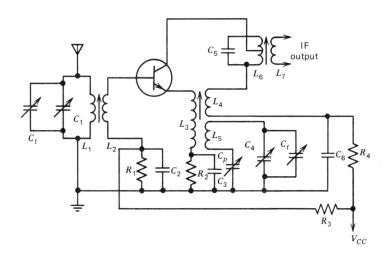

Figure 7-7 Converter circuit.

kHz, and FM at 10.7 MHz, are in *series*. The coil of the FM tank is zero impedance at 455 kHz and the capacitance of the AM tank is zero impedance at 10.7 MHz.

Occasionally the technical literature refers to the mixer or converter stage as the *first detector*. This implies that the audio detector stage is a *second detector*. Fortunately most of the literature is consistent in using *mixer* and *detector* as the titles of the two functions.

7-11
Dial
Tracking
Another problem associated with the LO is frequency *tracking*. This refers to the ability of the LO to change its frequency exactly in step with the tuning dial. As the RF amplifier tunes through the 550 to 1600 kHz broadcast band, the LO variation should be 1005 to 2055 kHz. If there is a change in this differential between the two signals the difference frequency will not be 455 kHz. This in turn results in a shift of the IF carrier and a distorted output.

Actually it is impossible to keep the RF and LO tuning exactly in step. In practice they are designed to be in step at either end and the center of the broadcast band. Such alignment is accomplished with *trimmer* capacitors mounted on the gang capacitor and a *padder* capacitor associated with the LO. The deviation in alignment between the ends and center point is minimized and acceptable. Figure 7-7 shows a basic converter that includes trimmer capacitors C_t across C_1 and C_4. The trimmer capacitors are mounted on each of the gang capacitor sections and are electrically in parallel with each section. The padder capacitance (C_p) is in series with the oscillator coil L_5. At the high frequency end of the dial the gang capacitance is a minimum (30 pF) and the adjustment of C_t is significant. At the low frequency end of the dial, the gang capacitor is fully meshed (300 pF) and the oscillator frequency is adjusted by means of the padder capacitor (C_p).

7-12
IF
Amplifier
The choice of the fixed frequency for the IF amplifier is a compromise. A higher or lower frequency has both advantages and disadvantages, for AM and FM, respectively. The IF frequency for broadcast AM is 455 kHz, the equivalent FM IF frequency is 10.7 MHz, and present-day television IF is 45.75

MHz. Some high frequency communications receivers use an IF of 2 MHz and microwave receivers usually operate with an IF of 30 MHz.

The IF amplifiers are always the *high gain* stages of the receiver because they are *fixed-tuned* and compactly designed and shielded. If the choice of IF frequency is *too* high, the response curve is too broad, and the unwanted adjacent channels are not rejected sufficiently. A high IF also requires the LO to operate at higher frequencies, which in turn results in tracking difficulties. Adjacent channel selectivity is accomplished in the IF stage.

A choice of a low IF makes image-frequency rejection more difficult. In addition the frequency response bandwidth becomes *too narrow* and cuts off some of the sidebands. If this condition is compensated for by lowering the Q of the coils, the stage gain is lowered as well. In general the IF frequency is usually selected below the lowest tuning range of the receiver.

The number of IF stages required depends on the service and design. *Inexpensive* AM broadcast receivers use a *single* stage. FM receivers use two to four stages. TV receivers use three or four stages. Communications receivers use two or three stages.

Solid state IF amplifiers are designed with *double-tuned* tanks that are tapped on one or both coils, or a single-tuned tank that is transformer or capacitive coupled. The stages may be neutralized, but this is not always the case. Figure 7-8 is typical of a two-stage neutralized IF amplifier.

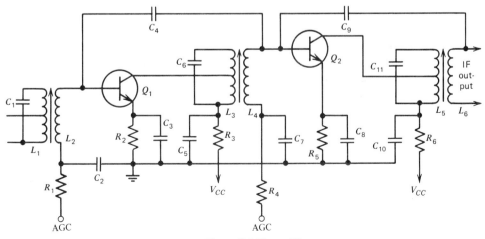

Figure 7-8 IF amplifier.

IF amplifiers are designed with transistors, FETs, and ICs. As a rule transistorized IF sections require more stages than the equivalent vacuum-tube IF section. This results from the use of high impedance tanks for vacuum-tube amplifiers. Note that both stages are provided AGC. The AGC lines are decoupled with R_1-C_2 and R_4-C_7 filter networks. The neutralizing signal is derived from the secondary of the tank and coupled back to the base through C_4 and C_9, respectively.

7-13 AM Detector   The diode detector (Sec. 7-4) is almost universally used as the AM detector. The major disadvantages of the diode detector are compensated for in previous stages. These disadvantages are lack of gain, low sensitivity, and poor selectivity. These failings are made up in the IF amplifier. The major advantage of using the diode detector is fidelity. It is also inexpensive and simple to include in the design of AGC (Sec. 7-14).

The simplest detector circuit is shown in Fig. 7-9a. The reactance of C at IF frequencies should be no greater than $0.1 \times R_L$. The forward resistance of the diode should be negligible compared to R_L. One other consideration is that R_L is in parallel with one or more circuits that act as shunt loads and reduce the effective R_L.

Figure 7-9b shows a more sophisticated filter. R_1 is part of the π filter, but it is also part of the R_1-R_L voltage divider. The portion of the signal developed across R_1 is lost to R_L where the *useful* portion of the signal is created. The problem thus becomes one of making R_1 large enough to provide IF filtering, but small enough to have most of the signal appear across R_L.

Note that the diode detector requires an input signal that is substantially greater than the turn-on voltage of the diode.

Historically, many other types of detectors were used, primarily amplifier types. These accomplished amplification in addition to detection. In general, fidelity deteriorates as the amplification increases. Some of the types of detectors are listed

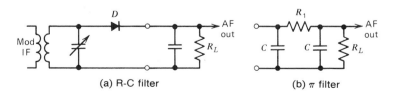

Figure 7-9 AM detector.   (a) R-C filter   (b) π filter

without further comment and in no particular order: plate detector, grid-leak detector, regenerative detector, superregenerative detector, square-law detector, and infinite impedance detector.

7-14
Automatic
Gain
Control (AGC)

The diode detector readily provides an *automatic gain control* (AGC) voltage. A typical AGC circuit is shown in Fig. 7-10.

The time constant R_3-C_6 is sufficiently long to smooth out the waveshape of Fig. 7-2b and develop a pure dc voltage. The level of the dc voltage is proportional to the peak value of the RF carrier. The AGC voltage can be positive or negative depending on the polarity of the diode.

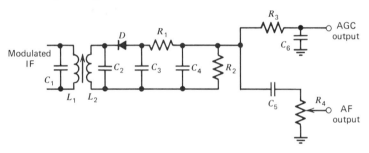

Figure 7-10 AGC circuit.

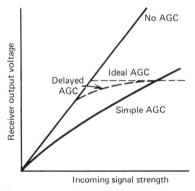

Figure 7-11 AGC systems.

AGC can be applied to the IF and RF stages. The number of stages controlled determines the degree of control. If additional control is required, the AGC voltage can be amplified. This is called *amplified AGC*.

AGC application carries a built-in penalty that causes a reduction of output even for weak RF inputs. This feature can be minimized by withholding the AGC until the input carrier voltage is a specified minimum value. This is called *delayed AGC*.

It is possible to approach an *ideal* AGC system with a combination of delayed and amplified AGC.

All these variations are summarized in Fig. 7-11.

7-15
Receiver
Specifications
Tests

A high-quality receiver is identified by standard specifications and the test for the more common ones will now be considered.

Sensitivity is the ability of a receiver to amplify weak signals. Specifically it denotes the strength of the input RF carrier required for a standard power measured at the *output* terminals. A *high quality* receiver may have a sensitivity of less than 1 μV and an economy model as poor as 150 μV. It is well to bear in mind that a receiver cannot cope with a signal that is smaller than the noise developed internally at its input. Also included in the sensitivity specification are percent modulation of the carrier input, the frequency of the audio modulation, the type of network to be used for coupling the carrier to the receiver input (dummy antenna), and the output load across which the output power is to be developed.

Selectivity is the ability of a receiver to reject unwanted adjacent signals. Selectivity is determined primarily by the IF section. The frequency response of the RF and mixer sections are too broad to contribute to selectivity. The procedure for checking the selectivity is to feed a signal in at carrier frequency and note the receiver output. The input signal is then varied to either side noting the additional signal strength required to bring the receiver output back to the original output level. The ratio of the resonance and off-resonance voltages are plotted in decibels.

Miscellaneous other specifications that may be included in the manufacturer's spec sheets include frequency response, hum level, cross modulation, input and output impedances, loudspeaker characteristics of frequency, power and impedance, and still other more exotic specifications.

7-16
Beat
Frequency
Oscillator (BFO)

If an *unmodulated* carrier is received by a conventional broadcast receiver, there is *no* output from the detector stage. In order to receive Morse code or interrupted continuous wave (ICW), a communications receiver is required. This differs from the broadcast receiver by the addition of a *beat frequency oscillator* (BFO) (Fig. 7-12).

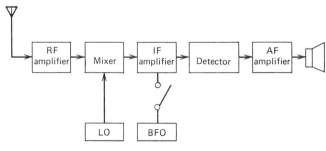

Figure 7-12 Beat frequency oscillator (BFO).

The BFO operates at the IF frequency, but is slightly adjustable. If the BFO is set at a frequency 1 kHz above or below the IF, and mixed with the IF signal, the detector output is an audible 1 kHz whenever CW is present.

7-17
Double-Heterodyne
Receiver

It is not practical to heterodyne a signal 30 MHz or higher down to 455 kHz IF. The LO and the input signal are too close in frequency. A more practical approach is the *double-heterodyne receiver* of Fig. 7-13.

This receiver has the advantage of a broad tunable frequency range and a narrow frequency IF for selectivity.

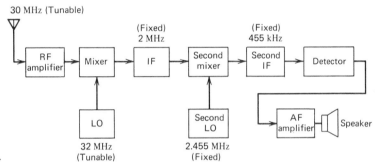

Figure 7-13 Double heterodyne receiver.

7-18
Miscellaneous
Features of a
Communications
Receiver

There are several other features that may be included in a communications receiver. You are unlikely to find *all* of these features in any *one* communications receiver.

Bandspread permits fine tuning of a receiver by adjusting a small tuning capacitor that is in parallel with the main tuning capacitor. This enables the selection of a signal in a crowded frequency spectrum.

S meter is a meter that indicates the strength of the input carrier signal. This enables fine tuning of the input signal.

Squelch circuit, also called *muting* circuit, cuts off the audio output whenever there is no carrier signal input. This is a useful feature because without a carrier signal input, no AGC is developed. This results in maximum gain in the RF and IF stages. The only signal present is internal noise, and this appears at the output.

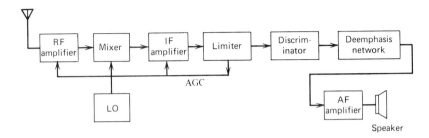

Figure 7-14 FM receiver.

7-19
FM
Receiver The FM receiver resembles the AM receiver in many respects. The unit operates in the 88 to 108 MHz range instead of 0.5 to 1.6 MHz. This requires a more critical fabrication, with short leads and smaller components. The block diagram is shown in Fig. 7-14.

The blocks that are unique to the FM receiver are the *limiter*, *discriminator*, and *deemphasis network*. The limiter function is to clip the peaks of the IF signal and present a uniform peak amplitude to the discriminator. The discriminator function is the conversion of the FM-IF to audio. The deemphasis network function is to compensate for the preemphasis introduced at the FM transmitter.

7-20
FM
Limiter The function of the limiter is to clip or suppress the noise impulses that have been imposed on the original FM transmission. These noise impulses are due to atmospheric disturbances and man-made noise. Limiters are usually designed as two cascaded stages. Figure 7-15 shows a typical two-stage cascaded limiter using FETs.

Note that the only bias is *grid-leak* bias. Grid-leak bias results in the positive peak of the input signal driving the FET gate *positive*. This automatically *clips* the positive peaks. By operating the drain at a *low* (V_{DD}) voltage, the bias is set *beyond* the cutoff

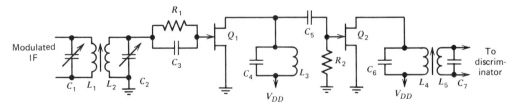

Figure 7-15 FM limiter.

point. This results in *clipping* the *negative* peaks. The method requires an input signal of 5 to 10 V for proper operation. This makes necessary a minimum of two IF stages preceding the limiters. A single limiter stage will *not* result in *complete* clipping. The second limiter stage operates with the advantage of the gain of the first limiter stage and this results in *complete* limiting.

7-21 Slope Detection A crude form of FM detection is the *slope detector*. This converts the FM-IF to AM-IF, which in turn can be detected by conventional AM detectors. This method depends on misaligning a standard tank circuit. The center of the *slope* is tuned to the FM-IF input frequency. This type of detector is obviously of low quality, because the slope is a nonlinear curve. It is subject to AM noise distortion. Nevertheless the slope detector is used for inexpensive narrow-band low quality receivers. The operation is shown in Fig. 7-16.

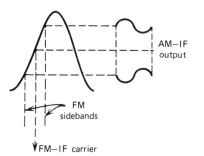

Figure 7-16 Slope detection.

7-22 Travis Detector The *Travis detector*, also called the *balanced slope detector*, is more linear than the slope detector. However the alignment of the unit is cumbersome. Each secondary tank is tuned to opposite ends of the bandwidth (Fig. 7-17).

The input tank C_1-L_1 is the output of the preceding IF amplifier and is tuned to the FM-IF (10.7 MHz). The top half of the secondary tank L_2-C_2 is tuned to the top of the upper sideband (10.7 MHz + 75 kHz). Similarly the L_3-C_3 tank is tuned

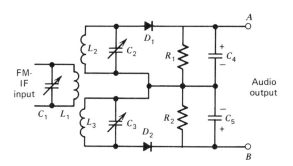

Figure 7-17 Travis detector.

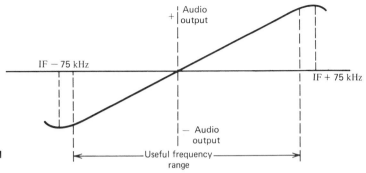

Figure 7-18 *S* characteristic curve of FM detector.

to 10.7 MHz − 75 kHz. Upper sideband frequency deviations cause D_1 to conduct and make the output terminal *A* positive. Similarly lower sideband frequency deviations cause D_2 to conduct and make the output terminal *B* positive.

The output of the *A*-*B* terminals is the audio output. The variation of audio output with frequency deviation is shown by Fig. 7-18. This is the standard *S* curve used for all FM detectors. This detector is also subject to AM noise distortion.

7-23
Foster-Seeley
Discriminator

Historically the Travis detector was replaced by the *Foster-Seeley discriminator*. This detector is still a widely used FM detector. The alignment is simpler than the double-tuned detector, with both primary and secondary tanks tuned to the FM-IF carrier frequency.

The Foster-Seeley discriminator is the FM detector with the highest fidelity and the greatest output voltage. The most obvious disadvantages are the requirement for limiting and the inability to generate AGC voltage. The schematic of the Foster-Seeley discriminator is shown in Fig. 7-19.

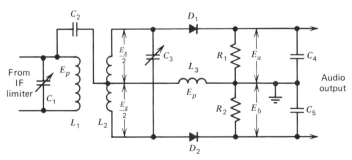

Figure 7-19 Foster-Seeley discriminator.

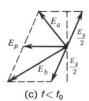

(a) $f = f_0$ (b) $f > f_0$ (c) $f < f_0$

Figure 7-20 Phasor relationships of discriminator signals.

The operation of the Foster-Seeley discriminator depends on the basic theory of a double-tuned tank. This can be shown to produce a 90° phase shift between the primary and secondary sides of the transformer. As the IF frequency deviates from the carrier frequency, the 90° become either a smaller or larger phase shift. The primary voltage (E_p) is coupled through C_2 to choke L_3. One half of the secondary voltage ($E_s/2$) is generated across each half of the secondary coil.

If we discount the voltage drops across the diodes D_1 and D_2, the vector sum ($E_s/2 + E_p$) appears as voltages E_a and E_b, respectively. The capacitors C_4 and C_5 function as IF frequency filter capacitors across load resistors R_1 and R_2. The audio output voltage is the difference voltage of E_a and E_b. Figure 7-20a shows the zero output voltage for the input frequency (f) equal to IF carrier frequency (f_0). $E_a = E_b$, and the audio output is zero. Figure 7-20b shows the vector relationships for $f > f_0$. This results in $E_a > E_b$, and an audio output. Figure 7-20c shows the opposite polarity of audio output voltage with $f < f_0$. The S figure of Fig. 7-18 also applies to the Foster-Seeley discriminator.

The AGC voltage for the FM receiver using a Foster-Seeley discriminator is derived from the IF stage. The IF signal is coupled to a standard AM detector. This unit ignores the frequency variation and creates a dc voltage proportional to the strength of the carrier. Obviously the limiter stage output signal cannot be used for this purpose.

7-24
Ratio
Detector

The *Ratio detector* is widely used. It is commonly used as the FM audio detector in TV receivers. The *quality* of the Ratio detector *is less* than the Foster-Seeley discriminator. Also the *output voltage is lower*. However the ratio detector *does not require* as much *limiting* and *can provide* an *AGC* voltage.

The schematic of the ratio detector is shown in Fig. 7-21. The diodes D_1 and D_2 are connected in *series*. The secondary voltage

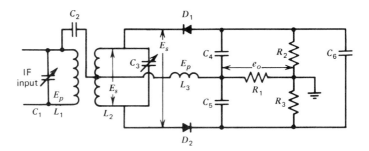

Figure 7-21 Ratio detector.

(E_s) and the primary voltage (E_p) across L_3 are applied across the capacitors C_4 and C_5. The total voltage is maintained at a constant value by the *swamping* capacitor C_6 ($\approx 5~\mu$F). However this voltage is divided across the capacitors C_4 and C_5. The difference of these two capacitor voltages varies with frequency deviation. This difference voltage determines the output audio voltage, e_o.

Theoretically the ratio detector requires *no* limiter, but in practice the manufacturer usually includes one limiter stage. A ratio detector circuit that provides AGC voltage is shown in Fig. 7-22.

The primary coupling to the choke L_3 is through magnetic coupling. The AGC output is determined by the total (carrier) voltage rather than the ratio voltage. The resistors and capacitors of the ratio detector are frequently provided as an integrated circuit. Indeed, entire sections of AM and FM receivers are being manufactured as an integrated circuit.

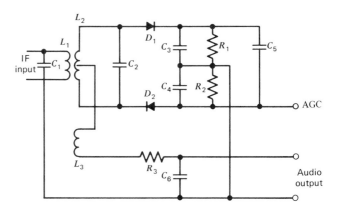

Figure 7-22 Ratio detector with AGC.

7-25 Automatic Frequency Control (AFC) The necessity of *automatic frequency control* (AFC) for the FM receiver becomes apparent when the operating frequency and bandwidth is considered. An FM receiver operating at 100 MHz (LO at 110.7 MHz) would have to drift 75 kHz to be completely out of the range of the IF amplifiers and discriminator. This order of frequency drift is only

$$\frac{0.075}{110} \times 100 = 0.068\%$$

To prevent LO frequency drift, the detector output is filtered and converted to dc. This dc correction voltage is applied to a varactor diode (Sec. 6-11) or a reactance transistor modulator (Sec. 6-12) and brings the LO back to center frequency.

An FM receiver may include an *AFC defeat* feature. This is a switch that opens the AFC circuit to permit the operator to tune in a *weak* signal adjacent to a strong signal. This is difficult to accomplish with AFC because the LO tends to lock on the stronger signal.

7-26 Deemphasis Circuit The FM transmitter provides an artificial amplification for the high audio frequencies with a preemphasis circuit (Sec. 6-9). This is compensated in the FM receiver with a *deemphasis* circuit (Fig. 7-23).

Note that the *R-C* time constant, τ

$$\tau = RC = 75 \times 10^3 \times 1000 \times 10^{-12} = 75 \ \mu s$$

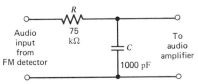

Figure 7-23 Deemphasis circuit.

7-27 FM Receiver Specifications The FM receiver is usually subjected to the same gamut of tests as the AM receiver. These include sensitivity, selectivity, dial tracking error, image frequency rejection, hum, cross-modulation and various other parameters.

The FM receiver may also be tested for sensitivity by checking the 20 *dB quieting*. This sequence consists of checking the noise output with no signal input (i.e., no AGC developed). An input signal is then increased until the AGC is sufficient to lower the gain (quiet the receiver) and decrease the noise output 20 dB. The value of this input signal is the 20 dB quieting sensitivity.

**7-28
Stereo
Receiver** Stereo *transmission* is described in Sec. 6-10. The *stereo receiver* reverses the process. The $L + R$ signal confined in the 0 to 15 kHz frequency range is directed to a low-pass filter. The $L - R$ signal contained in the 23 to 53 kHz frequency range is extracted by an appropriate bandpass filter. The 19 kHz pilot carrier is extracted by an appropriate filter and converted to 38 kHz in a frequency doubler. The 38 kHz carrier is mixed with the $L - R$ signal in an AM demodulator. Here it functions as the carrier for the $L - R$ double sidebands. The output of the AM demodulator is the $L - R$ audio signal. This output is combined with the $L + R$ audio and mixed in a matrix and deemphasis network. The outputs of this stage are the original L and R channels information. The block diagram of this section of the stereo receiver is shown in Fig. 7-24.

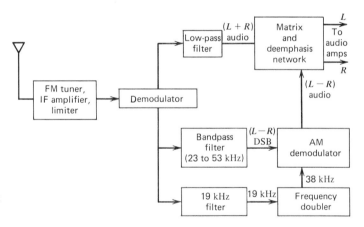

Figure 7-24 Block diagram of multiplex section of a stereo receiver.

**7-29
Summary** The early days of AM receiver technology used crystal detector and TRF receivers. These were superseded by the superheterodyne receiver, the basis of all modern receivers. The FM receiver requires limiting amplifiers and either the Foster-Seeley discriminator or the ratio detector.

Now return to the objectives and self-evaluation questions at the beginning of this chapter and see how well you can answer them. If you cannot answer certain questions, place a check next to each of them and review appropriate parts of the text. Then answer the questions and solve the problems below.

7-30
Questions

Q7-1 Referring to Fig. 7-1 explain the operation of the crystal head-set receiver.

Q7-2 Describe the TRF receiver.

Q7-3 Referring to Fig. 7-4 define the function of each block of the superhet receiver.

Q7-4 What advantage does the RF amplifier provide to the superhet receiver?

Q7-5 What are the advantages and disadvantages of a choice of a high IF frequency?

Q7-6 Referring to Fig. 7-6a indicate the effect on the operation of the following malfunctions:

    a. Open R_1.   **b.** Shorted C_2.

    c. Open C_4.   **d.** Shorted L_7.

    e. Open R_3.   **f.** Shorted C_6.

Q7-7 What advantage does the circuit of Fig. 7-6b offer over the circuit of Fig. 7-6a?

Q7-8 In addition to economy of dimensions, what advantage does the IC offer as a converter?

Q7-9 What components are involved in the adjustment for tracking?

Q7-10 Referring to Fig. 7-7 indicate the effect on the operation of the following malfunctions:

    a. Open L_4.   **b.** Shorted L_5.

    c. C_2 open.   **d.** C_2 shorted.

    e. C_p open.   **f.** C_p shorted.

Q7-11 Which section of the receiver provides most of the gain?

Q7-12 Are transistorized IF stages always neutralized?

Q7-13 Referring to Fig. 7-8 indicate the effect on the operation of the following malfunctions:

    a. C_4 open.   **b.** R_4 shorted.

    c. C_1 open.   **d.** R_6 shorted.

    e. C_3 open.   **f.** L_4 shorted.

Q7-14 Define the advantage of delayed AGC over simple AGC.

Q7-15 Referring to Fig. 7-10 compare the relative time constants of R_1C_4 and R_4C_5 and R_3C_6.

Q7-16 List four miscellaneous receiver specifications.

Q7-17 Define function of limiter stage of FM receiver.

Q7-18 Compare AM and FM broadcast receivers as to:
    a. Frequency range.   **b.** Bandwidth.
    c. Transmission range.   **d.** IF frequency.
    e. Frequency range of local oscillator.

Q7-19 What is the significance of the *S* characteristic curve of the FM detector?

Q7-20 Explain the operation of the Travis detector.

Q7-21 Compare the advantages and disadvantages of the Foster-Seeley discriminator and the ratio detector.

Q7-22 Define the function of AFC.

Q7-23 Define the function of the deemphasis network.

**7-31
Problems**

P7-1 An AM receiver is tuned to 500 kHz and the IF is 400 kHz. Calculate the image frequency and LO frequency.

P7-2 An FM receiver is tuned to 88 MHz. Calculate the image frequency and LO frequency.

P7-3 A TRF receiver covers the frequency range 30 to 50 MHz, and requires a bandwidth of 40 kHz. Assume the receiver bandwidth is appropriate at 30 MHz. Calculate the bandwidth of the receiver at 50 MHz.

P7-4 For P7-1, assume the *Q* of the input tank is 80. Calculate the image frequency rejection.

P7-5 For P7-2, assume the *Q* of the input tank is 170. Calculate the image frequency rejection.

Chapter 8 # Transmission Lines

8-1
Objectives

To learn:

1. The basic characteristics of a transmission line.
2. The types of losses in a transmission line.
3. Electrical equivalent of a transmission line.
4. Characteristic impedance of a transmission line.
5. Standing wave characteristics.
6. Reflection coefficient of a transmission line.
7. Effect of a load on a transmission line.
8. Properties of quarter and half-wavelength transmission lines.
9. Transmission line instrumentation.

8-2 Self-Evaluation Questions

Test your prior knowledge of the information in this chapter by answering the following questions. Watch for the answers to these questions as you read the chapter. Your final evaluation of whether you understand the material is measured by your ability to answer these questions. When you have completed the chapter, return to this section and answer the questions again.

1. Define the function of a transmission line.
2. How are the parameters of a transmission line defined?
3. Define the *characteristic impedance* of a transmission line.
4. Define a *lossy* line.
5. Identify two types of transmission lines, give an example of its use, and define the impedance range for each.
6. Define *standing waves* on a transmission line.
7. Define *node* and *antinode* points for an ideal lossless transmission line.
8. What does *viswar* mean?
9. Define reflection coefficient.
10. What loading conditions will result in the transfer of maximum power from the transmission line to the load?
11. How does the impedance measured at a distance $\lambda/4$ from the load relate to the load impedance?
12. Define the function of a balun.

8-3
Definition
of a
Transmission
Line
A *transmission line* is a device for accomplishing the transfer of high frequency energy from one area to another. One common example of this function is the line that accepts broadcast energy at the transmitter and delivers it to the transmitting antenna. A transmission line differs from any ordinary wire because of the restriction (placed on the transmission line) for *efficient* transfer of energy. In order to appreciate which parameters govern efficiency, an evaluation of the *losses* encountered in the transmission line must be considered.

Low frequency energy (60 Hz power) is transmitted to receptacles in the home or industry. This wiring is *not* defined as a transmission line. A house is simply *wired*, and the wire used is a common power cable. The load at the receptacle outlet is accommodated only by the current rating of the cable feeding the outlet. But an identical length of wire used in an RF, VHF, UHF, or microwave system must be a carefully designed transmission line.

8-4
Basic
Principles
The single feature that distinguishes the *power cable* from *transmission line* is the relative wavelength of the power frequency compared to RF. The equation for wavelength λ is related to the speed of light (v_c, a constant) and the frequency of the current in the line, or

$$\lambda = v_c / f \qquad (8\text{-}1)$$

where: λ (lambda) is the wavelength or distance covered by one
        cycle in meters (m)
    f is the frequency, in hertz (Hz)
    v_c is the velocity in meters per second
  v_c is the speed of light. Unless specifically indicated otherwise, it is assumed that the medium of transmission is air and v_c is constant at 300×10^6 meters per second (3×10^8 m/s $= 3 \times 10^{10}$ cm/s).

Example 8-1
Calculate the number of wavelengths (WLs) represented by the 240 m of power cable used to wire a home for 60 Hz power. (Assume the velocity of 60 Hz current is the same as the speed of light.)

Solution

$$\lambda = v_c/f = \frac{3 \times 10^8 \text{ m/s}}{60 \text{ c/s}} = 5 \times 10^6 \text{ meters/cycle (m/c)} \quad (8\text{-}1)$$

Therefore 240 m represents

$$\text{Number of WLs} = \frac{240 \text{ m}}{5 \times 10^6 \text{ m/s}}$$

or **48×10^{-6} wavelengths** (1 cycle $= 1$ WL)

Example 8-2
Repeat 8-1 for a UHF frequency of 500 MHz.

Solution

$$\lambda = v_c/f = \frac{3 \times 10^8 \text{ m/s}}{500 \times 10^6 \text{ c/s}} = \textbf{0.6 m/c} \quad (8\text{-}1)$$

The number of wavelengths represented by 240 m is

$$\frac{240 \text{ m}}{0.6 \text{ m/c}} = \textbf{400 wavelengths}$$

These two examples show the relationship between length of line and wavelength. The length of power cable is an insignificant fraction of a power wavelength. The result of this condition is that the *phase* of the voltage applied throughout the house wiring is essentially in phase with the source voltage at the fuse box. But if the line length is a significant fraction of a wavelength or even many wavelengths (Ex. 8-2), the voltage seen at different points along the line differ in phase with each other and with the source voltage. This principle is further explained in this chapter.

8-5
Losses in
Transmission
Lines

Three major types of energy loss occur in a transmission line. Two of these are similar to the power loss in any wiring system, the third is unique to a transmission line, that is, a line *many* wavelengths long at the specified frequency. These losses are:

a. *Copper loss*, or I^2R loss, or conductor effective resistance loss. At high frequency this loss differs from the calculations for power loss at low frequency because of the *skin* effect. The skin effect results from the self-inductance of the wire. At high frequency the current is forced to flow along the outer circumference, or *skin* of the wire, rather than uniformly distributed throughout the wire. The current behaves as though the wire is a tube without a solid core. Therefore, the copper in use represents a smaller cross section area and has a higher effective resistance.

b. *Dielectric loss* is a power loss in the dielectric material separating the conductors. This loss increases severely at high frequencies. It can be minimized by proper selection of the dielectric material used in the line. If the dielectric is air the power loss is minimal.

c. *Radiation loss* is the loss unique to transmission lines and results because the length of the line is a significant part of a wavelength or many wavelengths. This is the same "loss" that *radiates* energy in a well-designed antenna. The major distinction is that radiation in an antenna is desirable while in a transmission line it is to be avoided or minimized. Precisely how radiation loss is developed and what steps are taken to prevent it, is the major theme of this chapter.

8-6
Electrical
Equivalent
of a Line

Any pair of wires regardless of configuration must contain these four parameters: *series resistance*, *self-inductance* or inductance, a *shunting resistance* (or conductance) between the wires, and (distributed) *capacitance* between the wires.

Any unit of length of wire contains all four parameters, R, L, G and C. It is conventional to express the parameters on a *unit length* basis, such as 50 picofarads per meter or 0.1 microhenry per meter.

The transmission line can be represented by lumped constants valued on a unit length basis. This is seen in Fig. 8-1.

At UHF and microwave frequencies, the series inductive reactance (X_L) is much greater than the series resistance (R). Similarly the shunting susceptance of the capacitance (B_c) is

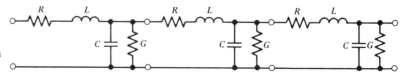

Figure 8-1 Electrical equivalent of a transmission line.

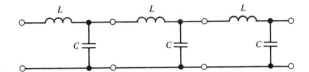

Figure 8-2 Lossless transmission line.

much *smaller* than the shunting conductance (G) of the line. If the R and G of the line are deleted as being too small and too large, respectively, the electrical equivalent results in a *lossless* line as shown in Fig. 8-2.

The lossless line representation is sufficiently accurate for the calculations of this chapter and this type of line is assumed throughout this work.

8-7
Characteristic
Impedance
Assume a transmission line that is *infinite in length* with a signal inserted at the input that never arrives at the output. The impedance measured at the input of this infinite line is the *characteristic impedance* of the line expressed in *ohms* and represented by the symbol Z_0. In a more practical vein, the *characteristic impedance* of a line is the impedance measured at the input of a *finite* length of line that is *terminated* in an impedance equal to the characteristic impedance.

8-8
Calculations of
Characteristic
Impedance
Mathematically the characteristic impedance, Z_0, can be related to the line parameters as follows:

$$Z_0 = \sqrt{\frac{Z}{Y}} = \sqrt{\frac{R+jX_L}{G+jX_c}} = \sqrt{\frac{R+jw_L}{G+jw_C}} \qquad (8\text{-}2)$$

where: Z is series impedance (ohms/meter) (Ω/m)
Y is shunt admittance (siemens/meter) (S/m)
R is series resistance (ohms/meter) (Ω/m)
L is series inductance (henry/meter) (H/m)
G is shunt conductance (siemens/meter) (S/m)
C is shunt capacitance (farads/meter) (F/m)

Equation (8-2) represents a transmission line containing *resistive* elements, called a *lossy* line. Relating the equation to a lossless line by deleting the resistive (G and R) elements, the characteristic impedance equation reduces to

$$Z_0 = \sqrt{L/C} \qquad (8\text{-}3)$$

Example 8-3

Given a *lossless* transmission line with inductive and capacitive values of 0.1 μH/m and 100 pF/m, calculate the characteristic impedance.

Solution

$$Z_0 = \sqrt{\frac{L}{C}} = \sqrt{\frac{0.1 \times 10^{-6}/\text{m}}{100 \times 10^{-12}/\text{m}}} = \textbf{31.62 } \boldsymbol{\Omega} \qquad (8\text{-}3)$$

Example 8-4

A transmission line with a characteristic impedance of 72 Ω, has a self-inductance of 0.1 μH/m. Determine the unit capacitance.

Solution

$$Z_0 = \sqrt{L/C} \quad \therefore C = L/Z_0^2$$

$$C = \frac{0.1 \times 10^{-6}}{(72)^2} = \textbf{19.29 pF}$$

The most common transmission lines used in industry and around the home are the *coaxial* cable and the parallel wire or *twinex* or *twin-lead*. Both types are used to connect a TV roof antenna to a receiver. The coaxial cable is also used as the input lead for high frequency oscilloscopes, signal generators, counters, and many other types of high frequency or fast rise time signals. The geometry of the two types of transmission line is shown in Fig. 8-3.

The characteristic impedance of the parallel wire transmission line is defined by its *geometry* and the dielectric material

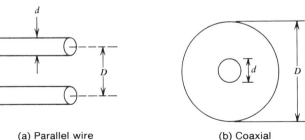

Figure 8-3 Common types of transmission lines.

(a) Parallel wire   (b) Coaxial

surrounding the conductors. It is generally used to connect a 300 Ω *folded dipole* antenna to a TV receiver with an input impedance of 300 Ω. In that case a 300 Ω transmission line is used. In practice, twinex line is available with selected characteristic impedances from 150 to 600 Ω. The relationship of geometry of line and parallel wire characteristic impedance is:

$$Z_0 = 276 \log 2D/d \quad \text{ohms } (\Omega) \tag{8-4}$$

where D and d are defined in Fig. 8-3a and must be in the same units. Since the dielectric is normally air for parallel-wire lines, the effects of the air dielectric are already included in the constant coefficient 276.

Example 8-5

Given a parallel wire transmission line with a spacing of 2 cm and a Z_0 of 300 Ω, calculate the diameter of the wire.

Solution

$$Z_0 = 276 \log 2D/d \tag{8-4}$$

$$d = \frac{2D}{\text{antilog} \dfrac{Z_0}{276}} = \frac{2 \times 2}{\text{antilog} \dfrac{300}{276}} = \frac{4 \text{ cm}}{\text{antilog } 1.087}$$

$$= \frac{4 \text{ cm}}{12.22} = \mathbf{0.3273 \text{ cm}}$$

Example 8-6

Determine the spacing required for parallel wire transmission lines if the wire size is 0.01 cm and the characteristic impedance is **a.** 600 Ω and **b.** 150 Ω.

Solution

$$Z_0 = 276 \log 2D/d$$

$$D = \frac{d \times \text{antilog} \dfrac{Z_0}{276}}{2}$$

a. $D = \dfrac{0.01 \times \text{antilog} \dfrac{600}{276}}{2} = \dfrac{0.01 \times \text{antilog} \, 2.174}{2}$

$= \dfrac{0.01 \times 149.3}{2} = \mathbf{0.7465 \, cm}$

b. $D = \dfrac{0.01 \times \text{antilog} \dfrac{150}{276}}{2} = \dfrac{0.01 \times \text{antilog} \, 0.5435}{2}$

$= \dfrac{0.01 \times 3.495}{2} = \mathbf{0.01748 \, cm}$

Note that the design for a characteristic impedance of 150 Ω is not a practical configuration. Two conductors of 0.01 cm diameter are touching if the distance between centers is 0.01 cm. For $D = 0.0175$ cm, the separation is 0.0075 cm. In order to accomplish the 150 Ω impedance, a much smaller diameter conductor is required.

The parallel-wire line Z_0 is also influenced by such additional variables as: proximity of ground or metal plane, metal shielding around wire and whether the line is in the horizontal or vertical plane relative to the ground.

The coaxial cable characteristic impedance Z_0 is defined as follows:

$$Z_0 = \frac{138}{\sqrt{k}} \log \frac{D}{d} \qquad \text{ohms (Ω)} \qquad (8\text{-}5)$$

where D and d are defined in Fig. 8-3b and k is the dielectric constant of the material between the shield and center conductor. Typical values of k are 1.2 to 2.5 with some materials running as high as 8. Z_0 can vary between 50 and 150 Ω. It is commonly used for the simple TV *dipole* antenna, connecting the 75 Ω antenna to the 75 Ω input of the TV receiver.

Example 8-7

Given a coaxial cable with an inner diameter of 0.03 cm (centimeters) and an outer diameter of 1 cm and a dielectric constant of 2, calculate the characteristic impedance.

Solution

$$Z_0 = \frac{138}{\sqrt{k}} \log \frac{D}{d} = \frac{138}{\sqrt{2}} \log \frac{1}{0.03} \qquad (8\text{-}5)$$

$$= 97.6 \log 33.3 = 97.58 \times 1.523$$

$$= 148.6 \ \Omega$$

Example 8-8
Given a coaxial cable with a dielectric of 1.2, determine the required ratio of outer diameter to inner diameter to produce a characteristic impedance of 72 Ω.

Solution

$$Z_0 = \frac{138}{\sqrt{k}} \log \frac{D}{d} \ \Omega$$

$$\frac{D}{d} = \text{antilog} \ \frac{\sqrt{k} \ Z_0}{138} = \text{antilog} \ \frac{\sqrt{1.2} \times 72}{138}$$

$$= \text{antilog} \ 0.5715$$

$$= 3.729$$

The significance of the D/d ratio is the relationship of the ratio to power handling capability. The inner conductor limits the current carrying capacity and the thickness and quality of the dielectric determines the voltage flashover. The 0.75 cm cable used with high frequency oscilloscopes is limited to a few watts, whereas a 25 cm cable can handle megawatts. Another consideration in the use of coaxial cable is the minimization of shunt capacitance. This can vary from 15 to 470 pF/m depending on the diameter, wire size, and quality of bead supports for inner conductor.

**8-9
Standing
Waves**
A transmission line that is *infinitely* long would have a strange reaction to a signal imposed on the sending or generator end of the line. Obviously, by definition the signal would never arrive at the end of the line. If the signal was observed at the generator, it would appear as any high frequency sinusoidal signal. The

voltage would vary from positive peak to negative peak and contain all the values inbetween. If the point of observation was moved a few kilometers down the transmission line, away from the generator, the same sinusoidal signal would be apparent, although attenuated, with smaller peaks. On the other hand, if the transmission line is a *lossless* line, no attenuation would occur and the signal would have the same voltage peaks as measured at the generator. If this analogy is carried to its ultimate conclusion, at infinity the *lossy* line signal has been *attenuated to zero*, with all the energy consumed by (copper and dielectric) losses. The lossless line, on the other hand, demonstrates the *same* signal strength at infinity as measured at the generator.

The practical world consists of transmission lines of finite length with attenuation. This chapter will concentrate on the finite length and ignore the losses. Assuming a line length of several wavelengths at the UHF frequency in question, what will happen to the signal when it arrives at the end of the line?

For a lossless line the signal will have the same strength at the end as it had at the generator. If it is further assumed that the line is not terminated, but is left open, the signal arrives at the end, and in the absence of a power-absorbing load, *bounces* or is *reflected* back. We thus find a *forward* (or incident signal) *wave* and a reflected or *backward wave*. The signal at the open end is obviously a *zero current* point with the voltage at a maximum. As the reflected signal returns toward the generator at different points along the line, it may add to the incident wave, increasing the signal strength. Similarly, it also cancels the incident wave at *other* points, resulting in a *minimum* signal strength.

It can be further stated that for the open-circuited line the minimum or *node voltage* points occur at the same place along the transmission line as the maximum or *antinode current* points and vice versa. This formation of peaks and nodes for voltage vs. current is called a *standing wave* and is shown in Fig. 8-4. Figure 8-4 demonstrates the relationship of the standing wave to the wavelength of the generator signal as well as the node to antinode relationship of the voltage and current. For an *ideal* (lossless) line the peak voltage of the SW envelope would build up to a value of twice the peak of the incident wave and at the cancellation points the voltage would be exactly zero volts. Theoretically this would result in a peak-to-node ratio of *infin-*

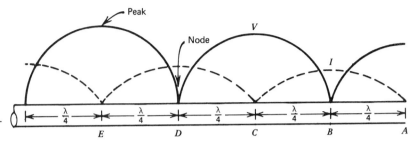

Figure 8-4 Standing waves on an open-circuited transmission line.

ity. This figure applies to a peak-to-node comparison of either the voltage or current waves. Actually the losses in the line prevent the complete buildup at the peaks and result in incomplete cancellation at the nodes. The result is a peak-to-node ratio of *less than infinity*. This ratio is called the *standing wave ratio* (SWR). In particular the voltage points are the more common parameters of interest. In that case it is specified as the voltage standing wave ratio (abbreviated VSWR, and pronounced *viswar*). The line is then said to be *resonant*.

The true significance of standing waves is that for the first time we are confronted with a phenomenon where the signal is determined by the place (along the line) rather than exclusively by the timing of a signal. The waveshape of the SW indicates the maximum amplitude the signal can attain at a particular point on the line. However, at any instant the *actual* amplitude is varying at the UHF rate of the signal source.

Another significant parameter that can be derived from an inspection of the standing wave pattern is the impedance seen at any point along the line. Since impedance at any point must satisfy Ohm's law, the impedance is V/I. Figure 8-4 shows maximum voltage, minimum current at points A, C, and E. These points correspond to a maximum impedance. Similarly points B and D show maximum current, minimum voltage, and, therefore, minimum impedance. Since it can also be shown that at these lettered points the voltage and current are in phase, the impedance seen is purely resistive.

It can also be shown that the impedance measured any place between the open end, point A, and the resistive point B, has a value between the maximum impedance of point A and the minimum impedance of point B and is *capacitive*. Similarly the impedance measured between the two resistive points B and C is inductive. These impedance relationships are repeated *every half wavelength* measured from the open end. The implication of all of these impedance relationships is that an open-ended transmission line presents a resistive, inductive, or capacitive impedance depending on the distance from the end the measurement is made.

The VSWR is obviously related to the amount of incident signal reflected back. The ratio of reflected signal to incident signal is called the *reflection coefficient* and is expressed:

$$\Gamma = V_r / V_i \qquad (8\text{-}6)$$

where Γ (gamma) is the reflection coefficient

V_r is the amplitude of the reflected voltage (volts)

V_i is the amplitude of the incident voltage (volts)

For a lossless line Γ approaches unity. Obviously there is a relationship between Γ and SWR. This is expressed:

$$\Gamma = \frac{\text{SWR} - 1}{\text{SWR} + 1} \qquad (8\text{-}7)$$

Example 8-9

A transmission line has a VSWR of 2.5, determine the reflection coefficient.

Solution

$$\Gamma = \frac{\text{VSWR} - 1}{\text{VSWR} + 1} = \frac{2.5 - 1}{2.5 + 1} = \frac{1.5}{3.5} = \textbf{0.4286}$$

Example 8-10

A transmission line has a reflection coefficient of 0.6. Calculate the SWR.

Solution

$$\Gamma = \frac{\text{SWR} - 1}{\text{SWR} + 1}$$

Using equation manipulation,

$$\text{SWR} = \frac{1 + \Gamma}{1 - \Gamma} = \frac{1 + 0.6}{1 - 0.6} = \frac{1.6}{0.4} = \textbf{4}$$

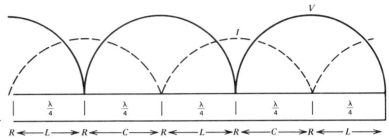

Figure 8-5 Standing waves on a short-circuited transmission line.

A transmission line terminated in a short circuit also presents a load that consumes no energy. Here the reflected signal is maximum and the VSWR is theoretically infinity. In all these respects the results are similar to those of an open-ended line. The differences between the two conditions are indicated in Fig. 8-5.

The positions of maximum current and voltage are reversed and the types of reactance between the resistive points are reversed. Otherwise the *same* theory applies. The calculation of viswar, reflection coefficient, resistance, and reactance is the same.

Two other types of loading of a transmission line result in a similar total reflection of energy. These are the idealized (no resistance) pure inductance and capacitance. A pure reactance cannot dissipate energy. It can only store energy for half a cycle and return it to the source during the other half cycle. Here again the SWR and Γ are maximum. The V and I at the load are, of course, 90° out of phase, with current leading for capacitive loading and lagging for inductive loading.

8-10
Resistive/Reactive
Loaded
Transmission
Lines

A transmission line terminated in a resistor load will transfer some portion of the energy to the load. To accomplish maximum power transfer from a source to a load, impedances must be *matched*. This is true for dc power from a battery, RF power from an amplifier through a double-tuned tank into another amplifier or, as in this case, a transmission line into a load. Since the internal impedance of the line is its characteristic impedance, for maximum power transfer, the load should be equal to Z_0. This type of loading results in zero energy reflection. This in turn offers a SWR of unity and a Γ of zero. There will be no standing waves and no radiation loss. The line is then described as a *flat* or *nonresonant* line. The voltage and current measured any place along the line will be the customary rms values of an uncomplicated signal source. The current and voltage at the load would be in phase and the same phase relationship would be true along the line.

On the other hand, if the load is a pure resistance that is not equal to Z_0, the energy transfer is incomplete. There will be partial absorption of energy within the load and partial reflection back to the line. This in turn results in SWR more than one (or unity) but less than the short or open circuit load conditions.

It can be shown that the SWR is directly related to the degree of mismatch between load and Z_0 regardless of which term is larger.

$$\text{SWR} = \frac{R_L}{Z_0} \quad \text{or} \quad \frac{Z_0}{R_L} \tag{8-8}$$

It is customary to use Eq. (8-8) to provide a SWR always greater than unity rather than a fraction.

Example 8-11

Given a VSWR of 4 and a transmission line with a characteristic impedance of 300 Ω, determine the two possible resistive loads.

Solution

$$\text{VSWR} = R_L/Z_0 \quad \text{or} \quad Z_0/R_L$$
$$R_L = \text{VSWR} \times Z_0 \quad \text{or} \quad Z_0/\text{VSWR}$$
$$= 4 \times 300 \quad \text{or} \quad 300/4$$
$$= \textbf{1200 } \boldsymbol{\Omega} \quad \text{or} \quad \textbf{75 } \boldsymbol{\Omega}$$

It is possible to compensate for the load mismatch, and the methods for accomplishing this are explored further in Sec. 8-11. If the load is greater than Z_0, the resulting behavior of the system begins to approach that of an open line, where Z_L is infinite. The reverse is true for a Z_L less than Z_0 where the system behavior approaches a short-circuited line.

If the load is a complex impedance, the methods of accomodating the mismatch and returning the system to an efficient nonradiating line are more involved. The calculations are normally accomplished with the aid of special charts.

8-11 Properties of Quarter and Half Wavelength Lines Reference to Figs. 8-4 and 8-5 show that the impedance measured at a quarter wavelength distance ($\lambda/4$) from the load is the reciprocal of the load impedance, Z_L.

The open-circuit load that presents a high impedance load ($Z_L = \infty$) at the open end results in a *low* impedance at a distance $\lambda/4$ away from the load. Similarly the short-circuited load ($Z_L = 0$) results in a *high* impedance at a distance $\lambda/4$ away from the load. In addition all impedances are *resistive* at the $\lambda/4$ distance point.

Since the open circuit appears to be *minimum* impedance at a point $\lambda/4$ from the load, it can be said that the *open-circuited $\lambda/4$ section* is acting as a *series-resonant circuit*. Similarly, the *short-circuited $\lambda/4$ section* is acting like a *parallel-resonant circuit*.

If the open or shorted lines are made slightly longer or shorter, the result is the same as if the frequency had been increased or decreased, respectively while keeping the line at constant length. A *series*-resonant circuit behaves *capacitively* at a *lower* frequency and *inductively* at a *higher* frequency. The reverse is true for a *parallel*-resonant circuit, which is *inductive* at *lower* frequencies and *capacitive* at *higher* frequencies. The significance of all this is that *a given length of transmission line is a frequency sensitive device*. It acts one way at proper length or frequency and much different at an adjacent frequency, possibly even for a sideband frequency. These conditions are summarized in Fig. 8-6.

The logical conclusion to be drawn about the quarter wavelength section is that if you don't like the impedance or reactance at any specified point on a transmission line, move over a

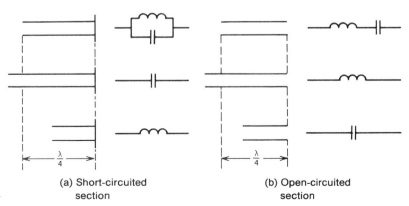

Figure 8-6 Quarter-wavelength sections.

(a) Short-circuited section

(b) Open-circuited section

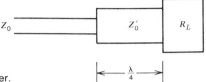

Figure 8-7 Quarter-wavelength transformer.

few centimeters in the appropriate direction where the impedance or reactance is more to your liking.

The half wavelength section is more straightforward in its application. Since the impedance repeats every $\lambda/2$, it is possible to measure the impedance of an inaccessible load by measuring the impedance seen at a point that is some multiple of $\lambda/2$ away from the load.

The quarter wavelength section can be used to match an improper resistor load to a transmission line. The method is indicated in Fig. 8-7.

The problem reduces to one of avoiding standing waves on the main transmission line Z_0. This is critical, since the line may be many kilometers long and any standing waves result in great *radiation* loss in addition to copper and dielectric losses. However, the load, R_L, is *not* equal to Z_0. By transformer theory it can be shown that inserting a $\lambda/4$ section of appropriate characteristic impedance results in efficient transfer of energy to the load with no standing waves on the main, lengthy, transmission line. The characteristic impedance required of the inserted $\lambda/4$ section is Z_0' given by:

$$Z_0' = \sqrt{Z_0 \times R_L} \qquad \text{ohms } (\Omega) \qquad (8\text{-}9)$$

where Z_0' is the characteristic impedance of the $\lambda/4$ section inserted between the main line and the load.

Example 8-12

Given a transmission line with a characteristic impedance of 200 Ω and a load of 120 Ω, calculate the characteristic impedance of the quarter wave transformer to accomplish the impedance match.

Solution

$$Z_0' = \sqrt{Z_0 \times R_L} = \sqrt{200 \times 120} = \mathbf{154.9 \ \Omega} \qquad (8\text{-}9)$$

Example 8-13
Given the transmission line Z_0 of 75 Ω, and the $\lambda/4$ matching transformer Z_0' of 100 Ω, determine the value of load resistance that was matched.

Solution

$$Z_0' = \sqrt{Z_0 \times R_L} \qquad (8\text{-}9)$$

$$R_L = \frac{(Z_0')^2}{Z_0} = \frac{(100)^2}{75} = 133.3 \ \Omega$$

If the load is a complex impedance the calculations are more involved, and it is common practice to utilize various charts and tables to simplify the calculations.

**8-12
Transmission
Line
Accessories**
There are many *accessories* used in making transmission line measurements. Manufacturers provide a family of *signal generators* covering the VHF and UHF frequency ranges. Some generators may cover a wide range of frequencies in a single generator using many bands or relatively few bands. Instruments range from extremely accurate, expensive, and stable units to do-it-yourself hobbyist kits. Some of the characteristics you may be concerned with are the output impedance, power output, ruggedness (for field work), portability, internal versus external power supply, temperature stability under load changes, long term stability, resolution of the frequency dial, resolution of the output attenuator, harmonic generation, and a host of other criteria specified for the unit. Note that a well-manufactured UHF signal generator can be used as a highly accurate *secondary* frequency standard for many years without need of repair, adjustment, or recalibration.

Another device commonly used in transmission line measurements is the *SWR Detector*. This unit is available in many designs and modes of operation. It may be a simple *crystal detector*. It may contain internal amplifiers designed for a *specific* frequency such as 1 kHz modulation or 30 MHz IF frequency. The *sensitivity* of the detector is a prime consideration.

The *slotted line* (Fig. 8-8) is the device that enables either measurement of SWR or the impedance along the transmission

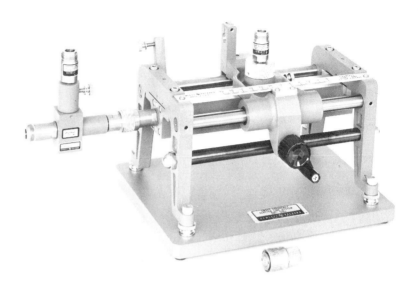

Figure 8-8 Slotted line.

HP Model #817B

line, or the frequency of the signal or the impedance of the load. It is a rigid coaxial line with a slot along its length. A movable carriage can slide in a trough above the slot. A *detector probe* is mounted on the carriage and extends partially into the slotted line, approaching (but not touching) the inner conductor. By this means, energy is coupled from the inner conductor to the detector probe without changing the SWR pattern within the slotted line. There is a centimeter scale running the length of the slotted line so that a signal at one position can be correlated to a signal at another location in the slotted line. The slotted line *must match* the characteristic impedance of the transmission line. Once the probe has picked up energy, the detected signal can be treated in any number of ways. Depending on the mode of modulation, an unmodulated carrier may use a detector designed for a superheterodyne system. It may be a simple detector reading output in decibels, volts, watts or amperes.

A *balun* (Fig. 8-9) is a device used to connect a *bal*anced system to an *un*balanced system. A twinex cable is an example of a balanced system. The coaxial line is an unbalanced system because the impedance to ground differs for the shield compared to the inner conductor. A common use for a balun is to connect a coaxial cable to a folded dipole TV antenna. The balun depends on the principles of $\lambda/4$ and $\lambda/2$ matching

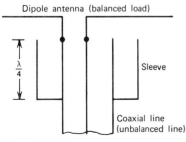

Figure 8-9 Balun.

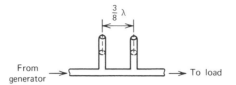

Figure 8-10 Double-stub matcher.

sections for its operation. Just as these sections are frequency sensitive, so is the balun. As a result the selected frequency for operation must be a compromise in the TV band. It is commonly selected as the geometric mean of the frequency band.

Multistub matching units are used to increase the frequency band over which an impedance match is accomplished. Each stub has a *sliding short* that can be adjusted for length of the stub. The spacing between stubs is fixed. The unit may be two, three or four stubs depending on the band requirements (Fig. 8-10).

There are a number of other devices used in transmission line measurements that are listed here without further identification: directional couplers, attenuators, phase shifters, multi quarter-wavelength sections, sweep oscillators, filters (high, low, band-pass, band-reject), adapters, counters, synthesizers, modulators, noise-measurement equipment, reflectometer bridge, and a multitude of other devices.

The Smith chart (Fig. 8-11) is used in the design of transmission line sections and attenuation calculations. The determination of SWR and the degree of impedance mismatch with changing frequency can also be done with the Smith chart. A variety of transmission line problems and the solutions using the Smith chart are shown in Appendix B.

8-13 Summary A transmission line transfers signal energy from one device to another in an efficient manner with minimal losses. An improperly terminated transmission line results in standing waves and radiation losses. The basic types of transmission lines are the coaxial cable and the parallel wire cable. The coaxial cable characteristic impedance is a nominal 75 Ω, the parallel wire cable, 300 Ω. The $\lambda/4$ section has unique characteristics that make the normalized input impedance to the line the reciprocal of the normalized load impedance. The $\lambda/2$ section presents an input impedance equal to the load. An unmatched load can be accommodated with the $\lambda/4$ matching transformer or the shorted stub techniques.

IMPEDANCE OR ADMITTANCE COORDINATES

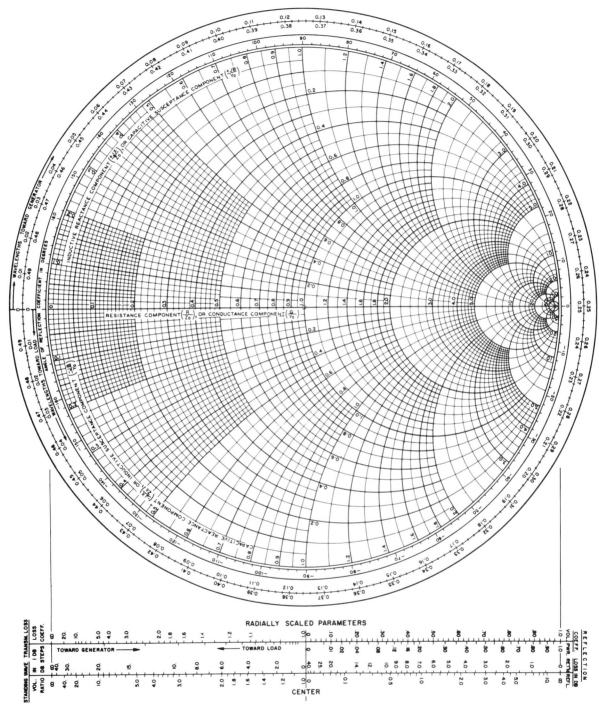

Figure 8-11 Smith chart.

Now return to the objectives and self-evaluation questions at the beginning of this chapter and see how well you can answer them. If you cannot answer certain questions, place a check next to each of them and review appropriate parts of the text. Then answer the questions and solve the problems below.

8-14
Questions

Q8-1 List three types of power loss in a transmission line.

Q8-2 Define skin effect and explain its significance.

Q8-3 Indicate an approach to minimize *each* of the three types of power loss described in Q8-1.

Q8-4 Define a *lossless* line.

Q8-5 Assuming the ratio of inner and outer diameters of a coaxial cable is maintained, what is the significance of increasing the *outer* diameter?

Q8-6 Define under what conditions a transmission line is:
a. Resonant?
b. Flat?

Q8-7 What is the phase of the impedance measured at the node and antinode points on a lossless transmission line?

Q8-8 Compare the impedance and node relationships of an open-ended line and a line with a short-circuited load.

Q8-9 What is the result of terminating a transmission line with a pure reactance load?

Q8-10 For a nonresonant line what is the node/antinode relationship?

Q8-11 What is the significance of terminating a transmission line in a purely resistive load whose value is *not* equal to the characteristic impedance of the line?

Q8-12 What basic law of electronics determines the impedance measured at any point along a transmission line regardless of whether the line is flat or resonant?

Q8-13 What changes would be observed along the transmission line as the load resistance is varied from a value less than the characteristic impedance to a value greater than the characteristic impedance?

Q8-14 At a $\lambda/4$ distance from the load what impedance is measured for the following loads?
a. Open-circuit load.
b. Short-circuit load.

Q8-15 What type of reactance is measured on a transmission line for a short-circuit load at a distance from the following load?
a. Less than $\lambda/4$.
b. Slightly more than $\lambda/4$.

Q8-16 What type of reactance is measured on a transmission line for an open-circuit load at a distance from the following loads?
a. Less than $\lambda/4$.
b. Slightly more than $\lambda/4$.

Q8-17 What impedance is measured on a transmission line at a distance from the load of $\lambda/2$?

Q8-18 Describe a method that used the characteristics of a $\lambda/4$ section to match an unequal pure resistance load to a transmission line.

Q8-19 List 10 parameters that might be specified in the purchase order of a UHF signal generator.

Q8-20 Define the function of a calibrated UHF attenuator.

Q8-21 Define the function of a SWR detector, and list the units it may be calibrated in.

Q8-22 Describe the construction of a slotted line and define its function.

Q8-23 List 10 types of equipment that might be used in transmission line measurements.

**8-15
Problems**

P8-1 Calculate the number of wavelengths represented by the 600 m of power cable used to wire an airplane for 400 Hz power.

P8-2 Repeat Prob. 8-1 for a VHF frequency of 210 MHz.

P8-3 A lossless transmission line has the following parameters: inductance of 0.22 μH/m and capacitance of 55 pF/m. Calculate the characteristic impedance.

P8-4 Given a lossless transmission line with a characteristic impedance of 150 Ω and a capacitance of 25 pF/m, calculate the inductance, L.

P8-5 Given a parallel-wire transmission line with a spacing of 0.75 cm and a characteristic impedance of 220 Ω, calculate the diameter of the wire.

P8-6 Given a 300 Ω parallel wire transmission line with a wire size of 0.005 cm, determine the wire spacing.

P8-7 Given a coaxial cable with an inner diameter of 0.015 cm, an outer diameter of 0.08 cm and a dielectric constant of 1.8, calculate the characteristic impedance.

Chapter 9

Waveguides and Other Devices

To learn:

1. The characteristics of rectangular waveguides.
2. The characteristics of circular waveguides.
3. TE and TM modes.
4. Field patterns.
5. Methods of generating modes.
6. Waveguide accessory devices.

9-2
Self-Evaluation
Questions Test your prior knowledge of the information in this chapter by answering the following questions. Watch for the answers to these questions as you read the chapter. Your final evaluation of whether you understand the material is measured by your ability to answer these questions. When you have completed the chapter, return to this section and answer the questions again.

1. Define the dimensions of a *rectangular waveguide* in terms of wavelength.
2. Why are the interior walls of a waveguide highly polished silver or gold plating?
3. Define *guide wavelength* of a signal.
4. Define *group velocity* of a signal.
5. Define the *dominant mode* of a signal.
6. Define *cutoff wavelength*.
7. Define *characteristic wave impedance*.
8. What are the advantages of a *circular waveguide* over a rectangular waveguide?
9. Define *polarization* of a signal.
10. Define the function of the *hybrid-ring junction*.
11. Define *nonreciprocity* of a microwave ferrite device.
12. Explain the operation of a *microwave* ferrite isolator.

9-3
Rectangular
Waveguide
Theory

The coaxial transmission line has a theoretically useful upper frequency limit of 18 gigahertz (GHz). In more practical terms, the commonly accepted limitation is just under 1 GHz (Fig. 9-1). The frequency concepts made popular by TV usage is a good rule of thumb. VHF extends to 216 MHz and UHF bands of TV end just below 1 GHz, the practical useful limit of coaxial cable (Fig. 9-1).

Microwave frequencies continue from 1 GHz to the frequencies represented by infrared light at approximately one terahertz (1 THz). Actual developmental research in the microwave region is still restricted below 150 GHz.

Why is it necessary to develop equipment to operate in the microwave region? The answer is a voracious public. The FCC has allocated to the *entertainment media* (AM, FM, and TV) practically the entire frequency spectrum from 0.5 MHz up to 1 GHz. This leaves any future expansion of communication frequencies to the microwave regions exclusively. For example, recent developments in the fields of laser/maser research, are aimed at using *visible light*, approximately 500 THz, for communications (Fig. 9-1).

Research into microwaves began with use of radar about the time of World War II. Radar began with 1 GHz in the *L*-band and progressed through the *S*-band ($\approx$3 GHz), *C*-band ($\approx$6 GHz), and *X*-band ($\approx$10 GHz). Now there is considerable use made of the various *K* bands covering 18 to 26.5 GHz. A recent domestic addition to commercial appliances is the radar microwave oven (10 GHz). Where we go from here is limited only by the human imagination.

The first commonly used microwave device is the *rectangular waveguide*. A *cable* conducts a signal along its inner wire conductor. Broadcast transmission in space is a signal that is *unguided* in the sense that it uses unbounded space. Aside from frequency considerations, waveguides introduce *less loss* than conventional wire lines and have greater power handling ability. The term waveguide implies a device that guides the path or movement or *propagation* of a signal or *wave*. To appreciate the significance of the term *wave*, we return to dc theory.

A simple closed dc battery circuit causes a current in a wire. The current creates a *magnetic field* that envelops the wire in a circular manner and each magnetic line is a closed loop. The net configuration is a *magnetic* field *perpendicular* to the wire and a

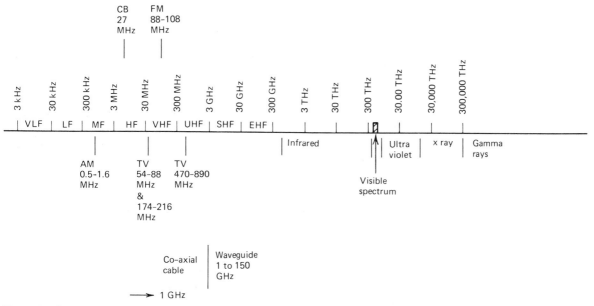

Figure 9-1 Frequency spectrum.

voltage gradient or *electrical* field that extends *along* the wire. Therefore the two fields, electric and magnetic, are *perpendicular to each other* and also mutually at right angles (orthogonal) to the *current*.

Energy is sent off into space or *radiated* as a result generally of *standing waves* on a (resonant) antenna. This energy represents both the (transverse) electric and magnetic fields. The signal travels by progression of the two fields maintaining their perpendicular relationship to each other in flight. A mathematical analysis of this electromagnetic (EM) signal is defined by the set of equations termed *Maxwell* equations, after James Maxwell the Scottish physicist who developed them. This same electromagnetic (EM) signal can also be inserted into a waveguide. The rules that govern the progression (propagation) of the signal down the length of the waveguide are of specific interest to us.

A rectangular waveguide can be thought of as a narrow box approximately twice as wide as it is high. The width should have a minimum dimension equal to a half wavelength where the wavelength is the *free space* wavelength ($\lambda = v_c/f$). Refer to Fig. 9-2.

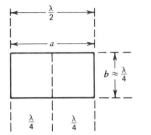

Figure 9-2 Cross section of rectangular waveguide.

You will note that the two sides are $\lambda/4$ away from the center of the waveguide. A short circuit at each side $\lambda/4$ distance from the center makes the *center* a *high impedance* point. As a result the signal can travel down the *center* of the waveguide with *minimum attenuation*. This relationship is true for a waveguide width that is any whole number multiple of half wavelengths.

To minimize attenuation, the internal walls of the waveguide are highly polished and have a thin plating of low resistance silver, gold, or copper. The base material of the waveguide is commonly aluminum or brass for strength, rigidity, weight, economy, or any combination of these advantages. The internal width is determined by the frequency, and the height is normally half the width (Fig. 9-2). The depth of the waveguide interior low resistance wall plating (silver, gold, or copper) depends on the requirement of carrying signal current as *skin effect*.

**9-4
Calculations of
Rectangular
Waveguide**

The signal is inserted into the waveguide in such a manner that it hits the side at a slight angle and is reflected back toward the center (Fig. 9-3). This process of reflections results in a zigzag progression that slows down the propagation of the signal. This in turn results in a measured wavelength along the length of the waveguide or *guide wavelength* (λg) that is *longer* than the free space wavelength (λ). The velocity of the wave (v_g), or *group velocity* as measured along the length of the waveguide must be slower than it would be if the signal propagated directly (v_c) without the reflections. The velocity at which the signal changes phase (v_p) or *phase velocity* is greater than v_c and is related to v_c and v_g.

The *lowest* frequency that can be accommodated by a specific waveguide relates to its wavelength compared to the long dimension, or *width* (a) of the waveguide. Another factor that comes into consideration is the number (m) of half wavelengths of the propagated signal to be accommodated by dimension a of

Figure 9-3 Reflections in a rectangular waveguide

Direction of propagation of wave

the waveguide, Eq. (9-1) below. This factor (*m*) is one component making up the *mode* of the signal. When *m* equals one, it is called the *dominant* mode. Section 9-5 is devoted to a discussion of modes in rectangular waveguides. The wavelength of this lowest useful frequency is referred to as the cutoff wavelength (λ_0) and is related to both *a* and *m*.

All the terms discussed in this section can be outlined in a few equations.

$$\lambda_0 = 2\,a/m \tag{9-1}$$

where: λ_0 = cutoff wavelength (cm)
  a = waveguide width (cm)
  m = number of half wavelengths of voltage fields along the *a* dimension

$$\lambda_g = \frac{\lambda}{\sqrt{1-(\lambda/\lambda_0)^2}} \tag{9-2}$$

where: λ_g = guide wavelength, wavelength of signal as measured along the length of the waveguide (parallel to direction of propagation) (cm)
  λ = free space wavelength (cm)

$$v_c^2 = v_g v_p \tag{9-3}$$

where: v_c = free space velocity (3×10^{10} cm/s)
  v_g = velocity of signal in the direction of propagation (cm/s)

$$v_p = \frac{v_c}{\sqrt{1-(\lambda/\lambda_0)^2}} \tag{9-4}$$

where: v_p = velocity with which the signal changes phase in the direction of propagation (cm/s)

$$v_g = v_c\sqrt{1-(\lambda/\lambda_0)^2} \tag{9-5}$$

where: v_g = velocity of signal in the direction of propagation (cm/s)

$$Z_0 = \frac{377}{\sqrt{1-(\lambda/\lambda_0)^2}} \quad \text{or} \quad 377\sqrt{1-(\lambda/\lambda_0)^2} \tag{9-6}$$

where: Z_0 = characteristic wave impedance, ohms (Ω)

The significance of the above equations is shown in the following examples.

Example 9-1

A 4 GHz signal is propagated in a rectangular waveguide with internal dimensions of 5 cm × 2.5 cm. Assuming the dominant mode, calculate:

a. Cutoff wavelength, λ_0.
b. Guide wavelength, λ_g.
c. Velocity of signal in direction of propagation (v_g).
d. Phase velocity (v_p).
e. Characteristic wave impedance (Z_0) of the waveguide.

Solution

a. $\lambda = v_c / f$ (8-1)

$$= \frac{3 \times 10^{10}}{4 \times 10^9} = \textbf{7.5 cm} \text{ (free space wavelength)}$$

$\lambda_0 = 2a/m$ (9-1)

$$= \frac{2 \times 5}{1} = \textbf{10 cm} \text{ (cutoff wavelength)}$$

Since the cutoff wavelength is longer than the free space wavelength, the signal will propagate in this waveguide.

b. $\lambda_g = \dfrac{\lambda}{\sqrt{1 - (\lambda/\lambda_0)^2}} = \dfrac{7.5}{\sqrt{1 - \left(\dfrac{7.5}{10}\right)^2}}$ (9-2)

$$= \frac{7.5}{\sqrt{1 - 0.5625}} = \frac{7.5}{0.6614} = \textbf{11.34 cm} \text{ (guide wavelength)}$$

c. $v_g = v_c \sqrt{1 - (\lambda/\lambda_0)^2} = 3 \times 10^{10} \times 0.6614$ (9-5)

$$= \textbf{1.984} \times \textbf{10}^{\textbf{10}} \textbf{ cm/s}$$

d. $v_p = \dfrac{v_c}{\sqrt{1 - (\lambda/\lambda_0)^2}} = \dfrac{3 \times 10^{10}}{0.6614} = \textbf{4.536} \times \textbf{10}^{\textbf{10}} \textbf{ cm/s}$ (9-4)

e. $Z_0 = \dfrac{377}{\sqrt{1 - (\lambda/\lambda_0)^2}} = \dfrac{377}{0.6614} = \textbf{570 } \Omega$ (9-6)

Example 9-2

A rectangular waveguide has internal dimensions of 3.76 cm × 1.88 cm.

a. Assuming a dominant mode, determine the lowest frequency that can be propagated in the waveguide.

b. Assuming a frequency of 9 GHz, what is the highest mode that can be accommodated?

c. Assuming $f = 11$ GHz and $m = 2$, calculate cutoff wavelength (λ_0), guide wavelength (λ_g), group velocity (v_g), phase velocity (v_p), and characteristic wave impedance (Z_0).

Solution

a. $\lambda_0 = 2a/m = 2 \times 3.76/1 = \mathbf{7.52}$ **cm** $\hspace{3cm}$ (9-1)

Lowest frequency will be higher than

$$f = v_c/\lambda = \frac{3 \times 10^{10}}{7.52} = \mathbf{3.989 \ GHz} \hspace{3cm} (8\text{-}1)$$

b. At 9 GHz, free space wavelength

$$\lambda = v_c/f = \frac{3 \times 10^{10}}{9 \times 10^9} = \mathbf{3.333 \ cm} \hspace{3cm} (8\text{-}1)$$

Therefore the dominant mode, ($m = 1$), can be accommodated. For $m = 2$, $\lambda_0 = 7.52/2 = 3.76$ cm, this mode can also be accommodated. For $m = 3$, $\lambda_0 = 7.52/3 = 2.507$ cm. Since this is smaller than 3.333 cm, this mode *cannot* be propagated.

c. At $f = 11$ GHz, $\lambda = 3 \times 10^{10}/11 \times 10^9 = \mathbf{2.727}$ **cm** for $m = 2$, $\lambda_0 = 3.75$ cm;

$$\lambda_g = \frac{\lambda}{\sqrt{1 - (\lambda/\lambda_0)^2}} = \frac{2.727}{\sqrt{1 - \left(\frac{2.727}{3.76}\right)^2}} \hspace{2cm} (9\text{-}2)$$

$$= \frac{2.73}{\sqrt{1 - (0.7253)^2}} = \frac{2.73}{\sqrt{1 - 0.526}}$$

$$= \frac{2.73}{\sqrt{0.474}} = \frac{2.73}{0.6885} = \mathbf{3.965 \ cm}$$

$$v_g = v_c\sqrt{1 - (\lambda/\lambda_0)^2} \hspace{3cm} (9\text{-}5)$$

$$= 3 \times 10^{10} \times 0.6885 = \mathbf{2.066 \times 10^{10} \ cm/s}$$

$$v_p = \frac{v_c}{\sqrt{1 - (\lambda/\lambda_0)^2}} \qquad (9\text{-}4)$$

$$= \frac{3 \times 10^{10}}{0.6885} = 4.357 \times 10^{10} \ \text{cm/s}$$

$$Z_0 = \frac{377}{\sqrt{1 - (\lambda/\lambda_0)^2}} = \frac{377}{0.6885} = 547.6 \ \Omega \qquad (9\text{-}6)$$

9-5
TE and TM
Modes
in Rectangular
Waveguides
The two types of waves, TE and TM, are differentiated by which signal has the electric field perpendicular to the direction of propagation (TE), and which signal has the magnetic field perpendicular to the direction of propagation (TM). Another type of identification within each category is the number of half wavelengths of electric fields and magnetic fields. These groupings determine the *mode* of the specific TE or TM signal.

9-5.1
TE Modes in
Rectangular
Waveguides
The TE (*transverse electric*) mode in a rectangular waveguide refers to a signal propagated so that the electric field is in a plane perpendicular to the direction of the progression or travel of the signal. Since the wave travels the *length* of the waveguide, the electric field must be in the *vertical* plane. Ignoring the magnetic field for the moment, the electric field is shown for two different modes $\lambda/2$ and λ ($m=1$, and $m=2$) in Fig. 9-4 (Recall that m is the number of half wavelengths across dimension "a")

Figure 9-4a shows the variation in *electric field strength* (intensity) in the cross-sectional cut of the waveguide. The maximum signal strength, indicated by the crowding of the lines, (as well

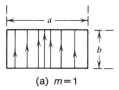

(a) $m=1$

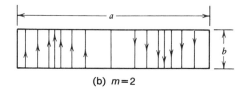

(b) $m=2$

Figure 9-4 The transverse electric (TE) fields or TE modes in a rectangular waveguide.

as by the height of the arrowheads) occurs at the center of the *a* dimension.

The variation follows the standard standing wave ratio pattern noted in Sec. 8-9. Figure 9-4b shows a complete wavelength with the SWR format, and phase reversal for the second half wave. This corresponds to a TE mode of $m=2$. Note that the point of least crowding now occurs in the center. These formations are maintained during the progression down the length of the waveguide.

The $TE_{m,n}$ mode refers to a signal in which the electric field is perpendicular to the direction of propagation, the *m* indicates the number of electric fields half wavelengths in the width, *a*, and the *n* is the number of magnetic field half wavelengths in the height, *b*.

9-5.2 TM Modes in Rectangular Waveguides The TM (transverse magnetic) wave has its magnetic field mutually perpendicular to the direction of propagation and also the electric field. The electric field has a component parallel to the direction of travel. The mode of the TM wave is defined by the subletters *m* and *n* that relate to the number of half wavelengths, as was true for the TE wave. If we ignore any associated electric fields for the moment, the cross-sectional view of a TM mode is shown in Fig. 9-5.

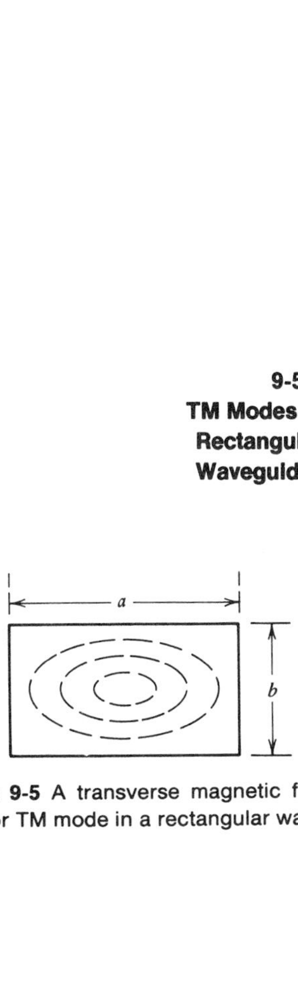

The combined electric and magnetic fields are designated $TE_{m,n}$ or $TM_{m,n}$ where the *m* and *n* represent the respective TE and TM modes. The universal equation for cutoff wavelength (λ_0) is

Figure 9-5 A transverse magnetic field (TM) or TM mode in a rectangular waveguide.

$$\lambda_0 = \frac{2}{\sqrt{(m/a)^2 + (n/b)^2}} \qquad (9\text{-}7)$$

The cutoff wavelength is dependent on both the *a* and *b* dimensions and the *m* and *n* modes. Once cutoff wavelength λ_0 is determined, the other waveguide equations remain valid. For the special condition of *n* equal to zero, Eq. (9-7) reduces to Eq. (9-1). This equation holds for either TE or TM modes of propagation.

Example 9-3

Given an 8 GHz signal, a rectangular waveguide 7.22×3.40 cm propagating in the $TE_{1,1}$ mode. Calculate:

a. Cutoff wavelength (λ_0).
b. Guide wavelength (λ_g).
c. Velocity of signal in direction of propagation (v_g).
d. Phase velocity (v_p).
e. Characteristic wave impedance (Z_0).

Solution

a. $\lambda = v_c/f = 3 \times 10^{10}/8 \times 10^9 = \mathbf{3.75}$ **cm** $\hspace{2cm}$ (8-1)

$$\lambda_0 = \frac{2}{\sqrt{(m/a)^2 + (n/b)^2}} \hspace{2cm} (9\text{-}7)$$

$$= \frac{2}{\sqrt{(1/7.22)^2 + (1/3.40)^2}} = \frac{2}{\sqrt{(0.1385)^2 + (0.2941)^2}}$$

$$= \frac{2}{\sqrt{0.01918 + 0.08651}} = \frac{2}{\sqrt{0.1057}} = \frac{2}{0.3251} = \mathbf{6.152}\ \mathbf{cm}$$

b. $\lambda_g = \dfrac{\lambda}{\sqrt{1 - (\lambda/\lambda_0)^2}} \hspace{2cm} (9\text{-}2)$

$$= \frac{3.75}{\sqrt{1 - \left(\dfrac{3.75}{6.152}\right)^2}} = \frac{3.75}{\sqrt{1 - (0.6096)^2}}$$

$$= \frac{3.75}{\sqrt{1 - 0.3716}} = \frac{3.75}{\sqrt{0.6284}} = \frac{3.75}{0.7927} = \mathbf{4.731}\ \mathbf{cm}$$

c. $v_g = v_c\sqrt{1 - (\lambda/\lambda_0)^2} \hspace{2cm} (9\text{-}5)$

$$= 3 \times 10^{10} \times 0.7927 = \mathbf{2.378 \times 10^{10}}\ \mathbf{cm/s}$$

d. $v_p = \dfrac{v_c}{\sqrt{1 - (\lambda/\lambda_0)^2}} \hspace{2cm} (9\text{-}4)$

$$= \frac{3 \times 10^{10}}{0.7927} = \mathbf{3.785 \times 10^{10}}\ \mathbf{cm/s}$$

e. $Z_0 = \dfrac{377}{\sqrt{1 - (\lambda/\lambda_0)^2}} = \dfrac{377}{0.7927} = \mathbf{475.6}\ \mathbf{\Omega} \hspace{1cm} (9\text{-}6)$

The TM mode introduces a variation in characteristic wave impedance from the equations already discussed. The value of characteristic wave impedance is given by the empirical relationship.

$$Z_0 = 377\sqrt{1 - (\lambda/\lambda_0)^2} \tag{9-9}$$

A comparison of Z_0 in the TE and TM modes indicates that the TE mode characteristic wave impedance is greater than 377 Ω and the Z_0 for TM is less than 377 Ω. As the Z_0 equation approaches *free space* conditions, the TM value approaches *zero* and the TE value approaches *infinity*.

A waveguide using a dielectric other than air will have its cutoff wavelength *increased* by a factor equal to the square root of the dielectric constant of the new material. This new value of λ_0 affects all the other equations. In addition the dielectric constant is specifically included in some of the other equations. Finally, there is the possibility that the value of the dielectric may be a complex term, which complicates the equations to varying degrees.

The attenuation contributed by a rectangular waveguide is expressed in decibels per meter (dB/m). The equations for attenuation are quite complex. However values can be derived from appropriate graphs. In general, attenuation varies with type of coating on the interior walls of the waveguide, the dimensions of the waveguide, and the frequency of operation. All the parameters appear in nonlinear form.

9-6 Field Patterns in Rectangular Waveguides The generation of the higher modes of propagation presents some problems. In practice, therefore, only the lower order modes are used. A representative sampling of the modes commonly used with rectangular waveguides is given below. The electric field is represented by solid lines. The magnetic field is represented by dotted lines. In general the TE mode is generated with a *vertical* probe (or antenna) and the TM mode with a *horizontal* antenna. This subject is discussed in more detail in Sec. 9-9. The lines of the two fields are *orthogonal*, intersecting at right angles. These principles are shown in Fig. 9-6.

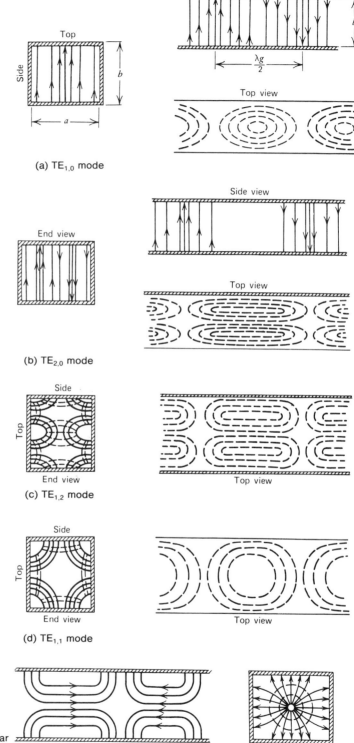

(a) TE$_{1,0}$ mode

(b) TE$_{2,0}$ mode

(c) TE$_{1,2}$ mode

(d) TE$_{1,1}$ mode

Figure 9-6 Field patterns in rectangular waveguides.

(e) TM$_{1,1}$ mode

9-7
Rectangular
Rigid Waveguide
Standards
Many companies manufacture *rigid* rectangular waveguides. A tabulation of a *partial* list available commercially as standard items is included in Table 9-1. The column headings are mostly self-explanatory. The one exception is the JAN RG column, which stands for Joint Army Navy.

Table 9-1
Rectangular Rigid Waveguide Standards

Band Desig- nation	Frequency Range (GHz)	JAN RG Desig- nation	Inside Dimension Width (cm)	Height (cm)	Cut- off Freq (GHz)	Atten- uation (dB/100 meters)	CW Power (kW)
L	1.12– 1.70	69	16.510	8.255	0.908	1.353	11,800
	1.70– 2.60	104	10.922	5.461	1.375	2.492	5,200
	2.60– 3.95	48	7.214	3.404	2.080	4.711	2,180
G	3.95– 5.85	49	4.755	2.215	3.16	8.849	941
C	4.90– 7.05		4.039	2.019		10.15	754
J	5.85– 8.20	50	3.484	1.580	4.29	12.54	554
H	7.05–10.00	51	2.850	1.262	5.26	22.78	355
X	8.20–12.40	52	2.286	1.016	6.56	27.45	206
P	12.40–18.00	91	1.580	0.790	9.49	40.92	119
K	18.00–26.50	53	1.067	0.432	14.1	87.51	43
R	26.50–40.00	96	0.711	0.356	21.1	145.4	23
	40.00–60.00		0.478	0.2388	31.4	127.3	10
	60.00–90.00	99	0.3099	0.1549	48.4	256.9	4

9-8
Circular
Waveguide
Theory
The circular (cross-section) waveguide is used whenever a *rotating* element, such as a radar antenna, has to be connected to a microwave system. In practice, lengthy runs of pipe use *rectangular* waveguide. The rectangular waveguide usually has its load end formed into a circular waveguide that is connected to the rotating antenna system at a ball/sleeve-bearing joint. This bearing joint must satisfy the mechanical requirements of strength and ease of rotation as well as impedance matching and a minimum of discontinuity. The electrical requirements are usually satisfied by *flanges* designed on the principle of $\lambda/4$ sections (discussed in Chap. 8) that act as electrical "chokes."

In general, the circular waveguide requires a *greater* cross-sectional area than the equivalent rectangular waveguide for the same frequency signal. Some of the signal modes commonly used with rectangular waveguides are *not* suitable for the circular waveguide because of a tendency of the magnetic/electric fields to rotate during the passage along the tube. Manufacture of the circular unit is simpler and the connections of sections is an easier task. However, the design of circular waveguides is somewhat more complicated than its rectangular counterpart.

The same $TE_{m,n}$ and $TM_{m,n}$ designations are used for circular waveguides, but with a different significance. In the circular unit *m* refers to the number of *full* period variations of the field in the angular direction around the *perimeter*. The *n* subscript indicates the number of *half* period variations of field along the radial direction.

The circular waveguide *dominant* mode, as in the case of the rectangular waveguide, is the mode with the *longest cutoff wavelength* and is designated $TE_{1,1}$. This corresponds to the $TE_{1,0}$ mode in the rectangular waveguide. The dominant mode is *not* symmetrical about the center. A discontinuity in the "pipe" will encourage rotation of the field pattern with resulting problems at the load end of the system. The two symmetrical modes are $TE_{0,1}$ and $TM_{0,1}$. These modes present no rotation problem. However, since they are *not* the dominant modes, they are susceptible to the generation of spurious signals that must be suppressed.

The attenuation equations are similar to those of the rectangular waveguide. There are slight variations for each mode. Basically the attenuation (dB/m) varies inversely with diameter and in a more complicated manner with the ratio of frequency to cutoff frequency.

The addition of a dielectric in the circular waveguide increases the guide wavelength. This in turn permits use of the waveguide at lower frequencies. The dielectric can be used in the design of a fixed attenuator. A circular waveguide is an *automatic attenuator* for frequencies *lower* than cutoff frequency. The amount of attenuation varies with length of the pipe. The $TE_{0,1}$ mode has lower attenuation than the other modes. It is the only mode in which attenuation varies inversely with increasing frequency, and the most likely candidate for long runs.

**9-9
Calculations
of Circular
Waveguides** The design of the circular waveguide involves the parameters of diameter and the mode. Except for the cutoff wavelength (λ_0), all the rectangular waveguide formulas apply to the circular waveguide. The cutoff wavelength is determined by

$$\lambda_0 = \frac{\pi d}{\mu_{m,n}} \quad \text{cm} \quad (9\text{-}10)$$

where λ_0 = cutoff wavelength (cm)
d = diameter (cm)
$\mu_{m,n}$ = term derived from the roots of a Bessel function
Table 9-2 is a listing of the values of $\mu_{m,n}$ for the commonly used modes of circular waveguides.

Table 9-2
Values of ($\mu_{m,n}$) for the Principle Modes in Circular Waveguides

TE		TM	
Mode	$\mu_{m,n}$	Mode	$\mu_{m,n}$
$TE_{0,1}$	3.832	$TM_{0,1}$	2.405
$TE_{1,1}$	1.841	$TM_{1,1}$	3.832
$TE_{2,1}$	3.050	$TM_{2,1}$	5.136
$TE_{0,2}$	7.016	$TM_{0,2}$	5.520
$TE_{1,2}$	5.330	$TM_{1,2}$	7.016
$TE_{2,2}$	6.710	$TM_{2,2}$	8.420
		$TM_{0,3}$	8.654

Example 9-4
Given a circular waveguide used for a signal at a frequency of 11 GHz propagated in the $TE_{0,1}$ mode. The internal diameter is 4.5 cm. Calculate:
a. Cutoff wavelength (λ_0).
b. Guide wavelength (λ_q).
c. Velocity of signal in direction of propagation (v_g).
d. Phase velocity (v_p).
e. Characteristic wave impedance (Z_0).

Solution

a. $\lambda = v_c/f = \dfrac{3 \times 10^{10}}{11 \times 10^9} = 2.727$ **cm** $\quad (8\text{-}1)$

$\lambda_0 = \dfrac{\pi d}{\mu_{m,n}} = \dfrac{\pi \times 4.5}{3.832} = 3.689$ **cm** $\quad (9\text{-}10)$

b. $\lambda_g = \dfrac{\lambda}{\sqrt{1-(\lambda/\lambda_0)^2}} = \dfrac{2.727}{\sqrt{1-\left(\dfrac{2.727}{3.689}\right)^2}}$ $\qquad$ (9-2)

$\qquad = \dfrac{2.73}{\sqrt{1-0.5465}} = \dfrac{2.73}{0.6735} = \textbf{4.054 cm}$

c. $v_g = v_c\sqrt{1-(\lambda/\lambda_0)^2}$ $\qquad$ (9-5)

$\qquad = 3\times10^{10}\times0.6735 = \textbf{2.021}\times\textbf{10}^{\textbf{10}}\textbf{ cm/s}$

d. $v_p = v_c\big/\sqrt{1-(\lambda/\lambda_0)^2}$ $\qquad$ (9-4)

$\qquad = 3\times10^{10}\big/0.6735 = \textbf{4.455}\times\textbf{10}^{\textbf{10}}\textbf{ cm/s}$

e. $Z_0 = 377\big/\sqrt{1-(\lambda/\lambda_0)^2} = 377/0.6735 = \textbf{559.8 }\Omega$ $\qquad$ (9-6)

Example 9-5

Given a circular waveguide with an internal diameter of 12 cm, operating with a 8 GHz signal that is propagating in the $TM_{2,2}$ mode. Calculate:

a. Cutoff wavelength (λ_0).
b. Guide wavelength (λ_g).
c. Characteristic wave impedance (Z_0).

Solution

a. $\lambda = v_c/f = \dfrac{3\times10^{10}}{8\times10^9} = \textbf{3.75 cm}$ $\qquad$ (8-1)

$\qquad \lambda_0 = \pi d/\mu_{m,n} = \dfrac{\pi\times12}{8.420} = \textbf{4.477 cm}$ $\qquad$ (9-10)

b. $\lambda_g = \lambda\big/\sqrt{1-(\lambda/\lambda_0)^2}$ $\qquad$ (9-2)

$\qquad = \dfrac{3.75}{\sqrt{1-\left(\dfrac{3.75}{4.477}\right)^2}} = \dfrac{3.75}{\sqrt{1-0.7016}} = \dfrac{3.75}{\sqrt{0.2984}}$

$\qquad = \dfrac{3.75}{0.5463} = \textbf{6.865 cm}$

c. $Z_0 = 377\sqrt{1-(\lambda/\lambda_0)^2} = 0.5463\times377 = \textbf{206 }\Omega$ $\qquad$ (9-9)

9-10
Field Patterns
in Circular
Waveguides

The field patterns for the common modes used in circular waveguides are shown in Fig. 9-7.

Note the angular and radial symmetry of the $TE_{0,1}$ and $TM_{0,1}$ modes. These modes present no problem to the receiver or load if rotation occurs during the propagation of the signal. The other modes will change the plane of *polarization* and will not be received properly. This results in reflected energy, standing waves, and inefficiency.

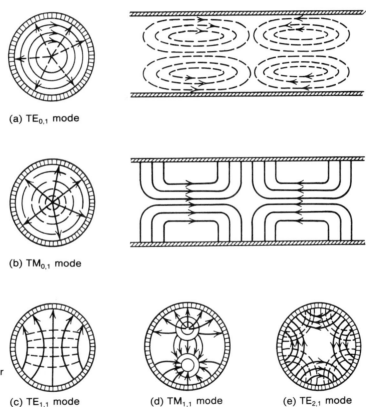

(a) $TE_{0,1}$ mode

(b) $TM_{0,1}$ mode

(c) $TE_{1,1}$ mode   (d) $TM_{1,1}$ mode   (e) $TE_{2,1}$ mode

Figure 9-7 Field patterns in circular waveguides.

9-11
Methods of
Generating Modes
in Waveguides

The generation of specific modes in a waveguide can be accomplished by inserting appropriate probes or antennas. In general an antenna *coincident* (parallel) with the axis would tend to set up TM waves, and a small loop *normal* (perpendicular) to the axis would be more likely to set up TE waves. These principles are illustrated by Fig. 9-8.

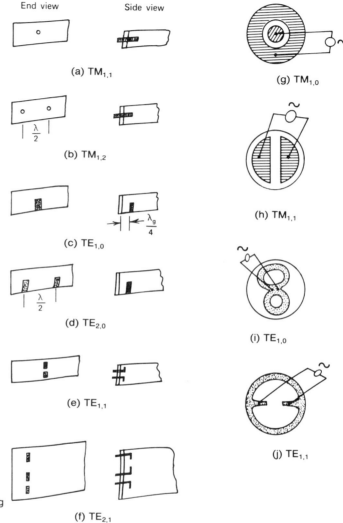

Figure 9-8 Methods of generating modes in waveguides.

Figures 9-8a and 9-8b have the antenna parallel to the direction of propagation in the rectangular waveguide and result in TM waves. The single antenna (Fig. 9-8a) develops a single field pattern.

The *double* antenna (Fig. 9-8b) develops a *double* field pattern. Figures 9-8c to 9-8f show the antenna perpendicular to the direction of propagation and result in TE waves. The single antenna of Fig. 9-8c results in a simple single field pattern. The multiple antennas of Figs. 9-8d, 9-8e, and 9-8f result in more complex field patterns.

A similar analysis of the circular waveguide antenna positions of Figs. 9-8g, 9-8h, 9-8i, and 9-8j indicates that a simple field pattern is generated by the single elements of Figs. 9-8g and 9-8j. The double elements of Figs. 9-8h and 9-8i result in a more complex field pattern.

9-12
Power Handling
Capabilities
of Waveguides

The power handling capability of the rectangular waveguide using air as the medium and operating in the dominant TE mode, relates the modes, dimensions, frequency and the potential gradient at the center of the waveguide, E_{max} expressed in V/cm.

$$P = 6.63 \times 10^{-4} (E_{max}^2) ab \frac{\lambda}{\lambda_g} \text{ W} \qquad (9\text{-}8)$$

Example 9-6

Given a rectangular waveguide 2.29×1.02 cm, operating at a frequency of 11 GHz in the $TE_{1,0}$ dominant mode, calculate the maximum power handling capability of the waveguide if the maximum potential gradient of the signal is 5 kV/cm.

Solution

$$\lambda = v_c / f \qquad (8\text{-}1)$$

$$= 3 \times 10^{10} / 11 \times 10^9 = 2.727 \text{ cm}$$

$$\lambda_0 = 2a/m = \frac{2 \times 2.29}{1} = 4.58 \text{ cm} \qquad (9\text{-}1)$$

$$\lambda_g = \frac{\lambda}{\sqrt{1 - (\lambda/\lambda_0)^2}} \qquad (9\text{-}2)$$

$$= \frac{2.727}{\sqrt{1 - \left(\frac{2.727}{4.58}\right)^2}} = \frac{2.727}{1 - (0.5954)^2} = \frac{2.727}{\sqrt{1 - 0.3545}}$$

$$= \frac{2.727}{\sqrt{0.6455}} = \frac{2.727}{0.8034} = 3.394 \text{ cm}$$

$$P = 6.63 \times 10^{-4} E_{max}^2 ab \frac{\lambda}{\lambda_g} \qquad (9\text{-}8)$$

$$= 6.63 \times 10^{-4} \times (5 \times 10^3)^2 \times 2.29 \times 1.02 \times \frac{2.727}{3.394}$$

$$= 6.63 \times 10^{-4} \times 25 \times 10^6 \times 2.29 \times 1.02 \times 0.8035$$

$$= \textbf{31.11 kW}$$

Obviously the power handling capability of a circular waveguide is related to the internal diameter of the pipe. It also depends on frequency of propagation and cutoff frequency. The maximum power handling capability of the circular waveguide propagating in the dominant mode ($TE_{1,1}$) is given by

$$P_m = 0.498 \times E_{max}^2 \times d^2 \left(\frac{\lambda}{\lambda_g} \right) \quad W \qquad (9\text{-}11)$$

where: P_m = maximum power handling capacity in the $TE_{1,1}$ mode (watts)

E_{max} = maximum allowable field strength (V/cm)

Example 9-7

Given a circular waveguide operating in the $TE_{1,1}$ mode at a frequency of 9 GHz with a maximum field strength of 500 V/cm. The internal diameter is 4.75 cm. Calculate the maximum power.

Solution

$$\lambda = v_c/f = \frac{3 \times 10^{10}}{9 \times 10^9} = 3.333 \text{ cm} \qquad (8\text{-}1)$$

$$\lambda_0 = \pi d / \mu_{m,n} = \frac{\pi \times 4.75}{1.841} = 8.106 \text{ cm} \qquad (9\text{-}10)$$

$$\lambda_g = \frac{\lambda}{\sqrt{1 - (\lambda/\lambda_0)^2}} = \frac{3.333}{\sqrt{1 - \left(\frac{3.333}{8.106} \right)^2}} \qquad (9\text{-}2)$$

$$= \frac{3.333}{\sqrt{1 - 0.1691}} = \frac{3.333}{\sqrt{0.8309}} = \frac{3.333}{0.9116} = 3.656 \text{ cm}$$

$$P_m = 0.498 \times E_{max}^2 \times d^2 \left(\frac{\lambda}{\lambda_g} \right) \qquad (9\text{-}11)$$

$$= 0.498 \times (500)^2 \times (4.75)^2 \left(\frac{3.333}{3.656} \right)$$

$$= 0.498 \times 0.25 \times 10^6 \times 22.56 \times 0.9117$$

$$= 2.561 \times 10^6 \text{ W}$$

The power handling capability of a waveguide can be increased by filling the pipe with an appropriate gas under pressure. On the other hand, operation at reduced pressure, such as the relative vacuum at 30,000 feet of altitude (in aircraft), reduces the power handling capability drastically. Elevated temperature or slight imperfections in the waveguide, such as dirt or humidity, also lowers the power handling capability.

9-13 Waveguide Couplers The *waveguide coupler* has many functions and comes in various forms. The simplest couplers are the bends and twists. These accommodate either TE modes (E bends) or TM modes (H bends). Couplers physically change the *direction* of the signal. The more common types are shown in Fig. 9-9.

The E bend units (Figs. 9-9a and b) have the electrical fields change direction and the H bend units (Figs. 9-9c and d) change the direction of the *magnetic* field. The rounded bends are for

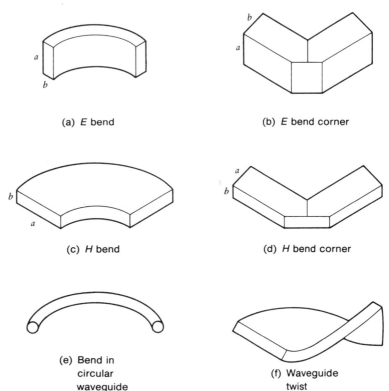

(a) *E* bend

(b) *E* bend corner

(c) *H* bend

(d) *H* bend corner

(e) Bend in circular waveguide

(f) Waveguide twist

Figure 9-9 Microwave bends and twists.

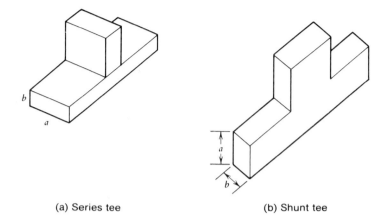

Figure 9-10 Tee junctions.

(a) Series tee

(b) Shunt tee

minor changes in direction whereas the *corner* bends are for *sharp* changes in direction. Corner bends are frequency sensitive because the dimensions relate to $\lambda_g/4$. The waveguide twist (Fig. 10-8f) results in a *reversal of polarization*. The longer the twist the more gradual is the change of plane and the better is the suppression of reflections.

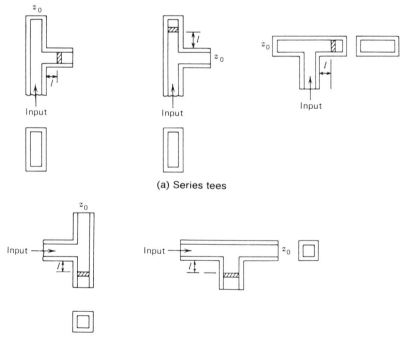

(a) Series tees

(b) Shunt tees

Figure 9-11 Impendance matching with tee junctions.

Another group of couplers includes the *tee junctions* (Fig. 9-10). The *series* or *E* plane tee has the right angle leg branching off the larger dimension. The *shunt* or *H* plane tee has the right angle leg branching off the smaller dimension. Refer to Fig. 9-10.

The impedance seen at the load end of a tee junction can be varied by the position of an inserted short a distance *l* relative to the center of the waveguide. In this manner the load impedance can be matched to the waveguide impedance, Z_0. Refer to Fig. 9-11.

Both the conductance (G) and susceptance (B) of the *series* tee and the resistance (R) and reactance (X) of the *shunt* tee can be varied by the distance *l*.

9-14 Directional Couplers The *directional coupler* is an important tool in microwave measurements. Inserted into the line, it permits the signal to continue as it couples (diverts) or samples some energy of the *forward* wave into appropriate detectors or measuring devices. At the same time it *rejects the reflected signal* returning from the load. The coupling may be a loop or probe inserted into the waveguide, or a slot or hole in the wall of adjacent waveguides. The main purpose of the directional coupler is to separate and isolate signals or to mix different signals. The coupler can be used for power monitoring, signal mixing, isolation of signal sources, swept transmission and reflection measurements, etc. A coupler can be waveguide or coaxial. Specifications usually include frequency band, directivity and coupling coefficient.

9-14.1 Coaxial Directional Coupler One type of coaxial directional coupler is shown in Fig. 9-12.

The coaxial directional coupler operates on the principle that any *reflected wave* from the load is *rejected* by the two coupling probes. All remaining *unwanted* reflected wave energy that arrives in the coupler is absorbed by the termination resistor. The *forward wave* energy is sampled and coupled to the detector or measuring equipment.

Depending on the user's requirements, a purchase requisition for a directional coupler would include at least these five parameters: *directivity*, *SWR*, *frequency range*, *coupling coefficient*, and *transmission loss*. The directivity is a measure of how well a coupler can isolate the forward from the reflected wave. This

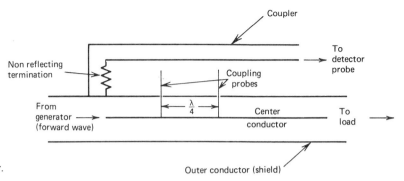

Figure 9-12 Coaxial directional coupler.

sets the limits on how accurately a coupler can perform a specific measurement. A low SWR minimizes mismatch errors, thereby improving the accuracy of the measurement. A wide frequency band will minimize the number of couplers required to cover a frequency range. The coupling coefficient of a coupler is usually an engineering compromise with directivity and frequency. Commercially a −20 dB coupling coefficient is commonly used. With this rating the coupler will extract only one percent of available power. Transmission loss is the total loss in the main line resulting from insertion of the coupler. It includes both insertion loss and coupling loss. This becomes particularly important at high frequencies where the available power is small. A transmission loss of −1 dB is commercially feasible for broadband couplers.

9-14.2
Hybrid-Tee
Coupler

A form of *multiport coupler* is the *hybrid-tee* junction shown in Fig. 9-13.

The relationship of electric and magnetic fields in Fig. 9-13 is such that the following sequence results. For the dominant

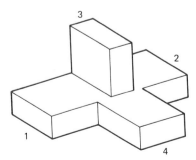

Figure 9-13 Hybird-tee junction.

mode, a signal applied to port 4 appears at 1 and 2 but not at 3. Also a signal applied to port 3 will appear at 1 and 2 but not 4. This assumes the ports are properly terminated.

9-14.3 Hybrid Ring Coupler Another multiport coupler is the *hybrid-ring* junction or ratrace. Refer to Fig. 9-14

The hybrid ring junction operates on the principle of length of travel of the signal. The signal travels around the ring in both directions and will either cancel or reinforce at a particular port. Input signals at port 1 divide between 2 and 4 but are out of phase with each other. Input signals at port 3 divide between 2 and 4, and are in phase. It becomes apparent that the hybrid junction can be used for either the *division* of a signal or the *mixing* of two signals. The hybrid ring is quite frequency sensitive.

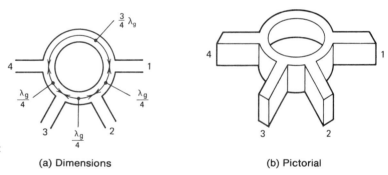

Figure 9-14 Hybrid-ring junction (rat race).

(a) Dimensions

(b) Pictorial

9-15 Impedance Matching Devices The impedance presented by a waveguide at any point can be adjusted by a *window* or *iris* inserted in the waveguide. The waveguide window can be a thin metal coated with some energy absorbing material. Figure 9-15 shows some commonly used waveguide windows.

Figure 9-15a indicates a method of creating a shunt inductive susceptance. The magnitude and polarity of the susceptance varies linearly with the size and location of the window. Figure 9-15b shows a *sequence of windows* placed along the waveguide. The susceptance will vary with the distance S between windows. Figure 9-15c represents a *shunt capacitance*, while Fig. 9-15d

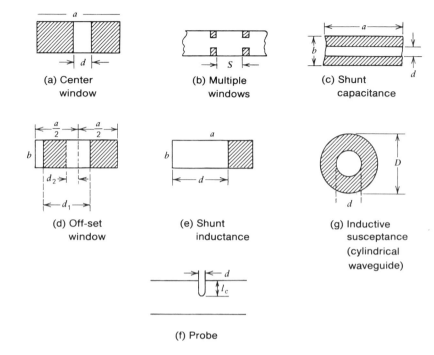

Figure 9-15 Waveguide windows.

(f) Probe

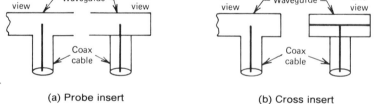

Figure 9-16 Methods of matching waveguide to coaxial cable

(a) Probe insert

(b) Cross insert

represents a *shunt inductance*, whose value is determined by window *size* and *assymetry of location*. Figure 9-15e represents a *shunt inductance* varying with the *a* and *d* dimensions. Figure 9-15g represents an *inductive susceptance* in a circular waveguide whose value is determined by dimensions *D* and *d*. Figure 9-15f represents an inserted cylindrical probe resulting in a *shunting capacitive reactance*.

Figure 9-16 shows two methods of matching a waveguide to a coaxial cable.

9-16
Electrical and
Mechanical Couplings

In waveguide usage either electrical or mechanical coupling or a combination of both may be used.

9-16.1
Coupling Coaxial
Cable to Waveguide

Two methods of coupling a coaxial cable to a waveguide are shown in Fig. 9-16.

9-16.2
Mechanical
Couplers

Two common devices used to join successive sections of waveguide are the *butt flange* (Fig. 9-17a) and the *choke flange* (Fig. 9-17b). Butt joints depend on proper alignment, smooth end surfaces being tightly drawn together. If all these details are attended to, the butt joint introduces less discontinuity and reflections than the choke joint. However the choke joint is less critical than the butt joint. Some separation and misalignment is allowable, and even encouraged. The choke flange (Fig. 9-17b) makes possible an electrical short circuit whenever a mechanical short circuit is difficult to obtain. However, because the choke flange is designed around $\lambda_g/4$ sections, it is frequency sensitive and a limited bandwidth results.

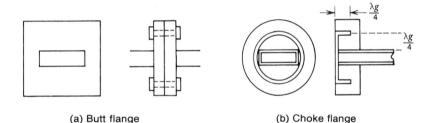

Figure 9-17 Flanges.   (a) Butt flange   (b) Choke flange

9-17
Waveguide
Attenuators

Attenuators for microwave systems (Fig. 9-18) are commercially available in many sizes and shapes. The attenuator may be either fixed, continuously variable (either mechanical or electrical) or *stepped*. It may be either *absorptive* or *reflective*, *calibrated* or *uncalibrated*, or even *programmable*. The *resistive element* may be either *lumped* or *distributed*, *pi* or *tee*. Attenuators are usually *tapered* to minimize reflections.

Some of the parameters to be considered in purchasing an attenuator are: frequency range, impedance, decibel range, average power rating, peak power rating, insertion loss, VSWR, temperature coefficient, and stability. The *resolution* must also

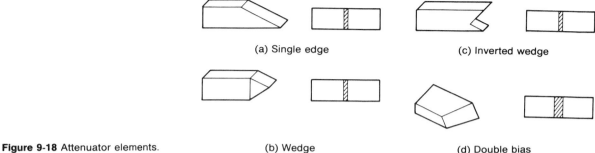

Figure 9-18 Attenuator elements.

(a) Single edge

(c) Inverted wedge

(b) Wedge

(d) Double bias

be specified if it is a variable or step attenuator. The size, shape, weight, required connectors, price, as well as some more subtle parameters, should also be specified.

A high-power attenuator is a separate unit and becomes a load or termination. It may dissipate a few watts or a megawatt. It may not require extra cooling or be air or water cooled. The unit may be a few cubic centimeters in volume or stand two meters high. It may be a high voltage unit or a high current device. Likewise the impedance may be a few ohms or a few kilohms. In ordering a dummy load the specifications should include power, frequency range, VSWR, impedance, connectors, dimensions, and cost.

9-18
Detectors
and Mixers
A *crystal detector* is a general purpose component. It is used for CW or pulsed power detection as well as frequency response testing of other microwave components. The original microwave detector was a point contact, "cat whisker," diode. Recent technology has the diode integrated with the other circuit elements such as the input matching resistor, RF bypass capacitor, and compensating elements. This fabrication minimizes stray reactance and improves performance at high frequency. The integrated assembly fabrication is used for the Low-Barrier Hot-Carrier Diode (LBHCD) detector. This fabrication using thin-film and semiconductor technology results in greater sensitivity, better performance, more rugged and improved heat dissipation properties. Refer to Fig. 9-19.

The diode is mounted so as to provide a complete dc path for rectification. At the same time it cannot upset the RF field in the waveguide. In essence it is across the waveguide for RF but

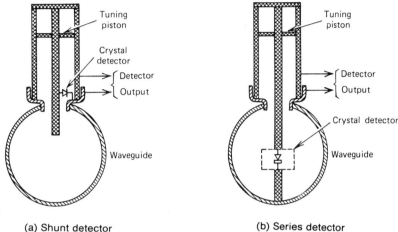

Figure 9-19 Crystal detector probe arrangements in a waveguide.

(a) Shunt detector   (b) Series detector

not for dc. In addition any reflections resulting from the presence of the diode must be minimized if not cancelled.

The diode construction usually includes a silicon wafer as the rectifier element. The body may be a ceramic cartridge type (useful up to 10 GHz), a coaxial type (useful above 10 GHz), or a tripolar diode with a built-in bypass capacitor that is useful over a *broad* frequency range.

Typical parameters required in purchase specifications for a crystal detector are broadband frequency coverage, flat frequency response, low SWR, and good square-law performance. The broadband frequency coverage minimizes the number of detectors required. A flat frequency response and low SWR results in more accurate measurements. The square-law performance results in an output voltage that is proportional to input RF power. Most microwave detectors operate on this principle. A typical crystal detector might have the following specifications: frequency range: 0.01 to 18 GHz; frequency response: 0.5 dB/octave; SWR: 1.5; low level sensitivity: 0.4 mV/μW; maximum input: 100 mW.

Microwave mixers accomplish the mixing function by a careful balancing of diodes. The mixer provides excellent suppression of the local oscillator and input frequencies at the output terminal. The mixer can be used as a phase detector, frequency doubler, current controlled attenuator, balanced modulator, amplitude modulator, or pulse modulator. The mixer operating power is obtained from the input signals and the maximum allowable input current at either input is specified. Typical specifications for a mixer include: frequency range, maximum input power, sensitivity, output impedance, and connectors.

**9-19
Ferrite
Waveguides**
Ferrite materials, commonly consisting of manganese ferrite, zinc ferrite, or a ceramic ferromagnetic oxide, originated in the communications field as powdered iron cores for RF transformers. Its function was the minimization of eddy current and heat losses. This led to its use in pulse transformers for the same reasons. The advent of the core memory of computers used the same material in a signal storage function.

Microwave use of a ferrite depends on another characteristic of the material. In the presence of a magnetic field, the ferrite can be made to interact with RF waves propagating along a transmission line or in a waveguide. The result is a low loss experienced by the wave propagating in one direction and high loss for reverse signals. This property of the ferrite is called *nonreciprocity*. It is used in UHF/microwave applications where energy tends to reflect as a result of irregularities in the line or improperly matched terminations.

A nonreciprocal device placed at the output of a generator can direct the reflected energy away from the generator and into a matched load for dissipation. There are two broad categories of use for the ferrite devices. As a *circulator*, the multiport device can direct the signal from one port to the adjacent clockwise terminal. As an *isolator* the ferrite can protect a port from signals coming from the wrong direction.

Figure 9-20 shows a simplified sketch of a ferrite device used as a circulator and isolator.

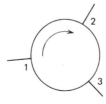

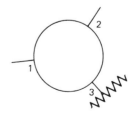

Figure 9-20 Ferrite devices.   (a) Circulator   (b) Isolator

In the circulator (Fig. 9-20a), a signal inserted at port 1 emerges at port 2, an input at port 2 emerges at port 3, and an input at port 3 emerges at port 1. If the device is used with port 3 terminated in a matched load, it becomes an isolator. An input signal at port 1 emerges at port 2 with low insertion loss. Signals reflected back from port 2 (as a result of improper termination at port 2) are diverted to the load at port 3.

Ferrite devices are used for intermodulation suppression, transmitter protection duplexing (radar), parametric amplifier load isolation, tunnel diode amplifiers, etc. A typical specification might be 600 to 900 MHz, 0.5 dB insertion loss, 20 dB isolation, maximum VSWR of 1.3, 50 W, 5 kW peak, connectors, dimensions and weight, and cost.

9-20 Miscellaneous Microwave Accessories A multitude of other components and equipment are used in microwave systems. Some of the widely used pieces are listed: frequency meter, modulator, noise source, filters (low, high, band), power sensors, slotted line, terminations, slide screw tuners, shorts, phase shifter, coaxial switch, adaptors, and a host of generators, spectrum analyzers, bridges, and frequency multipliers. Each device is identified by a list of specifications. An example of a specification for a miniature coaxial transfer switch would be insertion loss of 0.5 dB maximum, VSWR values of 1.5 maximum; impedance of 50 Ω, and isolation of 60 dB minimum. In addition the type of connector mechanical details, and the price per quantity would be added.

9-21 Microwave Measurements There are many parameters that can be measured in microwave systems. A description of the various techniques that are used to make these measurements would require an entire book. Obviously one section in one chapter can contain little more than a listing of some of the parameters.

9-21.1 Power Measurement The measurement technique used to measure power would depend on the frequency of the signal and the level of power (high vs. low), and the available measurement equipment (crystal detector, thermocouple, bolometer, flow calorimeter, etc.). The measurement of kilowatts or megawatts of pulsed power would be done with calorimeters. The measurement of microwatts would entail the most sensitive thermocuple bridge circuit meter available.

9-21.2
Attenuation
Measurement

Attenuation is a measure of the loss of signal power in a network or transmission line. There are two basic methods used for this measurement, *power ratio* method, and *substitution* method. The power ratio method consists of measuring the power delivered to a load with the unit inserted in the system, and then without the unit in the system. The power ratio of these two measurements, expressed in dBs, is the attenuation of the unit.

The substitution method consists of measuring the output power with the unit in the system and then replacing it with an adjustable calibrated attenuator that is adjusted for identical output. The attenuation of the unit is the reading on the calibrated attenuator.

9-21.3
Frequency
Measurement

Frequency is related to wavelength but, depending on the medium, will result in a wavelength different from free space wavelength. The frequency measurement is most readily done with a calibrated cavity wavemeter. The adjustment is a micrometer calibrated for frequency. The wavemeter is coupled to the waveguide via an appropriate coupling device (tee, ring, etc.) and adjusted for resonance. The wavemeter oscillation is indicated by the detector probe. The two types of wavemeters most commonly used are the *transmission* wavemeter and the *absorption* wavemeter.

9-21.4
Wavelength
Measurement

The *wavelength* can be measured with the waveguide equivalent of the slotted line (Fig. 8-8). It is then called *standing-wave detector*. The wavelength measurement is made by placing a short circuit at the load end of the line. The probe is moved away from the short-circuited end to the first voltage minimum position. This distance, as read off the calibrated length of the line, represents the waveguide half wavelength (λ_g). The free space wavelength and frequency can be calculated using Eqs. (9-2) and (8-1).

9-21.5
SWR
Measurement
The SWR measurement may be made directly using the standing wave detector. Adjust the SWR meter for full-scale deflection at the voltage maximum position, then note the reading at the voltage minimum position. High values of SWR indicate a low value of voltage at the minimum voltage position. If this minimum voltage point is difficult to pinpoint, two equal voltage points, either side of the minimum position can be determined. The actual minimum voltage position is assumed to be midway between the two points.

9-21.6
Impedance
Measurement
The impedance of an unknown load can be determined using the standing wave detector and a short-circuited load. The shift of the minimum voltage position as the short-circuited load is replaced by the unknown load, is noted and a sequence of calculations and Smith chart plots is made. This procedure is specifically defined in Appendix B, Sec. B-5, Exs. B-13 and B-14.

9-22
Summary
Operation at microwave frequencies requires the use of waveguides. Waveguides are either rectangular or circular. Signals are generated in either the TE or TM modes. Field patterns may be simple or complex. Waveguide accessories include couplers, attenuators, detectors, mixers, and ferrites.

Now return to the objectives and self-evaluation questions at the beginning of this chapter and see how well you can answer them. If you cannot answer certain questions, place a check next to each of them and review appropriate parts of the text. Then answer the questions and solve the problems below.

9-23
Questions
Q9-1 What is the highest frequency at which the use of coaxial cable is still practical?

Q9-2 What is the advantage of operating in the microwave region?

Q9-3 Identify the *L*, *S*, *C*, *X*, and *K* frequency bands.

Q9-4 Define propagation of a wave.

Q9-5 How do signals usually travel down a waveguide?

Q9-6 Define the TE mode.

Q9-7 Define the TM mode.

Q9-8 Name some of the parameters of a waveguide that affect attenuation.

Q9-9 Define the frequency range for the G, J, H, P, and R bands.

Q9-10 What are the disadvantages of a circular waveguide compared to a rectangular waveguide?

Q9-11 Why are some modes impractical for circular waveguides?

Q9-12 Which modes have circular symmetry?

Q9-13 How are TM modes generated?

Q9-14 How are TE modes generated?

Q9-15 Define the function of waveguide couplers.

Q9-16 Compare the series-tee and shunt-tee junctions.

Q9-17 Define the function of the directional coupler.

Q9-18 Explain the operation of the hybrid-tee junction.

Q9-19 Compare the butt flange and the choke flange.

Q9-20 How do the high-power waveguide attenuator specifications differ from those for the low-power waveguide attenuator?

Q9-21 List the parameters that should be specified in the purchase of a crystal detector.

Q9-22 List the functions that can be performed by a microwave mixer.

Q9-23 Explain the operation of a microwave ferrite circulator.

9-24
Problems

P9-1 A 5 GHz signal is propagated in a rectangular waveguide with internal dimensions of 4.5 cm $\times$ 2.25 cm. Assuming the dominant mode, calculate: λ_0, λ_g, v_g, v_p, Z_0.

P9-2 Given a rectangular waveguide with internal dimensions of 4 cm $\times$ 2 cm.

a. Assuming a dominant mode, determine the lowest frequency that can be propagated in the waveguide.

b. Assuming a frequency of 8.5 GHz, what is the highest mode that can be accommodated?

c. Assuming $f = 12$ GHz and $m = 2$, calculate: λ_0, λ_g, v_g, v_p, and Z_0.

P9-3 Given a 9 GHz signal, a rectangular waveguide 6.9 cm $\times$ 3.45 cm propagating in the $TE_{1,1}$ mode. Calculate λ_0, λ_g, v_g, v_p, and Z_0.

P9-4 Given a rectangular waveguide 2.4 cm $\times$ 1.2 cm, operating at a frequency of 10 GHz in the $TE_{1,0}$ dominant mode, calculate the maximum power handling capability of the waveguide if the maximum potential gradient of the signal is 4.6 kV/cm.

P9-5 Given a circular waveguide used for a signal at a frequency of 9 GHz propagated in the $TE_{1,1}$ mode. The internal diameter is 4 cm. Calculate λ_0, λ_g, v_g, v_p, and Z_0.

P9-6 Given a circular waveguide with an internal diameter of 10 cm operating with a 8 GHz signal that is propagating in the $TM_{1,1}$ mode. Calculate λ_0, λ_g, and Z_0.

P9-7 Given a circular waveguide operating in the $TE_{1,1}$ mode at a frequency of 11 GHz with a maximum field strength 700 V/cm. The internal diameter is 3.5 cm. Calculate the maximum power.

Chapter 10 Active Microwave Tubes

10-1
Objectives

To learn:

1. The operation of planar triodes.
2. The operation of the klystron amplifier.
3. The operation of the magnetron.
4. The operation of the traveling wave tube.
5. The operation of various solid state microwave amplifiers.

10-2
Self-Evaluation Questions

Test your prior knowledge of the information in this chapter by answering the following questions. Watch for the answers to these questions as you read the chapter. Your final evaluation of whether you understand the material is measured by your ability to answer these questions. When you have completed the chapter, return to this section and answer the questions again.

1. Which parameters limit the operation of vacuum tubes at microwave frequencies?
2. Which features of the *lighthouse tube* make it usable at microwave frequencies?
3. Explain the operation of a *two-cavity klystron*.
4. Explain the operation of a *reflex klystron*.
5. Explain the operation of a *magnetron*.
6. Explain the purpose of *strapping* in a *magnetron*.
7. Explain the operation of a *traveling wave tube*.
8. Which parameters limit the operation of *transistors* at microwave frequencies?
9. Explain the operation of a *varactor* diode.
10. Explain the operation of a *parametric amplifier*.

10-3
Lighthouse Tube

As the technology moved into the UHF and microwave regions, the *transit time* of the electron passage from cathode to anode in a vacuum tube became a new limitation in addition to interelectrode capacitance. Of equal nuisance value, the self-inductance

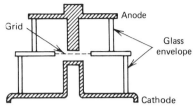

Figure 10-1 Lighthouse tube.

of the input leads created a skin effect that proved to be excessive. One solution was the *acorn tube* that depended on a reduction of element size and spacing and used parallel input leads. This extended the usable frequency spectrum considerably.

The next step was the development of the *lighthouse tube*, also called the *parallel-plane tube*, *planar tube* and *disk-seal tube*. This device raised the usable frequency spectrum into the microwave region. The construction of the lighthouse tube is shown in Fig. 10-1.

Connecting leads are *disks* that reduce self-inductance. The electrode spacing is very small, on the order of 0.2 millimeters, which minimizes the transit time problem. The small spacing unfortunately limits the power handling capacity and requires external cooling. The disk configuration lends itself to plugging into coaxial cavities. This permits one cavity feeding the input signal between grid and cathode and another cavity receiving the amplified output between the cathode and anode.

The frequency of operation is readily controlled by the design frequency of the cavities. An amplifier would use the same input and output frequencies. A frequency multiplier would have the input and output cavities designed for a multiple frequency. A feedback path from output cavity to input cavity would convert the unit to an oscillator. Tuning of the cavity is readily accomplished by mechanical adjustment of a diaphragm in one wall, screw, or post. The planar construction permits operation at 10 GHz with pulsed outputs of 10 kW. This magnitude of power requires external cooling. Operation is commonly performed in the grounded grid configuration.

10-4
Microwave
Cavities
At microwave frequencies, the tuned circuit can consist of a *cavity resonator*. The Q of the circuit (or cavity) is a measure of the ratio of the energy *stored* each cycle to the energy *lost* each cycle. The Q is also defined by the ratio of the *volume* of the cavity to the interior *area* of the cavity. If we assume that all other conditions remain the same, a larger cavity has a higher Q than a smaller cavity. The RF definition of Q, namely, the ratio of center frequency to bandwidth, is still proper for cavities. An

unloaded cavity may attain a Q of 100,000. Loading may reduce the Q to the 1000 to 50,000 range. A cavity resonator may be considered to be an *enclosed waveguide* and can be spherical, rectangular, or cylindrical. The dimensions *must be related* to the *half wavelength*. A properly excited cavity can function as a *microwave oscillator*. Furthermore, it can oscillate at a *harmonic* frequency. Unwanted harmonic oscillation is commonly avoided by using oddly shaped cavities, called *reentrant resonators*. This construction has one of the walls reenter the resonator shape. These designs are more complex than standard cavities. The usual procedure is to develop the basic design, construct a unit, and note the frequency discrepancy between actual and desired resonant frequencies. The dimensions of the cavity are then modified for the required frequency. The energy can be coupled to the cavity by means of a loop, probe, or slot. An additional method is the electron beam coupling that will be detailed in Sec. 10-5.

10-5 Velocity Modulated Tubes The major distinction between the low frequency vacuum tubes and the specialized microwave tubes is the treatment of the *electron beam*. The vacuum tube offers a *constant velocity* electron stream with a *variable quantity* of electrons depending on modulation. The microwave tube offers a *constant quantity* of electrons with *variable velocity* determined by the modulating RF. This is called *velocity modulation*. If the period of interaction of the beam and the RF is a cycle or less, it is called *local interaction*. This is the case for the *klystron*. If the interaction continues over many cycles, it is called *extended interaction*. This is the case for the *traveling wave tube* (TWT). The *magnetron* combines *both* methods of interaction.

If an oscillator changes frequency because of a variation in the dc voltages applied to the unit, the oscillator is said to be *pushed*. If the frequency variation is a result of change of *load*, the unit is said to be *pulled*. These conditions can be minimized by the use of regulated voltages and buffers. A more sophisticated alternative would use AFC systems for frequency control. On the other hand some units lend themselves to FM generation by varying the applied voltages.

10-6
The
Two-Cavity
Klystron

The *klystron* (Fig. 10-2) is a form of velocity-modulated micro-wave tube. The klystron was developed about the time of World War II and is used as a microwave oscillator or fixed-frequency amplifier. The klystron may be designed with one or more cavities.

The filament, cathode, and focusing electrodes constitute the *electron gun* of the klystron. They direct a high velocity electron beam toward the high potential anode. The *buncher cavity* receives the weak microwave input and sets up the RF field around the electron beam. Depending upon the polarity of the RF field at the instant the electron passes by the buncher cavity, the velocity of the electron either accelerates, decelerates, or is unchanged. During the passage in the drift space, the accelerated electrons catch up with the previously decelerated electrons. By the time the electrons reach the area of the catcher cavity, they have combined into a group or *bunch*. This process is called *bunching*. The bunch surrenders energy to the *catcher cavity* because as the bunch passes through, the RF polarity is such that the RF *decelerates* the electron; hence it receives energy from the electron bunches. Because the sequence of bunches corresponds to the RF signal, the catcher cavity receives energy at an RF rate. The ratio of difference in RF energy between the two cavities may be 1000. The bunching process is affected by the anode voltage. The anode voltage, beam current, cavity tuning, and load coupling must be properly adjusted for maximum microwave power output.

The klystron is inherently a high-Q narrow-band amplifier. It is possible to design *multicavity* (three or more) klystrons. If the cavities are tuned to the *same* frequency (*synchronous* tuning),

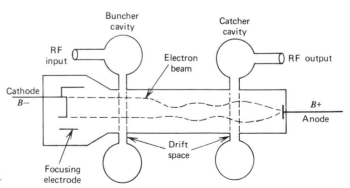

Figure 10-2 Two-cavity klystron amplifier.

the bunching is improved, resulting in *more* gain and efficiency but with a narrow BW. The cavities can be designed for *stagger* (asynchronous) *tuning*, which results in *wider* bandwidth. The two-cavity unit can also be designed as a fixed frequency oscillator with an appropriate feedback loop from catcher cavity to buncher cavity. The two-cavity klystron is not a practical variable frequency oscillator because it would necessitate adjustment of both of the cavities and of the anode voltage. This is not a reasonable approach to a variable frequency oscillator.

10-7 Reflex Klystron The *reflex klystron* (Fig. 10-3) is a modification of the two-cavity klystron. It can be used as a low-power, low-efficiency *variable* frequency oscillator because there is only a single cavity to be frequency adjusted.

The electron-gun construction is similar to the multicavity klystron. The single cavity is at a positive potential and acts as the anode. The same cavity serves both the buncher and catcher functions. The electron stream is directed past the cavity where it undergoes the velocity modulation or bunching process in the *forward* direction. The *repeller* is at a *negative* potential relative to the cathode. It repels the bunched electron beam *back* toward the cavity. The repeller voltage determines the *reflex* or turning *point*. The electrons reaccelerate toward the cathode surrender their energy to the cavity on passing through and fall into the positive potential wall of the tube. (It is usually common practice to operate the tube/cavity at ground potential, with the cathode and repeller voltages negative). The bunched stream surrenders more RF energy than it receives, and oscillation is sustained. The output power is determined by the completeness of the bunching process.

The frequency of a reflex klystron is readily adjusted by inserting a screw, post, or dielectric into the cavity, or varying a

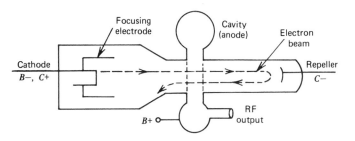

Figure 10-3 Reflex klystron.

diaphragm in the cavity wall (not shown in Fig. 10-3). In operation *the negative potential must be applied to the repeller before the positive voltage is applied to the anode*. Otherwise the electron beam strikes the repeller and destroys it. The magnitude of anode and repeller voltages have a slight effect on the frequency. For each specific frequency setting, there is an optimum setting of anode and repeller voltages for maximum RF output. These voltages control *transit time*, which in turn de-

Figure 10-4 Four-cavity klystron.

termines mode. The *shortest* transit time requires the *maximum* voltages and results in *maximum power* output. Common practice calls for the next smaller transit time at a different mode with moderate accelerating voltage and less power output.

The reflex klystron is available in lengths of five centimeters to three meters. It can deliver power outputs of a few milliwatts to a few watts. It can function in the UHF and microwave frequencies up to approximately 100 gigahertz (the EHF band). It can be used as the local oscillator in a superheterodyne receiver, signal generator or FM generator. It operates at efficiencies of ten to forty percent. Figure 10-4 is a four-cavity klystron operating at 12 GHz with a bandwidth of 6 MHz, a gain of 35 dB and 35 W output. It is a Varian type VKU-7792 A.

10-8 Magnetron The magnetron (Fig. 10-5) was the first *high-power* microwave oscillator. It is essentially a diode that functions on the interaction of electric and magnetic fields. It consists of a cylindrical cathode surrounded by the anode. The anode contains a number of resonant cavities.

External to the unit is a magnet with a pole at either end of the cathode, creating a magnetic field parallel to the axis of the cathode. The electrons emitted from the cathode without the influence of the magnetic field, follow standard vacuum technology and move radially to the anode. The magnetic field causes each electron to move angularly (in a curved path) in the *interaction space* (Fig. 10-5). As a given electron approaches the anode it releases energy to a cavity. It then falls towards the cathode and enters into a lower orbit. Gradually the electron again picks up energy (since it is repelled by the cathode). It reapproaches the anode and again surrenders energy to a cavity.

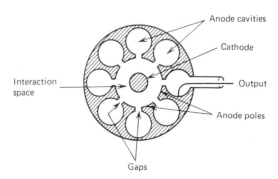

Figure 10-5 Magnetron.

The exact path is determined by the anode voltage and strength of magnetic field.

A *critical* magnetic field causes an electron to barely graze the anode before bending back. If the RF signal is peaking positive in the cavity as the electron approaches, they are in phase and energy is transferred. For proper oscillation the total phase shift around the interior periphery of the anode must be some multiple of 2π. The output signal is taken from one of the cavities through a coaxial line.

A particular electron may approach each cavity in turn or skip one or more between approaches to the anode. These are different modes of operation and can create different frequencies. If these frequencies are close together, there is a tendency for the magnetron to shift frequency continuously. The *dominant* mode, also called the π *mode*, refers to operation of a magnetron where adjacent poles have a phase difference of π radians. When properly adjusted, the electron will progress in the interaction space with the change in RF polarity from cavity to cavity. This is again a form of bunching and is called the *phase-focusing effect*.

In order to minimize the generation of spurious frequencies and prevent frequency shifting, a type of construction called *strapping* (Fig. 10-6) is employed.

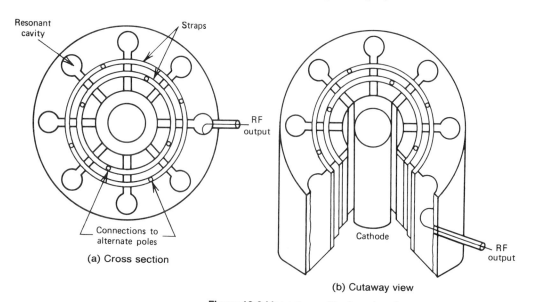

(a) Cross section

(b) Cutaway view

Figure 10-6 Magnetron with strapping rings.

The heavy strapping rings are connected to *alternate* poles (Fig. 10-6b) that keeps the alternate poles in the *same phase*. As a result adjacent poles are specifically out of phase with each other and each pair of poles represents a cycle. Any frequency other than the prescribed frequency finds the cavity signal out of phase and the delivered energy simply results in a current flow in the strapping rings. An alternative to strapping is the *rising sun* construction with alternate lengths of anode poles (not

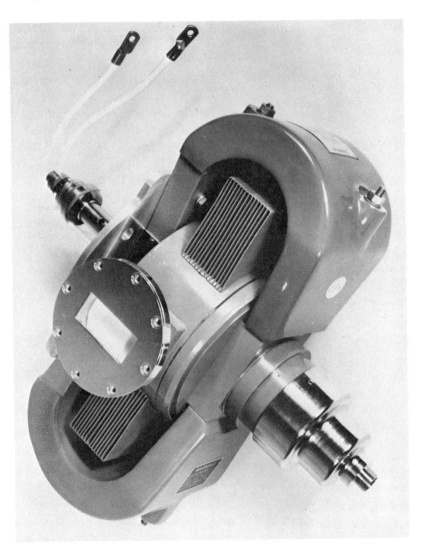

Figure 10-7 Coaxial magnetron.

shown). The choice of a proper combination of anode voltage and magnetic field is usually derived from *Rieke* diagrams (outside the scope of this text).

Mechanical tuning capability of a magnetron is approximately 5%. Voltage variation also provides minor tuning.

The magnetron is used both for CW and pulsed operations. As a pulsed oscillator a typical duty cycle is 0.001. Operation can be anywhere from 30 MHz (VHF) to 100 GHz (EHF). The peak output power may vary between megawatts at UHF to 10 kW at 100 GHz. As a CW oscillator, the magnetron may deliver 25 kW at low microwave frequencies. The magnetron is currently used as the basic oscillator of radar, various aircraft guidance beacons, and microwave ovens. An efficiency up to 70% is attainable depending on frequency. Figure 10-7 is a pulsed, mechanically tuned coaxial magnetron, Varian type SFD-313. It operates in the frequency range 5.45 to 5.825 GHz, output power of 1 MW. It is used in long-range search and tracking radars. Some variations on the basic construction are the *long anode structure* (for extra power), coaxial magnetron

Figure 10-8 Pulsed crossed-field amplifier.

and *crossed-field amplifiers* (CFA). Figure 10-8 is a pulsed crossed-field amplifier, operating at 3.1 to 3.5 GHz, peak power output of 125 kW, bandwidth of 400 MHz, a gain of 11 dB, and a 40% efficiency. It is Varian type SFD 243.

10-9 Traveling Wave Tube (TWT) Soon after World War II and subsequent to appearance of the magnetron and klystron, Varian developed the *traveling wave tube* (TWT). This improved the narrow bandwidth of the multicavity klystron amplifier and offered an improved noise figure (NF). The TWT extends the short time of interaction between the electron beam and the RF field. This results in a lower Q circuit with correspondingly broader bandwidth. The advantage of multicavities is obtained using a helical coil. Each turn of the helix offers the coupling advantage of a cavity. The TWT is shown in Fig. 10-9.

To obtain the advantage of extended interaction of beam and RF signal, the RF signal must be slowed down in the direction of progression of the electron beam. This is accomplished by having the RF travel in a helical path. By proper design of helix diameter and pitch, the forward motion of the RF signal is in step with the electron beam progression. Because the TWT is much longer than the klystron, the focused beam normally tends to diffuse along the way. This is controlled by an external magnetic field that concentrates the beam in the center of the helix. This can also be accomplished with a series of small permanent magnets. These are called *periodic permanent magnets* and are located along the length of the tube.

The beam first encounters the RF signal at the *beginning* of the helix, where the input signal is *weak*. There is beam/signal

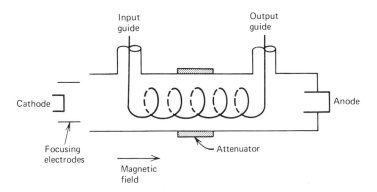

Figure 10-9 Traveling wave tube.

interaction, and the bunching process begins. At each turn of the helix the RF signal and the bunched beam are in phase and mutually supportive. This results in a continuous amplification during the travel. By the time the beam has arrived at the end of the helix, bunching is completed. The RF signal is greatly amplified and sent to the output waveguide. The electron beam continues to the positive anode.

Figure 10-10 Coupled-cavity traveling wave tube.

Oscillation is suppressed by means of an attenuator in the form of an RF absorbent material applied to the tube face and located near the beginning of the tube. This absorbs the weak reflected signal. It also prevents signal buildup with a negligible loss of forward signal and gain.

The helix structure offers the advantage of being *nonresonant*. There are also disadvantages, however. It has high frequency limitations by virtue of its structure, is quite noisy and also has definite power limitations. A poorly focused electron beam can cross the helix and melt the structure destroying the TWT.

The TWT can be used as a low-power, low-noise amplifier with gains of 30 dB, 30 mW output, and with an octave bandwidth. As a medium-power amplifier it can offer outputs of up to 25 W. High-power TWTs can handle 100 kW of pulsed power with 50 dB gain and 50% efficiency. The TWT can also be used as a broad band RF amplifier, repeater amplifier in communications links, and television links, radar, and communications satellites. The TWT may be pulse, frequency, or amplitude modulated.

Figure 10-10 is a coupled-cavity traveling wave tube operating between 1.75 and 1.85 GHz, with a CW output of 12.5 kW, and a gain of 30 dB. It is Varian-type VTL-6640A1, used for satellite communications.

10-10 Active Microwave Semiconductors The early transistors had a very limited frequency range. In time, there were improvements in power, voltage and current ratings, sensitivity, switching speed, noise figure, gain and temperature characteristics. In addition, frequency characteristics were improved and the frequency range was increased from audio to RF to VHF, UHF, and finally into the lower microwave region.

Microwave diodes were available about the time of World War II, but function was limited to detector applications. Recent developments in high frequency diodes have expanded their functions considerably. The operation and function of microwave diodes is discussed in Sec. 10-12.

10-11 Transistor Amplifiers The high frequency limitations of transistors are more complex than vacuum tubes. The junction capacitance, which is an obvious limitation, varies with depletion layer, which in turn is controlled by the (reverse) bias. The gain factors, h_{fb} and h_{fc}, acquire reactive components and become complex terms. These variables make it difficult to define parameters for practical use by designers. The high frequency limitations of lead inductance are similar to those of the vacuum tube. Shorter leads as well as the use of low inductance packaging are helpful.

Transit time in the transistor is governed basically by the same time of travel of the electron that is found in the vacuum tube. In the semiconductor the electron's passage is through a material rather than space. Electron travel time is determined by a combination of influences. The initial path is out of the emitter, which must lag the control signal. The base width must be crossed in addition to the opposition because of base impurities. Finally the collector depletion layer and the width of the collector must be crossed as well. This last rate is governed by the collector voltage, which determines drift velocity through the collector. The result of all these delays is a distorted output signal at UHF frequencies.

The upper frequency of operation of a transistor is defined either as a *gain-bandwidth* product or as a *maximum frequency* of oscillation. There are a variety of materials and methods of fabrication used in the list of commercially available microwave transistors. The latest trend is toward microwave integrated circuit (MIC) packaging where the circuit elements are included with the basic transistor as an IC package. In addition the trend is to parallel a number of transistors at the output to accomplish high power output at microwave frequencies.

Some typical values for commercially available transistors are the following: 8.5 W at 2.3 GHz, 6 W at 3.5 GHz, and 5 W at 4 GHz. A noise figure of 6 dB is typical as is a gain of 25 dB.

The reliability of the solid state microwave amplifier is of the utmost importance if the unit is to be used in a satellite or an underseas cable. The industry's goal is a MTF (mean time to failure) of an incredible 10^9 hours of operation. Compare this figure to an MFT of 10^3 hours for a vacuum tube, and we realize the advantages of solid state amplifiers. Added to this advantage is the dramatic dc power saving of the solid state device and the picture is complete. Recent developments have the solid state amplifier operating at 40 GHz. Undoubtedly, in due time, the integrated package will provide reasonable power at 100 GHz.

10-12 One of the family of voltage-variable capacitors (VVC), the
Varactor varactor diode operates on the principle that a reverse-biased
Diode junction exhibits capacitance across the junction.

$$C_t = C_0 / \sqrt{V_R} \qquad (10\text{-}1)$$

where: C_0 is maximum capacitance, which occurs at $V_R = 0.3$
V. Furthermore, this value of capacitance will vary with changes
in reverse bias. Of course, one limitation is the reverse bias
rating of the diode where avalanche occurs and the unit is
destroyed.

Nevertheless, a range of 40 to 400 pF is possible at VHF and
5 to 25 pF in the microwave region. This has resulted in the use
of the varactor diode in the TV tuner. The minimum capacitance and internal base resistance determine the maximum
usable frequency. Present technology has set the figure at approximately 100 GHz.

Varactor diodes are also used as frequency multipliers or
harmonic generators, in which case they are called *varactor
multipliers*. This application depends on the nonlinear variation
of capacitance with applied voltage. An RF signal applied to the
diode will generate harmonics at the output. The varactor is
commonly used as a doubler, tripler, or quadrupler, with output
power and efficiency decreasing inversely with multiplication.
Cascading a string of units will multiply the input frequency
accordingly. Efficiency varies from 25 to 75% depending on the
frequency and fabrication. The units have been used up to 100
GHz. Some typical values are:

200 mW input − 20 mW output at 11 GHz (10% efficiency)

1200 mW input − 100 mW output at 9.9 GHz (8.3% efficiency)

20 W input − 4 W output at 3.58 GHz (20% efficiency)

A variation of the varactor multiplier is the *step-recovery
varactor*. These units can multiply by twelve in a single stage
with efficiency varying inversely with multiplication factor. The
output power is less than the standard unit and varies inversely
with frequency. This is also known as *charge-storage diode* and
snap-off varactor. Energy is stored in its capacitance, and the
harmonics are generated by releasing a pulse of current. The

pulse of course is rich in harmonics and is a result of the return of stored carriers. Typical values are:

Times 6	2.5 GHz output	5 W 33% efficiency
Times 8	6.4 GHz output	0.25 W 25% efficiency

10-13
Parametric
Amplifier

The *parametric amplifier* presents another use for the varactor diode. In this application it is used as a low-noise *microwave amplifier*. The principle of operation depends on the relationship of a charge on a capacitor creating a voltage ($V = q/C$). If the charge is stored on the plates, and the capacitance is varied, the voltage represented by that charge will vary. The capacitance is varied by means of the varactor diode effect. Instead of a dc bias variation, an RF *pump* signal is used as the variable force. The weak input signal creates the initial charge and voltage across the diode. This is amplified by the pump signal that provides the energy for the signal buildup. The strength of the pump signal is the limitation on the amplification.

If the pump frequency is twice the input frequency, the system is operating in the *degenerate mode*. Any other relationship of input and pump frequencies results in a beat frequency called the *idler* frequency. This type of operation is the *nondegenerate* mode. In this mode, energy is contributed to both the input and idler frequencies by the pump source. Either frequency may be considered the output signal.

Because the parametric amplifier deals with extremely weak input signals and feedback from succeeding stages can cause increased noise, it is imperative to isolate the amplifier from succeeding circuitry. This is accomplished using a ferrite circulator (Sec. 9-19). Another approach lowers inherent noise in the amplifier by cooling the unit in a *cryogenic* system. Obviously this method is bulky and expensive and is used only under the most demanding conditions.

The basic parametric amplifier is a high-Q narrow-band device. A number of diodes cascaded using appropriate circuitry results in an amplifier with wide bandwidth. Parametric amplifiers are frequency limited in the sense that the pump source has limitations of power and frequency. The parametric amplifier has been operated at 30 GHz with power gain of 20 dB and noise figure of 0.3 dB.

10-14 The *tunnel diode*, also called *Esaki diode* after its inventor, is an
Tunnel excellent low-power microwave oscillator or amplifier. The
Diode fabrication includes a heavily doped, very thin junction of
germanium, gallium arsenide, or gallium antimide material. The
resulting diode characteristic curve includes a *negative resistance*
characteristic portion (Fig. 10-11).

The thin junction enables the carrier to *tunnel* its way through
to the negative resistance portion between points A and B of the
characteristic curve. The operation is restricted between the
peak voltage and current (V_p, I_p) of point A and the valley
voltage and current (V_v, I_v) of point B. Because the values are in
the milliampere and millivolt ranges, the maximum power output of the unit is in the microwatt range.

Using the tunnel diode in the microwave region with a high Q
cavity results in minimal loading and great stability. As an
oscillator, the only requirement is a low voltage, low current
power supply. Oscillation up to 100 GHz is possible. The
frequency of oscillation can be varied by adjusting the tuning
element (L-C) tank, cavity, etc.).

The negative-resistance characteristic of the tunnel diode also
permits operation as an *amplifier*, because it results in power
gain. The frequency limitation is due to junction capacitance
and internal resistance. The unit is inherently a low-noise device. It shares the problem of the parametric amplifier in the use

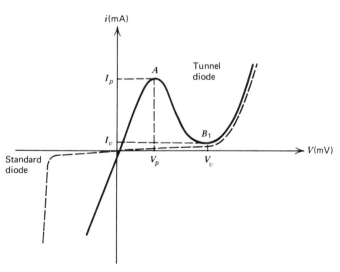

Figure 10-11 Tunnel diode characteristic
curve.

of a ferrite circulator for isolation from its load. A gain of 10 dB in the X band with a noise figure of 2.5 dB is a reasonable specification. At lower frequency the gain increases.

10-15
Miscellaneous
Diodes

A number of other diode devices have been developed in recent years and eventually will assume a position among the truly important microwave components.

The *Gunn diode*, named after the inventor, uses galium arsenide, indium phosphide, cadmium telluride, or indium arsenide. It is described as a *bulk effect* diode. The operation depends on the *transferred-electron effect* that results from setting up a high voltage gradient in the material. This produces a negative resistance characteristic that is used to create oscillations in a suitable circuit. Gunn diodes have been used as oscillators and amplifiers with power in milliwatts at frequencies as high as 25 GHz. Efficiency is very low at these frequencies.

The *LSA* (limited space-charge accumulation) diode is also a bulk effect diode. It is a modification of the Gunn diode that can operate at higher frequencies and possibly with higher power output. Operation at 90 GHz has been accomplished.

The *IMPATT* (impact avalanche and transit time) diode accomplishes a negative resistance characteristic by a combination of transit time and *avalanche current multiplication*. The power rating is between that of the Gunn and LSA diodes. These units can provide one watt in X band and 100 mW at 100 GHz.

The *PIN* (positive-intrinsic-negative) diode consists of a narrow p layer separated from a narrow n layer by an intrinsic layer. At high frequencies it becomes a variable resistance. Power capability depends on the material (germanium, silicon, or gallium arsenide). The unit is used for microwave power switching.

Other microwave diodes that may assume great importance in the future are the *Schottky barrier* diode and the *backward* diode. There is a great deal of government- and company-sponsored research in microwave semiconductors. Each year significant improvements in MICs are introduced.

10-16
Summary
The *high*-power microwave devices are the *klystron, magnetron,* and *traveling wave tube* (TWT).

The semiconductors are constantly being extended in frequency. These include transistor amplifiers, varactor diodes, parametric amplifier, tunnel diode, Gunn diode, limited space-charge accumulation diode, impatt-avalanche and transit-time diode, and positive-intrinsic-negative diode.

Now return to the objectives and self-evaluation questions at the beginning of this chapter and see how well you can answer them. If you cannot answer certain questions, place a check next to each of them and review appropriate parts of the text. Then answer the questions and solve the problems below.

10-17
Questions

Q10-1 Compare local and extended interaction in microwave tubes.

Q10-2 Define the terms *pushed* and *pulled* for microwave oscillators.

Q10-3 Explain the effect of voltage variation on the klystron.

Q10-4 What is the significance of the sequence in which the voltages are applied to a klystron?

Q10-5 Which devices use magnetrons as the source of frequency?

Q10-6 What is the significance of integrated packaging of microwave transistors.

Q10-7 Discuss the significance of reliability in the use of microwave transistors.

Q10-8 Explain the operation of a varactor multiplier.

Q10-9 What is the major distinction of the step-recovery varactor?

Q10-10 Define pump signal, idler frequency, and degenerate mode, as they pertain to the parametric amplifier.

Q10-11 How is noise figure reduced in a parametric amplifier?

Q10-12 Explain the operation of the tunnel diode.

Q10-13 Explain the operation of the Gunn diode.

Q10-14 Explain the advantage of the LSA diode over the Gunn diode.

Q10-15 List four additional diodes.

Chapter 11

VHF
Antennas

11-1
Objectives
To learn:

1. The functions of VHF antennas.
2. The parameters of the VHF antennas.
3. The basic theory of the VHF antenna.
4. The operation of and variations of the dipole antenna.
5. The effect of ground on the VHF antenna.
6. The characteristics of directional VHF antennas.

11-2
Self-Evaluation
Questions
Test your prior knowledge of the information in this chapter by answering the following questions. Watch for the answers to these questions as you read the chapter. Your final evaluation of whether you understand the material is measured by your ability to answer these questions. When you have completed the chapter, return to this section and answer the questions again.

1. Define the function of an antenna.
2. Define *gain* of an antenna.
3. Define a *resonant* antenna.
4. Define *directivity* of an antenna.
5. What is meant by *radiation pattern* of an antenna?
6. Define *beamwidth* of an antenna.
7. What is the significance of the *polarization* of an antenna?
8. Define *front-to-back* ratio of an antenna.
9. What is the approximate *input impedance* of a *dipole* antenna?
10. Explain the function of the *ground* in the operation of the Marconi antenna.
11. Describe the *Yagi* antenna and explain its function.
12. Describe the *folded dipole* and explain its function, input resistance, and radiation pattern.
13. Define the *log-periodic* dipole.

**11-3
Fundamentals
of the Antenna**

An antenna is a device designed to accommodate RF signals, usually in the form of *standing waves*. This is true for both the transmitting antenna terminating a transmission line, and the receiving antenna feeding a receiver. The antenna may be a few turns of wire wound around a ferrite core, a parabolic antenna 30 m in diameter, or an array laid out over an acre of land. The antenna may be located on the wing or body of a plane, on a mountain top, or in the hull of a submarine. The early days of radio required an antenna that was a length of wire that stretched across many tenement roof tops. Today that same function is performed by a tiny loop. Regardless of the location, size, shape, or weight, all antennas have the same basic function. Namely, it is to receive or transmit electromagnetic signals from or to space, respectively.

**11-4
Antenna Parameters**

**11-4.1
Frequency
Range**

The purchase specifications for a simple antenna are relatively straightforward. The *center frequency* or (possibly) the *frequency range* is an important consideration. If price is not a limitation, the material of fabrication and the type of terminal connections are specified. A more elaborate antenna obviously has more specifications. These parameters will be listed and discussed.

**11-4.2
Gain**

An antenna is said to have *gain* in the sense that more signal (power density) is radiated in a specific direction than for a *point-source* antenna (called an *isotropic* antenna) that radiates equally in all directions. The power measurement is always made with the same input power to the antennas, with the measurement equipment an equal distance from the antennas. This parameter is also called *directive gain* or simply *antenna gain*. The length of the antenna and the status of standing waves (*resonant antenna*) or the absence of standing waves (*nonresonant antenna*), determine *directive* gain. Typical gain figures for a *resonant* antenna are 1.5 for $\lambda/2$ length to 7 for an 8λ length.

The equivalent *directive* gain for the nonresonant antenna is 3 to 17.

The *directivity* of the antenna refers to the gain measured in the direction of major radiation. This is also called *maximum directive* gain.

11-4.3
Power
Gain

The *power gain* is a variation of maximum directive gain. An equal field strength is measured at a specified distance from a standard (reference) antenna and the antenna under test. The *comparison of the required antenna input power* as the variable constitutes the power gain. This can be expressed either as a power ratio or in dB.

$$\text{dB power gain} = 10 \log \frac{\text{power to reference antenna}}{\text{power to test antenna}} \quad (11\text{-}1)$$

Example 11-1

A power gain test of a reference antenna and a test antenna resulted in the following data: Input power to the reference antenna = 500 mW; input power to the test antenna = 125 mW. Calculate the power gain of the test antenna.

Solution

$$\text{Power gain} = 10 \log \frac{\text{power to reference antenna}}{\text{power to test antenna}} \quad (11\text{-}1)$$

$$= 10 \log \frac{500}{125} = 10 \log 4$$

$$= 10 \times 0.6021 = \textbf{6.021 dB}$$

Note: The lesser power required for the test antenna is a measure of its superiority.

11-4.4
Radiation
Resistance

The resistance of an antenna consists of two distinct parameters. The *radiation resistance* is the most significant resistance of the antenna. The loss of energy by radiation is equivalent to a like amount of energy dissipated in a resistance. The radiation resistance is referred to a specific input point. It is defined in terms of the current input at the reference point and the power dissipated in a resistor that is equivalent to the radiated power.

$$R_r = \frac{\text{radiated power}}{(\text{input current})^2} \; \Omega \qquad (11\text{-}2)$$

where: R_r = radiation resistance in ohms (Ω)

Example 11-2

An antenna radiates 15 W for an input current of 400 mA. Calculate the radiation resistance.

Solution

$$R_r = \frac{\text{radiated power}}{(\text{input current})^2} = \frac{P}{I^2} \; \Omega \qquad (11\text{-}2)$$

$$= \frac{15 \text{ W}}{(0.4 \text{ A})^2} = \frac{15}{0.16} = \mathbf{93.75 \; \Omega}$$

At high frequencies radiation resistance is practically the total resistance of the antenna. The balance of the antenna resistance comprises nonuseful losses: dielectric loss, eddy current loss, corona effect, and antenna to ground resistance. Within certain limitations of length and height above ground, the calculation of radiation resistance is given by Eq. (11-3).

$$R_r = 790 \left(\frac{l}{\lambda}\right)^2 = 790 \left(\frac{lf}{v_c}\right)^2 \qquad \text{ohms } (\Omega) \qquad (11\text{-}3)$$

where: R_r = radiation resistance in ohms (Ω)
l = length of antenna (cm)
λ = free space wavelength (cm)
f = frequency (MHz)
v_c = velocity of light = 3×10^{10} cm/s

Example 11-3

An antenna has a length of 15 cm, and is operating at 400 MHz. Calculate the radiation resistance of the antenna.

Solution

$$\lambda = v_c / f = (3 \times 10^{10}) / (400 \times 10^6) = 75 \text{ cm} \qquad (8\text{-}1)$$

$$R_r = 790 \left(\frac{l}{\lambda}\right)^2 \Omega \qquad\qquad\qquad (11\text{-}3)$$

$$= 790 \left(\frac{15}{75}\right)^2$$

$$= 790(0.2)^2 = 31.6 \ \Omega$$

11-4.5
Antenna Efficiency Antenna efficiency is related to a number of parameters. The condition of the antenna surface (oxidation) is a factor. In general it is determined by the relative values of the useful radiation resistance and the undesirable other nonuseful loss resistance. A well-designed antenna may have an efficiency of 90%. Frequency enters into the consideration of efficiency. At low frequencies the antenna may require an impractical long length. This necessitates other sophisticated methods of simulating length. A high frequency antenna is subject to the undesirable losses listed in Sec. 11-4.4.

11-4.6
Antenna Bandwidth The *bandwidth* of an antenna can mean different things under differing usages. A TV channel is allocated a 6 MHz band. It would be an oversimplification to say the antenna bandwidth requirement is 6 MHz. (This may be true for specialized commercial applications where a separate antenna is used for each TV channel.) The commonly used TV (dipole or rabbit-ears) antenna must cover the entire VHF band, 54 to 216 MHz. The extra little-loop antenna, seemingly added as an afterthought, must cover the UHF band, 470 to 1000 MHz. Obviously both these antennas are grossly inefficient. They function adequately only by virtue of a highly sensitive receiver combined with a strong transmitted signal. There are methods of broadening the bandwidth of an antenna, but common TV practice is to design the antenna for the *geometric mean* frequency f_m and hope for the best.

$$f_m = \sqrt{f_L \times f_H} \qquad \text{Hz} \qquad (11\text{-}4)$$

where: f_m is the geometric mean frequency (Hz)

f_L is the lower end of the frequency band (Hz)

f_H is the upper end of the frequency band (Hz)

Example 11-4

An antenna is to cover the TV-VHF frequency range from 54 to 216 MHz. Calculate the antenna length.

Solution

$$f_m = \sqrt{f_L \times f_H} \qquad (11\text{-}4)$$

$$= \sqrt{54 \times 216} = \textbf{108 MHz}$$

Antenna wavelength

$$\lambda = \frac{v_c}{f} = \frac{3 \times 10^8 \text{ m/s}}{108 \times 10^6 \text{ c/s}} = \textbf{2.778 m}$$

11-4.7 Radiation Pattern *Radiation pattern* refers to the signal strength radiated in each direction around an antenna. A point source (idealized) radiator located in outer space would have a radiation pattern that is a perfect sphere. This means that the *field intensity* measured at a given fixed distance from the radiator in *any* direction whatever has the *same* value, as shown in Fig. 11-1a. An antenna having a *horizontal radiation* has a pattern similar to a doughnut, with the antenna as an axis, as shown in Fig. 11-1b. Other antennas radiate in a very *narrow* region. Typical of these are the highly *directional* antennas, whose pattern is shown in Fig. 11-1c.

A radiation pattern indicates a specific (constant, given) field intensity measured in any direction. Figure 11-1c shows three points on the pattern, x, y, and z corresponding to field vectors of lengths l_1, l_2, and l_3. These are measured at angles zero, θ, and ϕ respectively. The same field intensity is measured at all three points, but point x is farthest from the radiating element and z is closest. The strongest signal therefore is measured along the *horizontal* line $o - x$. The radiation pattern may be described as the envelope (locus) of all points having equal values of field strength.

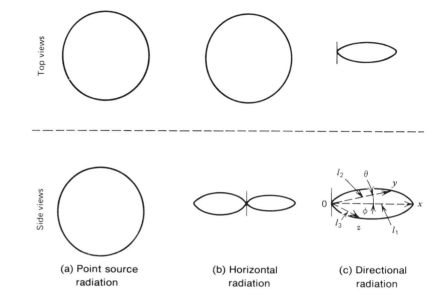

Figure 11-1 Radiation patterns.

(a) Point source radiation

(b) Horizontal radiation

(c) Directional radiation

11-4.8
Side Lobes *Side lobes* are another aspect of radiation pattern. In actual practice, a single radiation pattern (as those in Fig. 11-1) is difficult to attain. More commonly, a large *major* lobe, representing the desired pattern, is accompanied by one or more *side lobes* of smaller field intensity. This is shown in Fig. 11-2.

The significance of the side lobe for an antenna system is the dissipation of energy in *unwanted* directions. Similarly for a receiving antenna, the receiver is subject to undesired, interfering signals.

Figure 11-2 Side lobe radiation pattern.

(a) Two side lobes

(b) Four side lobes

(c) Six side lobes

11-4.9
Beamwidth The *beamwidth* of an antenna is defined in either of two ways. Referring to Fig. 11-3, angle θ is the (-3 dB or) *half-power-point* beamwidth. The radiation at points y and z is 3 dB less than at point x. Angle θ_0 is the *angle between first-nulls* beamwidth. This is the first smallest angle at which no radiation is measured. This no-radiation condition is repeated between each side lobe.

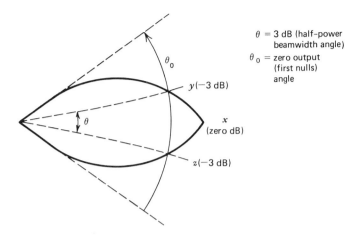

Figure 11-3 Beam widths.

11-4.10
Polarization Obviously a directional antenna may be positioned vertically, horizontally, or at some angle in between. The *polarization* of an antenna refers to the plane of the electric field, and this is parallel to the antenna. Usually *low* frequency antennas are *vertically* polarized because of their relationship to ground. Horizontally polarized signals meet with less noise interference. This is used for short length, high frequency antennas whenever it is practical.

11-4.11
Front to
Back Ratio *Unidirectional* antennas have maximum radiation in only one direction (Fig. 11-1c). For these antennas the *front to back ratio* is an important parameter. This is the ratio of the maximum power radiated in a specific direction to power radiated (180°) in the opposite direction. When used as a receiving antenna, it is a measure of the reduction in signal received when the signal approaches the antenna from the *reverse* direction.

11-5
Dipole
Antenna The simplest antenna, a familiar sight on rooftops, is the TV dipole antenna. A dipole is designed overall as a half wavelength ($\lambda/2$) long at the signal frequency (Fig. 11-4). The transmission line feeding the dipole antenna should have a characteristic impedance equal to the impedance measured at the center of the dipole. This is in the 75 to 300 Ω range and lends itself either to a coaxial transmission line or TV twinlead. The result

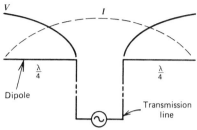

Figure 11-4 Standing waves on a dipole antenna.

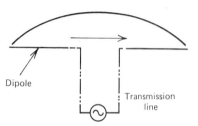

Figure 11-5 Dipole current distribution.

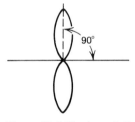

Figure 11-6 Dipole radiation pattern.

is a properly terminated transmission line and maximum transfer of energy to the dipole. The dipole follows the rules outlined in Sec. 8-9. Because it is a $\lambda/4$ long on each side and terminates in an open end, the standing wave pattern is a maximum *voltage* at the *ends* and maximum *current* at the *center*, as shown in Fig. 11-4.

The standing wave pattern of Fig. 11-4 shows that the input impedance to the dipole antenna is a high current, low voltage point. This implies a low impedance input or *current feed*. For this reason, it is common practice to designate the standing wave pattern on an antenna as a *current* standing wave pattern, with an arrow indicating direction. Figure 11-4, redrawn as Fig. 11-5, shows this.

The dipole radiation pattern corresponds to and follows the *peak current* points as shown in Fig. 11-6.

The pattern in Fig. 11-6 is the cross-sectional view of a doughnut shape using the dipole as an axis.

If the antenna length is increased to a full wavelength, there results changes in input impedance, standing wave pattern, radiation pattern, and directivity. This is shown in Fig. 11-7. Note that there are two lobes (corresponding to two half wavelengths), and the lobe angle has become more horizontal (54° instead of 90°).

Whenever the antenna is an *odd* multiple of $\lambda/2$, a center-fed input will be a low impedance, high current input. The reverse (high impedance, low current) is true for an antenna that is an *even* multiple of $\lambda/2$ lengths. The radiation pattern for an antenna $3\lambda/2$ is shown in Fig. 11-8. Note the three lobes corresponding to three half wavelengths. The main lobe is more horizontal (45°) and the center lobe is a minor lobe.

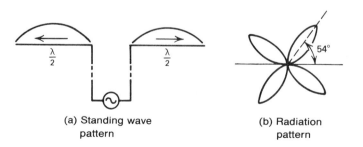

(a) Standing wave pattern

(b) Radiation pattern

Figure 11-7 One wavelength antenna.

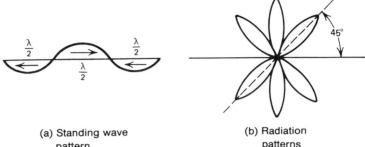

Figure 11-8 One and a half wavelength antenna.

(a) Standing wave pattern

(b) Radiation patterns

In general there are as many lobes as the number of *half* wavelengths. The angle off the axis becomes *smaller* with *added* length. The width of the main lobe narrows and it becomes *longer* and *more directional*. Some additional radiation patterns are shown in Fig. 11-9.

Note that for any of the dipoles there is no radiation whatever along the axis of antenna. Radiation patterns result from in phase and out of phase current combinations. These add to or subtract from the radiation strength in specific directions.

The dipole antennas discussed are all *resonant* antennas in the sense that there exists both a forward and reflected signal. These result in the standard standing wave patterns as defined in Sec. 8-9. An alternative use of an antenna is to feed the signal in at one end of the antenna and terminate the other end with a load resistor. The load absorbs the forward signal and prevents the generation of a reverse signal. This condition is described as a *nonresonant* antenna. The circuit and the resulting unidirectional radiation pattern are shown in Fig. 11-10. The directivity improves with antenna length. The radiation varies from 20 Ω at $\lambda/4$, to 80 Ω at $\lambda/2$, to 120 Ω at λ, flattening to 240 Ω at 6λ.

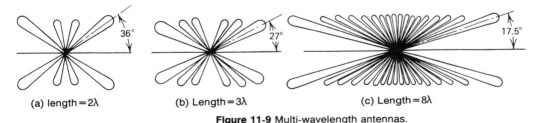

(a) length = 2λ

(b) Length = 3λ

(c) Length = 8λ

Figure 11-9 Multi-wavelength antennas.

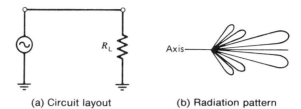

Figure 11-10 Nonresonant antenna. (a) Circuit layout   (b) Radiation pattern

**11-6
Antenna
Ground
Effects** The radiation patterns previously discussed assumed the antenna is located many wavelengths away from the ground. These are known as the *free space patterns* of the antennas. All radiation patterns are modified by reflection of radiated waves from the ground. The ground acts as a huge RF signal reflector. This is particularly true for low frequency broadcast in which a signal successively bounces off the ionosphere and the ground, to be received halfway around the world. The ground can act as the electric image or mirror of the actual antenna. As a result, the physical antenna behaves as though there is an identical antenna nearby.

**11-6.1
Horizontal
Antenna** The radiation pattern of a horizontal antenna is also affected by ground reflections. As a rule of thumb, antennas operating up to 14 MHz should be elevated at least a half-wavelength off ground. Antennas operating at frequencies above 28 MHz should be elevated at least one wavelength. Figure 11-11 shows the effect of height above ground on the radiation pattern of a horizontal antenna with a fixed length. Note the shift of radiation angle from the vertical at a height of $\lambda/4$, to the near

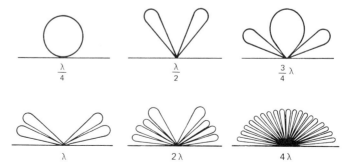

Figure 11-11 Effect of height above ground on the radiation pattern of a fixed-length horizontal antenna.

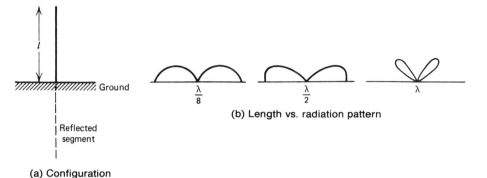

(a) Configuration

(b) Length vs. radiation pattern

Figure 11-12 Marconi antenna configuration and effect of length on radiation pattern.

horizontal at a height of λ. The radiation resistance varies with antenna length; the values are approximately 50 Ω at λ/4, 70 Ω at λ/2, 95 Ω at λ, and 140 Ω at 6λ.

11-6.2
Vertical
Antenna
Ground reflections result in a vertical antenna behaving as though it were one half of a complete antenna with the other half represented by ground. A grounded vertical antenna λ/4 long is called a *Marconi antenna* (Fig. 11-12a). This one behaves as if it were half of a complete λ/2 long antenna. The radiation pattern is identical to the pattern that results from the same segment of a complete antenna located far from ground.

The length of the Marconi antenna affects the radiation pattern. Increasing the length helps the horizontal directivity up to a length of one wavelength, after which the pattern becomes more vertical. This is shown in Fig. 11-12b.

The radiation resistance varies between 20 and 100 Ω in a complex manner depending on the ratio of antenna length to wavelength.

11-6.3
Grounding
Systems
Earth is not uniform in electrical quality. Some types of soil are poor conductors, resulting in a poor ground. This is true for major electrical installations as well as antenna installations. The approach to improved grounding takes various forms. One method is to sink a series of parallel 30 m pipes, until a

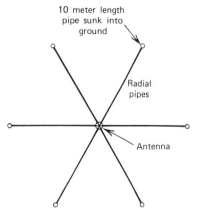

10 meter length
pipe sunk into
ground

Radial
pipes

Antenna

Figure 11-13 Antenna ground mat.

sufficient number have been sunk to give an electric ground with the specified (1 to 5 Ω) resistance. An *antenna* ground presents a somewhat different problem. In this case the requirement is a ground matting with the antenna at the center. A typical procedure is to lay down pipes running radially from center. At the perimeter each radial link is connected to a 10 m pipe that has been sunk into the ground (Fig. 11-13).

Grounding a system is not an exact science but careful design yields reasonably close results. If all else fails, the "salting" process may be used. This is a process of watering the area with brine (salt) solution. Sufficient salting lowers the ground resistance. Rocky soil that does not lend itself to the pipe sinking technique can be covered with a ground *mat*. This may consist of piping or mesh screen. It is laid out elevated slightly above ground.

11-7
High Frequency
Directional
Antennas

11-7.1
Basics
Low and medium frequency *vertical* antennas may require a (λ/4) length that is too long and impractical for construction on that location. A length less than λ/4 is an electrical mismatch with resulting inefficiency, low radiation resistance, and reactive input impedance. The solution is to add the required length but to put the addition in the *horizontal* plane. This results in an *inverted L* construction. The additional member may be centered, making the unit a T-construction. More elaborate extensions consisting of sophisticated star-shaped or mesh-screen arrays are also used. This general approach to increasing vertical antenna length is called *top loading* (Fig. 11-14).

Sometimes a vertical antenna is actually too long for a specified frequency. A unit longer than 5/8λ will present a radiation pattern that is not a true ground wave. The main lobe starts to elevate. Normally this is undesirable for line-of-sight use unless the system is designed for long distance communication using reflections from the ionosphere.

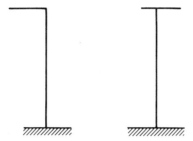

Figure 11-14 Top loading of vertical antennas.

(a) *L* configuration   (b) *T* configuration

The *effective length* of an antenna is *not* its physical length. Effective length includes the effect of dielectric materials in the antenna, top loading, diameter of radiating elements, nonideal standing wave pattern, velocity of wave on the antenna, and a host of other physical conditions. The effective length of an antenna for frequencies below 30 MHz is calculated from the empirical relationship

$$l_e = \frac{292}{f} \text{ wavelengths (m)} \tag{11-5}$$

where: l_e = effective electrical wavelength, m
f = frequency, MHz

Example 11-5
A vertical antenna is designed to operate at 12 MHz. Calculate the effective length.

Solution

$$l_e = \frac{292}{f} \text{ wavelength in meters (m)} \tag{11-5}$$

$$= \frac{292}{12} = 24.33 \text{ wavelengths} \quad \text{or} \quad 24.33 \text{ m}$$

Transmission line theory (Sec. 8-9) indicates that positions of peak current and node voltage, or peak voltage and node current are *pure resistance* points. All other positions represent a reactive impedance. The peak current, low resistance is measured at the center of a $\lambda/2$ antenna. The peak voltage, high resistance is measured at the end of the $\lambda/2$ antenna, or the center of a wavelength (λ) antenna. A signal applied at a low resistance point requires *current feed*, while the high resistance input is *voltage feed*.

Theoretically a transmission line whose characteristic impedance equals the input impedance of the antenna can be connected directly. Conversely a difference of impedance values requires an impedance matching device. In practice there is always some reactance present at the input to an antenna. This requires some form of tuning element, either capacitive, inductive, or both. One additional requirement may be the suppression of spurious frequencies, primarily harmonics. This is done with a simple π or L, "notch" or bandstop filter (wavetrap) or one of the host of more sophisticated high-pass or bandstop filters.

11-7.2
Arrays Television usage has seen the development of a steady progression of directional antennas. The dipole was joined by a *director* and *reflector* and became the *Yagi* (Yagi-Uda) antenna. Yagi element lengths and separation, and radiation pattern are shown in Fig. 11-15.

The Yagi antenna gain is approximately ($+7$) dB. The back lobe is significant in the reduction of "ghost" effects. Ghosts are signals reaching the antenna after being reflected by large structures, such as mountains. The *front to back ratio* and the input impedance depend on the proximity of the elements. The basic Yagi antenna was eventually expanded with more reflector and director elements that improved gain and directivity. In

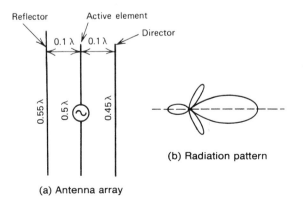

Figure 11-15 Yagi antenna.　　　(a) Antenna array

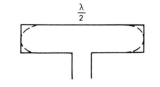

Figure 11-16 Folded dipole antenna.

areas that must receive TV signals from *different* source directions, the Yagi antenna is mounted on a servo-driven rotatable support. This points the director so that it is always perpendicular to the source.

Another common TV antenna is the folded dipole shown in Fig. 11-16.

The fabrication of the folded dipole antenna is usually a single aluminum rod, rounded on the ends as indicated. However it is possible to design the unit for different diameter front and back elements, with a provision for varying the separation. The radiation pattern of the folded dipole is similar to that of the basic dipole. The input impedance is multiplied by 4, making it approximately 300 Ω. The antenna is usually used with 300 Ω transmission line and a TV receiver that has a 300 Ω input impedance. The folded dipole has a greater bandwidth than the basic dipole. There are other variations of the dipole and the folded dipole, but they are not common.

The *rhombic* antenna is another broad-band directional antenna. This feature derives from its operation as a nonresonant (unidirectional current flow) antenna. Figure 11-17 shows the configuration and radiation pattern of the rhombic antenna.

The rhombic antenna is particularly useful below 30 MHz. The input impedance and appropriate terminating resistance is in the 600 to 800 Ω range. The directivity is governed by the length l and the angle ϕ. The length typically falls in the 2λ to 8λ range. A rhombic antenna with a length of 6λ and an angle ϕ of 70° has a beamwidth of 10°.

The log-periodic dipole array comprises a broad group of antennas. It is a Yagi-type structure with all dipoles active and each succeeding element longer. Figure 11-18 shows the configuration of a log-periodic antenna.

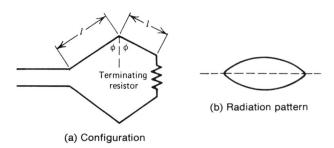

Figure 11-17 Rhombic antenna.   (a) Configuration   (b) Radiation pattern

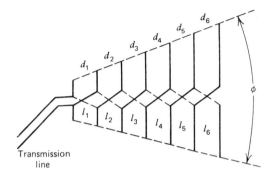

Figure 11-18 Log-periodic antenna.

The log-periodic antenna is very directional with directivity related to ϕ. The frequency coverage is broad, relating to the frequencies of the shortest and longest dipoles. The ratio of element separation (d) to dipole length (l) must be equal for each element. At one time this was a popular TV antenna and was also used by ham radio operators.

Other groups of directional antenna arrays are the *end fire* and *colinear* arrays. The end fire is a grouping of vertical antennas and the colinear is a series of horizontal antennas placed end to end. These are shown in Fig. 11-19. The directivity is determined by the number of elements, spacing, and in-phase/out-of-phase feed.

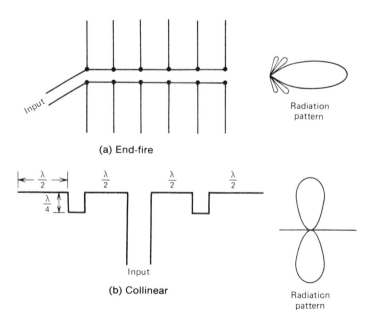

Figure 11-19 Antenna arrays.

There is a veritable multitude of antenna arrays, each one contributing directivity or gain or a combination of the two. The TV transmitter antenna commonly uses a *turnstile* antenna to accomplish omnidirectional transmission. A listing of the names of specialized RF and VHF antennas would require many pages.

**11-8
Summary** The antenna is the input source to the first stage of the receiver and the output termination at the last stage of the transmitter. It may be designed to transmit in all directions, in a specific plane, or in a highly directional beam. The antenna may be a simple length of wire or an elaborate gathering of elements. The antenna may be as big as your thumb or spread out over acres of land. For some installations the ground nearby the unit may be almost as important as the antenna.

Now return to the objectives and self-evaluation questions at the beginning of this chapter and see how well you can answer them. If you cannot answer certain questions, place a check next to each of them and review appropriate parts of the text. Then answer the questions and solve the problems.

**11-9
Questions**

Q11-1 Define *directive gain* of an antenna.

Q11-2 Define *power gain* of an antenna, and explain one method for measuring it.

Q11-3 Define efficiency of an antenna. What is meant by the radiation resistance of an antenna and how is it related to efficiency?

Q11-4 Which power components make up the *nonuseful* power in an antenna?

Q11-5 Define *bandwidth* of an antenna.

Q11-6 What is the significance of field intensity with respect to radiation pattern?

Q11-7 What is the significance of *side lobes* in a radiation pattern?

Q11-8 Explain the *standing-wave patterns* on a dipole antenna.

Q11-9 Describe the *radiation pattern* of a dipole antenna.

Q11-10 What is the result of increasing the *length* of a dipole?

Q11-11 What is the difference in fabrication between a *resonant* and *nonresonant* antenna?

Q11-12 How does ground influence the radiation pattern of a *horizontal* antenna?

Q11-13 Describe three methods of improving the quality of sandy soil for electrical installations.

Q11-14 What is the significance of *top loading* for an antenna?

Q11-15 Define *effective length* of an antenna.

Q11-16 Explain the function of a *rhombic antenna* with respect to impedance and directivity.

11-10
Problems

P11-1 Given a dipole antenna 12 cm long operating at 300 MHz. Calculate the radiation resistance of the antenna.

P11-2 Calculate the effective length of an antenna operating at 18 MHz.

P11-3 A dipole antenna has a radiation resistance of 25 Ω, and is operating at 350 MHz. Calculate the length of the antenna.

P11-4 A dipole antenna, 30 cm long, has a radiation resistance of 20 Ω. Calculate the operating frequency.

P11-5 A dipole antenna is to be used for TV-UHF. Calculate:
a. Geometric mean frequency.
b. Length of dipole.

P11-6 An antenna has a radiation resistance of 300 Ω. The effective resistance of the other losses is 20 Ω. Calculate the efficiency of the antenna.

P11-7 The radiated power of an antenna is 30 W. The current input is 400 mA. Calculate the radiation resistance.

Chapter 12 Microwave Antennas

12-1
Objectives

To learn:

1. The functions of microwave antennas.
2. The characteristics of the parabolic antenna.
3. The variations of parabolic antennas.
4. The characteristics of the horn antenna.
5. The variations of horn antennas.
6. The characteristics of helix antennas.
7. The variations of helix antennas.

12-2
Self-Evaluation
Questions

Test your prior knowledge of the information in this chapter by answering the following questions. Watch for the answers to these questions as you read the chapter. Your final evaluation of whether you understand the material is measured by your ability to answer these questions. When you have completed the chapter, return to this section and answer the questions again.

1. Explain the operation of the parabolic antenna.
2. Describe two methods of feeding a signal into a parabolic antenna.
3. Why is the parabolic antenna particularly useful in radio astronomy?
4. What techniques are used in the fabrication of a parabolic antenna that will be used in high winds?
5. Explain the distinction in function between the rectangular and conical horn antennas.
6. What is a typical bandwidth of a horn antenna in terms of the operating frequency?
7. Describe the discone antenna and list its advantages.
8. Describe a helix antenna.
9. What is a unique advantage of the helix antenna?
10. What are typical dimensions of the helix antenna?

**12-3
Microwave
Antenna
Basics**

At microwave frequencies, the wavelength is sufficiently small to permit arrays of many elements. This results in narrow beamwidth and high gain. Possibly the best known microwave antenna is the radar unit used and seen at airports. Similar units are used in weather forecasting. Occasionally a microwave antenna is located on top of a tall building in the heart of the business district.

**12-4
Parabolic
Antenna**

The *parabolic antenna* uses the same principles as the parabolic mirror. The antenna is shown in Fig. 12-1.

The physical relationships of the parabola are summarized on Fig. 12-1. The *directrix* is an imaginary plane from which the output signal rays originate. The x'-x plane (see Fig. 12-1) is the actual opening or mouth of the parabolic antenna. This is called the *aperture* plane. The y'-y plane (see Fig. 12-1) is an imaginary plane where all the output rays are in phase.

When functioning as a *receiving* antenna, signals arriving from a distant source approach the parabolic antenna in a plane perpendicular to the axis of the antenna. The signal is reflected from the parabolic surface to the *focus* (focal point). The focus is the physical as well as the electrical input to the receiver. Common practice terminates the rectangular or circular waveguide (that transports the received signal) in the shell of the parabolic antenna. The shell is penetrated by means of an appropriate connector. The center of the connector is connected

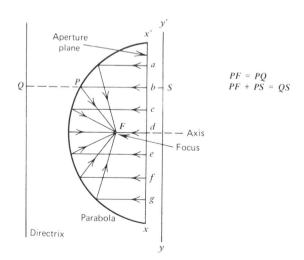

Figure 12-1 Parabolic antenna.

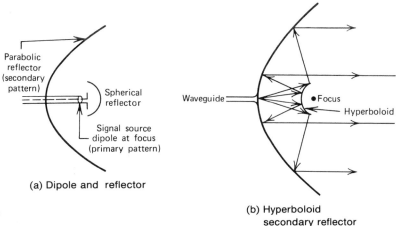

(a) Dipole and reflector

(b) Hyperboloid
secondary reflector

Figure 12-2 Methods of feeding a parabolic antenna.

to the isotropic or dipole antenna that performs the reception of the signal. The parabolic antenna, functioning as a transmitting element, reverses the sequence. The transmitted signal is provided to the element at the focus point and the parabolic antenna sends the wave out in a sharp beam of parallel rays.

The method of feeding the transmitter signal to the parabolic antenna is not simple. A point source or dipole antenna causes transmission in more than one direction. The theory of operation of a parabolic antenna requires that all transmitted energy be reflected by the parabolic surface. Any transmission in addition to this reflected energy results in undesirable side lobes. In practice a small dipole with a reflector (Fig. 12-2a) may be used, or a *hyperboloid secondary reflector* (Fig. 12-2b), or one of the directional microwave antennas.

In either case it becomes evident that the hypothetical symmetry of the parabolic signal must be slightly distorted. The radiation pattern of the source signal is called the *primary* pattern. The output signal is the *secondary* pattern (Fig. 12-2a). The radiation pattern of the parabolic antenna is highly directional. Figure 12-3 shows the radiation pattern for an antenna with a mouth diameter of 12λ. The amplitudes of the minor lobes are seen to be negligible. In practice there is a slight difference in directivity between the vertical and horizontal planes. The radiation field pattern is defined by a Bessel function.

A parabolic antenna used for a very weak signal, such as radioastronomy signals, has the receiver input stage located

Figure 12-3 Radiation pattern of a parabolic antenna.

directly at the focus point. In fact the input amplifier may be designed with a cryogenic system for low noise level. The main lobe beamwidth between first null points is defined by

$$\phi_0 = 70\frac{\lambda}{D} \qquad \text{degrees}(°) \qquad (12\text{-}1)$$

where ϕ_0 = beamwidth between first null points, degrees(°)
λ = free space wavelength, cm
D = diameter of parabola, cm

Example 12-1
Calculate the first null points beamwidth of a 15 cm parabolic antenna, operating at 10 GHz.

Solution

$$\lambda = v_c/f \qquad (8\text{-}1)$$

$$\lambda = \frac{3 \times 10^{10}}{10 \times 10^9} = 3 \text{ cm}$$

$$\phi_0 = 70\frac{\lambda}{D} \qquad (12\text{-}1)$$

$$= 70 \times 3/15 = 14°$$

The beamwidth between half-power points is defined by

$$\phi = 58\frac{\lambda}{D} \qquad (12\text{-}2)$$

Example 12-2
Calculate the half-power-points beamwidth of a 25 cm parabolic antenna, operating at 2 GHz.

Solution

$$\lambda = v_c/f \qquad (8\text{-}1)$$

$$\lambda = \frac{3 \times 10^{10}}{2 \times 10^9} = 15 \text{ cm}$$

$$\phi = 58\frac{\lambda}{D} \qquad (12\text{-}2)$$

$$= 58\left(\frac{15}{25}\right) = 34.8°$$

The power gain of the parabolic antenna, under ideal conditions of operation, is given by

$$A_p = 6\left(\frac{D}{\lambda}\right)^2 \qquad (12\text{-}3)$$

where: A_p = power gain with respect to a resonant half wave dipole.

Example 12-3

Given a parabolic antenna with a 2 m diameter and operating at 1.5 GHz. Determine the power gain as a ratio and in dB.

Solution

$$\lambda = v_c/f \qquad (8\text{-}1)$$

$$\lambda = \frac{3 \times 10^{10}}{1.5 \times 10^9} = \textbf{20 cm}$$

$$A_p = 6\left(\frac{D}{\lambda}\right)^2 \qquad (12\text{-}3)$$

$$= 6\left(\frac{200}{20}\right)^2 = \textbf{600}$$

$$A_p = 10\log 600 = 10 \times 2.778 = \textbf{27.78 dB}$$

Example 12-4

Determine the required diameter of a parabolic antenna operating at 5 GHz to result in a first null points beamwidth of 10°. Calculate half-power points beamwidth, and the power gain as a ratio and in dB.

Solution

$$\lambda = v_c/f \qquad (8\text{-}1)$$

$$\lambda = \frac{3 \times 10^{10}}{5 \times 10^9} = \textbf{6 cm}$$

$$D = 70\,\lambda/\phi_0 = 70 \times 6/10 = \textbf{42 cm} \qquad (12\text{-}1)$$

$$\phi = 58\frac{\lambda}{D} = 58\left(\frac{6}{42}\right) = \textbf{8.28}° \qquad (12\text{-}2)$$

$$A_p = 6\left(\frac{D}{\lambda}\right)^2 = 6\left(\frac{42}{6}\right)^2 = \textbf{294} \qquad (12\text{-}3)$$

$$A_p = 10\log 294 = 10 \times 2.468 = \textbf{24.68 dB}$$

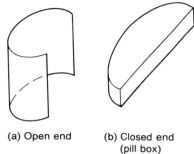

(a) Open end   (b) Closed end
(pill box)

Figure 12-4 Cylindrical parabolic antennas.

There are a number of variations of the basic parabolic antenna that are commonly used. The cylinder types of parabolic antennas restrict the radiation pattern into a narrower plane. These antennas have a parabolic curvature in one plane only. They offer a sharper radiation pattern with restrictions outside of the design angle. Some typical cylindrical antennas are shown in Fig. 12-4.

The antenna parabola may be a few centimeters in diameter or physically as large as a 10 story building. Whenever feasible, the antenna is protected in a nonmetallic weatherproof sphere. These are common sights at airports. If the exposed antenna must be subjected to unmanageable winds, the parabolic surface may be a mesh or screen construction.

12-5 Horn Antenna

Another broad type of microwave antenna is the *horn* antenna (Fig. 12-5). This is readily visualized as a *rectangular* waveguide with the load end flared out. The transmitted signal travels the length of the rectangular transmission line and is ushered smoothly out to the atmosphere with minimal discontinuity. A similar service is provided for the *circular* waveguide with a *conical horn* antenna (Fig. 12-5f).

The horn antenna may be flared in the horizontal plane, in which case it is a *sectoral H-plane horn* antenna (Fig. 12-5b). A unit flared in the vertical plane is a *sectoral E-plane horn* antenna (Fig. 12-5c). A horn antenna flared in both horizontal and vertical planes is a *pyramidal horn* antenna (Fig. 12-5d). A special case of rectangular horn may have the flare curved, in which case it is an *exponentially tapered pyramidal* horn antenna (Fig. 12-5a).

In a similar manner there are variations in the conical horn antenna. These include the *exponentially tapered conical horn* (Fig. 12-5e) and the *biconical horn* antennas (Fig. 12-5g).

The directivity of the horn antenna is not as high as the parabolic antenna. Obviously the fabrication is not complex and the connection to the waveguide is a simple matter. A waveguide may have a slot in the end or side for radiation. This is using a modification of a horn antenna, an antenna without length or flare. The biconical antenna offers omnidirectional radiation in a plane perpendicular to the plane of the antenna.

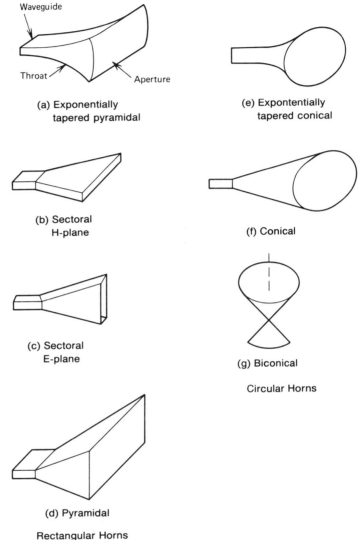

(a) Exponentially
tapered pyramidal

(e) Expontentially
tapered conical

(b) Sectoral
H-plane

(f) Conical

(c) Sectoral
E-plane

(g) Biconical

Circular Horns

(d) Pyramidal

Rectangular Horns

Figure 12-5 Rectangular and circular horn antennas.

The length of a horn antenna should be on the order of 8 to 10 wavelengths for effective directivity. The angle of flare in each plane relates to the length. Figure 12-6 shows the length and horizontal flare angle of a *pyramidal* horn antenna, and identifies the height and width dimensions.

The beamwidth is expressed in terms of the vertical and

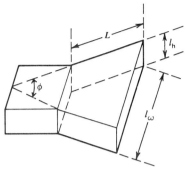

Figure 12-6 Pyramidal horn antenna dimensions.

horizontal aperture by:

$$D = 7.5 \frac{l_w}{\lambda} \frac{l_h}{\lambda}, \qquad \text{degrees}(°) \qquad (12\text{-}4)$$

where: D = beamwidth of pyramidal horn, degrees(°)
l_w = length of aperture in horizontal plane, cm
l_h = length of aperture in vertical plane, cm

The power gain over a $\lambda/2$ dipole is given by

$$A_p = 4.5 \frac{l_w}{\lambda} \frac{l_h}{\lambda} \qquad (12\text{-}5)$$

Example 12-5

Given a pyramidal horn antenna with aperture dimensions of 12×6 cm. The operating frequency is 5 GHz. Calculate:
a. Beamwidth.
b. Gain as a power ratio and in dB.

Solution

a. $\lambda = v_c / f$ $\qquad (8\text{-}1)$

$\lambda = \dfrac{3 \times 10^{10}}{5 \times 10^9} = \textbf{6 cm}$

$D = 7.5 \dfrac{l_w}{\lambda} \dfrac{l_h}{\lambda}$

$= 7.5 \times \dfrac{12}{6} \times \dfrac{6}{6}$

$= 7.5 \times 2 \times 1 = \textbf{15°}$

b. $A_p = 4.5 \dfrac{l_w}{\lambda} \dfrac{l_h}{\lambda}$

$= 4.5 \times 2 \times 1 = \textbf{9}$

$A_p = 10 \log(P_o / P_i) = 10 \log(9) = \textbf{9.542 dB}$

More universal solutions to design problems can be derived from graphs and nomograms that relate half-power beamwidth, length of horn, angle of flare, and aperture. Separate calculations must be performed for the E-plane and H-plane. The horn antenna bandwidth is approximately 10% of operating frequency. There are more complex horn antennas including the *Cass-horn* and *triply folded* horn, also called *hog-horn* antenna. These are low-noise antennas with gain and beamwidth comparable to the parabolic antenna. A specialized form of conical horn is the *discone* antenna. This is a conical antenna mounted on a disk that serves as a ground plane. It offers great bandwidth, on the order of 9:1 frequency ratio, and is omnidirectional. The discone antenna is particularly useful in the VHF and UHF bands.

12-6 Helix Antenna The *helix* antenna is highly directional and generates a *circular* polarization. A circular polarized signal may be received by either a horizontal or vertical antenna. This feature makes the helix particularly useful in satellite communication. Oddly enough, two helical antennas cannot communicate unless they are wound in the *same* direction. The helix antenna is defined by its dimensions. This is shown by Fig. 12-7.

The definition of the dimensions are summarized:

D = diameter of helix, cm
C = circumference in (πD), cm
s = spacing between turns measured along axis, cm
L = total length of helix (axial length), cm
n = number of turns = L/s
d = diameter of conductor, cm

The pitch of the winding relates to the diameter and spacing between turns. The half-power point and first null beamwidth of the helix antenna are defined by Eqs. (12-6) and (12-7).

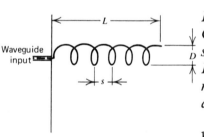

Figure 12-7 Helix antenna.

$$\phi = \frac{52}{\frac{\pi D}{\lambda}\sqrt{n\frac{s}{\lambda}}} \qquad \text{degrees}(°) \qquad (12\text{-}6)$$

where: ϕ = the half-power points beamwidth

$$\phi_o = \frac{115}{\frac{\pi D}{\lambda}\sqrt{n\frac{s}{\lambda}}} \qquad \text{degrees}(\geqslant) \qquad (12\text{-}7)$$

where: ϕ_o = the first nulls beamwidth

The maximum directive gain or directivity is defined by

$$D_{max} = \frac{15 \, ns(\pi D)^2}{\lambda^3} \tag{12-8}$$

Example 12-6

Given a helix antenna operating at 2 GHz, with the following dimensions: the spacing between turns is 5 cm, the diameter of helix is 10 cm, and the number of turns is 20. Determine the half-power points beamwidth, the first nulls beamwidth and directivity.

Solution

$$\lambda = v_c/f \tag{8-1}$$

$$\lambda = \frac{3 \times 10^{10}}{2 \times 10^9} = \textbf{15 cm}$$

The half-power points beamwidth is

$$\phi = \frac{52}{\frac{\pi D}{\lambda}\sqrt{n\frac{s}{\lambda}}}$$

$$= \frac{52}{\frac{\pi \times 10}{15}\sqrt{\frac{20 \times 5}{15}}} = \frac{52}{2.094\sqrt{6.667}} = \frac{52}{2.094 \times 2.582}$$

$$= \frac{52}{5.407} = \textbf{9.617}°$$

the first nulls beamwidth is

$$\phi_o = \frac{115}{\frac{\pi D}{\lambda}\sqrt{n\frac{s}{\lambda}}} \tag{12-7}$$

$$= \frac{115}{5.407} = \textbf{21.27}°$$

The directivity is

$$D_{max} = \frac{15 \, ns(\pi D)^2}{\lambda^3} \tag{12-8}$$

$$= \frac{15 \times 20 \times 5(\pi \times 10)^2}{(15)^3}$$

$$= \frac{1500 \times 987}{3375} = \textbf{438.7}$$

Figure 12-8 Tapered axial mode helical antennas.

A helix antenna with dimensions much smaller than λ approaches the characteristics of a dipole, with radiation in a plane perpendicular to the helix axis. More typically the helix dimensions are on the order of a wavelength. The gain and beamwidth vary with helix length.

The helical beam antenna has inherent broad-band properties, covering a wide, two-to-one frequency range, and an impedance on the order of 100 Ω. The helical antenna radiation pattern may be varied by tapering the helix. Some sample configurations are shown in Fig. 12-8.

Helical antennas can also be arranged in arrays of 2 to 10 mounted on a ground effect back plate. Depending on spacing and phasing of input signal, various gains and directivities can be accomplished. The helix is frequently used in VHF communications.

12-7
Summary

The microwave antenna enjoys certain advantages over the comparable low frequency antennas. The free space wavelength is small enough to permit arrays of elements in a reasonably small package. This in turn results in high gain and directivity. Some antennas are uniquely useful for satellite communications. Other antennas are logical extensions of waveguides.

Now return to the objectives and self-evaluation questions at the beginning of this chapter and see how well you can answer them. If you cannot answer certain questions, place a check next to each of them and review appropriate parts of the text. Then answer the questions and solve the problems below.

12-8
Questions

Q12-1 Define the aperture plane of the parabolic antenna.

Q12-2 Distinguish between the primary and secondary patterns of a parabolic antenna.

Q12-3 Describe two types of cylinder variations of the parabolic antenna.

Q12-4 Describe the fabrication of the following types of horn antennas: exponentially tapered pyramidal, sectoral H-plane, sectoral E-plane, and pyramidal.

Q12-5 Describe the biconical horn antenna.

Q12-6 How does the slot antenna relate to the pyramidal horn antenna?

Q12-7 Which parameters are included in graphs used for the design of horn antennas?

Q12-8 What category includes the hoghorn antenna? What advantages does it offer?

Q12-9 If the diameter of a helix antenna is made very much smaller than λ, what will the radiation pattern be?

Q12-10 What are the basic parameter advantages of a helix antenna?

**12-9
Problems**

P12-1 Given a 20 cm parabolic antenna operating at 6 GHz. Calculate the first null points beamwidth.

P12-2 Calculate the half-power points beamwidth of a 20 cm parabolic antenna operating at 5 GHz.

P12-3 Calculate the power gain of a parabolic antenna with an 80 cm diameter that is operating at 3 GHz.

P12-4 A parabolic antenna is operating at 8 GHz. It has a first null points beamwidth of 6°. Calculate
a. The power gain.
b. Half-power points beamwidth.

P12-5 Given a pyramidal horn antenna with aperture dimensions of 8×4 cm. The operating frequency is 8 GHz. Calculate
a. Directivity.
b. Power gain as a ratio and in dB.

P12-6 Given a helix antenna operating at 3 GHz with the following dimensions: spacing between turns = 3 cm, diameter of helix = 8 cm, number of turns = 15. Calculate
a. The half-power points beamwidth.
b. The first nulls beamwidth.
c. Directivity.

P12-7 A helix antenna is operating at 4 GHz. The directivity is 500. The spacing between turns is 4 cm, and the diameter of the helix is 8 cm. Calculate the number of turns.

P12-8 A pyramidal horn antenna operating at 4 GHz has a power gain of 25 dB and a width of 10 cm. Calculate the aperture height.

P12-9 A parabolic antenna operating at 3 GHz has a power gain of 26 dB. Calculate:

    a. The diameter of the parabolic antenna.

    b. The half-power points beamwidth.

P12-10 A parabolic antenna operating at 2 GHz has a first null points beamwidth of 10°. Calculate:

    a. The diameter of the parabolic antenna.

    b. The half-power points beamwidth.

Chapter 13 Miscellaneous Communications Systems

13-1
Objectives To become familiar with various miscellaneous communications systems, including:

1. Pulse modulation.
2. Single sideband systems.
3. Telemetry systems.
4. Radar systems.

13.2
Self-Evaluating
Questions Test your prior knowledge of the information in this chapter by answering the following questions. Watch for the answers to these questions as you read the chapter. Your final evaluation of whether you understand the material is measured by your ability to answer these questions. When you have completed the chapter, return to this section and answer the questions again.

1. What advantages does *pulse modulation* offer over *amplitude modulation*?
2. Define the characteristics of *pulse amplitude modulation* (PAM).
3. Define the characteristics of *pulse position modulation* (PPM).
4. Define the characteristics of *pulse code modulation* (PCM).
5. Indicate frequency range and number of channels in *citizen band* radio.
6. Define frequency limitations of *electromechanical* filters.
7. Define phase-shift method of *single sideband* (SSB) generation.
8. Define a *transducer*.
9. Define *frequency multiplexing*.
10. Define *time multiplexing*.
11. Define a *duplexer*.
12. Explain the operation of a *doppler radar*.
13. Explain the significance of a planned position indicator (PPI) display.

13-3
Pulse
Modulation
(PM)

A more specialized means of modulation is based on *sampling* the audio intelligence on a regular basis. This is called *pulse modulation* and is based on theory established in the 1920s. This states that if a signal is sampled at a rate that is twice the highest frequency included in the intelligence, the original signal can be reproduced. The inherent advantage of pulse modulation is the short period of RF transmission. There is carrier output only during the interval of the pulse. This in turn permits a greater *peak* power output, because the *average* power output is considerably smaller. This is similar to the operation of radar systems. In addition pulse signals can be "cleaned up" at the receiver with clippers.

13-3.1
Pulse Amplitude
Modulation (PAM)

Pulse amplitude modulation (PAM) is a mode of operation in which the amplitude of the pulse is varied in accordance with the modulating audio. The sequence is shown in Fig. 13-1.

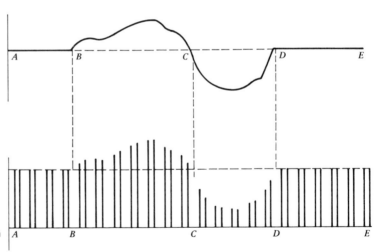

Figure 13-1 Pulse amplitude modulation (PAM).

13-3.2
Pulse Position
Modulation (PPM)

Another form of pulse modulation is *pulse position* modulation (PPM). This involves the shift of the pulse position to left or right in accordance with the modulating audio. This is also called *pulse time* modulation (PTM). The sequence of pulse shift is shown in Fig. 13.2.

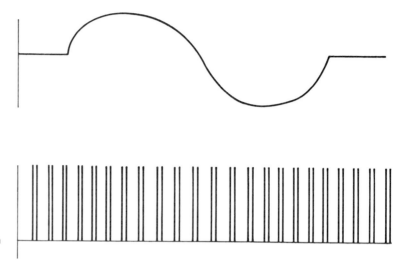

Figure 13-2 Pulse position modulation (PPM).

13-3.3
Pulse Duration
Modulation
Pulse duration modulation (PDM) is also called *pulse width modulation* (PWM). In this mode the audio signal is represented by the variation in the width of the pulse. This sequence is shown in Fig. 13-3.

There are many other variations of pulse modulation, such as *pulse code modulation* (PCM), that use a binary coding system for conveying intelligence. This process is called *quantization* and produces a quantized signal.

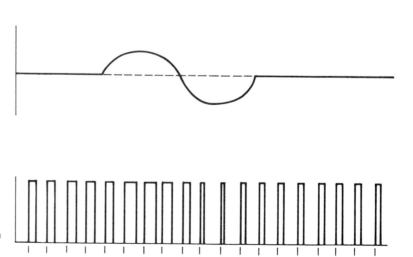

Figure 13-3 Pulse duration modulation (PDM).

13-4
Single Sideband
(SSB) Transmission

13-4.1
General
Requirements

The power savings of SSB transmission were discussed and calculated in Ch. 5. Also included were the calculations for single-sideband-suppressed carrier (SSBSC) transmission. The latter was proven to provide a minimum power savings of 75%. This figure increased with a decreasing index of modulation. Of even greater importance than the power savings, for a crowded frequency spectrum, is the savings in bandwidth. Halving the bandwidth will almost double the number of channels that can be used. Some transmission techniques exactly double the number of channels by means of SSB.

Citizens band transreceivers, which are presently riding a crest of popularity, use SSB to a great extent. Almost all 40 channels are assigned a bandwidth of 10 kHz. The 40 allocated channels lie in the frequency region of 26.965 MHz to 27.405 MHz, for a frequency span of 440 kHz. Other systems using SSB are *fixed radio-telephone service* and *aeronautical mobile service*.

13-4.2
Balanced Modulator
SSB Generation

The *balanced modulator* function has been described previously, and is used in many communications systems. It is one of the most widely used circuits for generating SSBSC transmission. The balanced modulator mixes the RF and the modulating audio. The outputs are the two sidebands without the carrier (DSBSC).

The sidebands are passed through a highly selective filter where one of the sidebands is eliminated. The filter may be an *L-C* configuration (π or T, constant k or m derived) crystal lattice network (piezoelectric principle) or an electromechanical (mechanical) filter. The mechanical filter is restricted in frequency (100 kHz to 500 kHz), but offers the best skirts (shape factor), attenuation, and packaging configuration.

It is possible to use two balanced modulators, each mixing the same carrier but a different audio signal. The outputs can then be treated with filters. The lower sideband of one is removed and the upper sideband of the other is removed. The remaining sidebands are combined to make up a double sideband transmission representing two distinct modulating signals.

To simplify the tuning problems at the receiver, some systems include a *weak (pilot)* carrier similar to the stereo FM system.

13-4.3
Phase Shift Method
of SSB Generation

A method of SSB generation that avoids the use of filters is the *phase shift method*. This makes use of two balanced modulators each feeds a carrier that has been phase shifted 90°. One of the balanced modulators is audio modulated directly. The second balanced modulator is modulated by an audio that has been phase shifted 90°. The outputs of the two balanced modulators are combined in an *adder*. The adder output is the required SSB signal. The major difficulty of this system is the problem of phase shifting a *range* of audio frequencies 90°.

There are other, less commonly used methods of SSB generation. One method uses *controlled carrier transmission*. The carrier is transmitted in bursts at times corresponding to lulls in the audio modulation. Another system is a modification of the phase shift method in which the audio is placed on an audio subcarrier before being phase shifted 90°.

13-4.4
SSB Receivers

There are a multitude of receiver types used for SSB reception. If a pilot carrier has been transmitted, the task is a simple heterodyning function with appropriate sideband filters for demodulation.

A fully suppressed carrier requires the creation of an artificial carrier at the receiver. This can be done with a beat frequency oscillator (BFO) but requires extreme frequency stability.

Some more complex SSB receivers use double conversion superheterodyne systems. Still other receivers incorporate a bank of frequency synthesizers.

13-5
Telemetry

13-5.1
Definition

If broadcasting is defined as the transmission of speech, music or video intelligence, telemetry can be defined as the transmission of a measurand (measurement). More formally, the definition involves the conversion of a measured magnitude into a representative electrical signal, transmission over a path, and reconversion for display, recording, or processing. The basic units of the telemetering system can be identified as a:

1. Transducer for converting the measurement to an electrical signal.
2. Transmitter for transmission of the signal.
3. Transmission path (wire or air link).
4. Receiver, to receive the transmitted signal.
5. Converter, to convert the electrical signal to an appropriate form for final use.

The transmitter/receiver link may be a few feet long as in some industrial uses, or millions of miles as in interplanetary probes. The measurement may be a continuous process or very occasional (per second, per minute, per hour, per day, etc.).

13-5.2
History of Telemetry Historically the first mention of transmitting a measurement was made in 1812 by a Russian. Progress was very slow in its development and was primarily used for military purposes. In 1874, telemetry was used for monitoring meterological conditions. Progress continued in the United States through 1940 with important installations at the Panama Canal and various power generating companies.

World War II was a period of feverish activity in the field of telemetry, primarily in aircraft, rockets, and guided missile systems. These wartime military developments refined the techniques of radio telemetry. Following the declassification of military developments, rapid strides were made in the use of telemetry in hazardous locations. The late 1950s saw the development of the Weather Information Telemetry System (WITS), which provided for many remote unattended positions transmitting meteorological information. The most recent dramatic progress was the use of telemetry to monitor the astronauts as they walked on the surface of the moon during the Apollo program. This led directly to the fully automated hospital, where *all* the vital parameters of *many* critically ill patients can be monitored *continuously* by one attendant observing a computer display.

13-5.3 Transducers The process of converting a measurement to an electrical signal is accomplished by a transducer. The WITS program, used for predicting weather, monitored the complete gamut of parameters required by the weather forecaster. The Apollo program required the monitoring of the biological parameters of individuals.

There are too many types of transducers to compile a comprehensive list. As a compromise some of the more significant *groupings* of electrical transducers will be listed.

1. Mechanical
   a. Velocity
   b. Acceleration
   c. Stress
   d. Pressure
   e. Linear position
   f. Rotary position
2. Weather
   a. Barometric pressure
   b. Wind velocity
   c. Wind direction
   d. Temperature
   e. Rainfall
3. Temperature (industrial)
4. Biological
   a. Temperature
   b. Cardiac (ECG)
   c. Pressure
   d. Brain waves (EEG)
   e. Muscle (EMG)
   f. Eye (ERG and/or EOG)
   g. Stomach

The chemical industry involves many dangerous processes that are monitored remotely and require transducers. Power distribution, steel mills, mining, food processing, atomic energy plants are industries involved with transducers. There are few modern industries that do not require a thickness, width, height, depth, speed, or some other parameter to be monitored and displayed automatically.

There are a variety of transducer types that can be used for any particular measurement. The transducer may operate on any of the following principles:

1. Variable resistance
2. Variable reluctance
3. Piezoelectric
4. Thermocouple
5. Thermistor
6. Photoelectric
7. Encoders
8. Synchros
9. Inductosyns
10. Bridge
11. Variable capacitance
12. Solar cell

There are many more modes of operation of transducers. Even purely electronic parameters may be converted to transducer output, such as frequency, period, sound level, resistance, and magnetic field intensity.

Some of the significant features of a transducer are:

1. Sensitivity
2. Range
3. Resolution
4. Repeatability
5. Accuracy
6. Stability

A transducer output is either a voltage or current. This output can be amplified or converted to another electrical parameter if required. The most common conversion is to digital form using an analog-to-digital (A/D) converter. At the receiver the reverse process is used with a digital-to-analog (D/A) converter.

13-5.4
Multiplexing The transmission of a measurement requires an entire system. If two transducers offered two signals for transmission, they could not be accommodated at the same time or an unacceptable scramble would result. However, if signal number one is transmitted and then discontinued, and this is followed by signal

number two, they would both arrive in an acceptable form. The only additional requirement would be an identifying signal that indicates the sequence. This identification is a synchronizing (sync) pulse. This alerts the receiver as to which signal will follow.

This method of interleaving transmitted signals is called *time multiplexing*. It is a form of *sampling* or *commutating*. In practice, many signals are included in a time multiplex system. It is usually done by first converting the signal to a pulse form. This may be PAM, PTM, PDM, or PCM. The group of pulses representing a measurement are transmitted, each group in turn, until all the transducer outputs have been transmitted as indicated by appropriate sync pulses.

Another form of multiplexing is to have each transducer output modulate an oscillator operating at a different frequency. These modulated oscillators in turn modulate a high frequency transmitter. Each of the original oscillators acts as a subcarrier for the high frequency carrier.

The subcarrier may contain double sidebands, but more likely one sideband has been filtered out before modulating the high frequency carrier, thus saving valuable frequency space and power.

This process is called *frequency multiplexing*. The process of subcarrier modulating a carrier can be carried on until one has gone beyond the frequency spectrum or, more likely, has used up the frequency allocation. The subcarrier and carrier may both use frequency modulation, in which case it is an FM-FM telemetry system. A combination of AM and FM is possible or a purely AM system may be used.

13-5.5
Telemetry Transmitter Some typical subcarrier band center frequencies (in kHz) are listed. The usual bandwidth is ±7.5%. The FM index of modulation is usually 5.

1. 0.4 kHz	**7.** 2.3	**13.** 14.5
2. 0.56	**8.** 3.0	**14.** 22.0
3. 0.73	**9.** 3.9	**15.** 30.0
4. 0.96	**10.** 5.4	**16.** 40.0
5. 1.3	**11.** 7.35	**17.** 52.5
6. 1.7	**12.** 10.5	**18.** 70.0

The higher bands may use a time multiplex arrangement and accommodate 2 to 10 transducers with appropriate synchronizing. This entire block of bands may frequency modulate a carrier at 5 MHz with different groups of blocks modulating 6 MHz, 7 MHz, etc. These in turn may then modulate a microwave carrier. The transmitter is thus able to accommodate hundreds of signals. The ultimate carrier would be the microwave frequency (assume 10 GHz), the next lower carrier, the RF (5 MHz) is the subcarrier, and the band (50 kHz) would then be subsubcarrier modulated by $\approx$6 transducer signals.

13-5.6
Telemetry Receiver

The telemetry receiver is in a frequency sense the mirror image of the transmitter. The 10 GHz signal is received and demodulated into its specific subcarrier bands of 5 MHz, 6 MHz, 7 MHz, etc. The next sequence of demodulation would reduce the signals to the band carrier 1 to 70 kHz. From these outputs, the original signals would be extracted and converted to the appropriate form for display, recording, viewing, listening, processing, etc.

Obviously great care must be taken in the design and operation of a telemetry system. Frequency stability of the carrier and the subcarrier is essential. Intermodulation distortion must be avoided and noise must be minimized.

13-6
Radar

13-6.1
History of Radar

Radar is a contraction of *radio detection and ranging*. It was developed shortly before World War II and was quickly refined for war use. After the war radar was modified for many non-military uses as well as more sophisticated military applications. A brief listing of *some* of the uses for radar includes:

1. Search
2. Tracking
3. Navigation
4. Satellite
5. Weather
6. Air traffic control
7. Vehicle speeding detection

13-6.2
Radar Basics The basic function of radar is the location of a distant object. This is accomplished by transmitting an RF signal of appropriate (UHF or microwave) frequency and noting the arrival of the *reflection* or *echo* of the transmitted signal.

The time lapse between the transmission and the reception is an indication of the range or distance of the target. The distance a transmitted signal travels in 1 μs is 300 m. Therefore 2 μs are required for the detection of a target 300 m distant.

13-6.3
Pulsed Radar The most common radar system uses a pulse modulation. Here the transmission is in the form of a well-defined, sharply shaped pulse. The time of transmission is noted and compared to the time of arrival of the echo. This time lapse, at the rate of 2 μs/300 m, indicates the distance of the target.

A *pulse duration* of 2 μs is commonly used in radar transmission. The pulse is carefully shaped before modulating the carrier so that the *width* and *skirts* of the pulse are *precisely* defined. As a result the exact instant of departure of the transmission can be recorded. Likewise the instant of arrival of the echo is readily detected because of the steepness of the leading edge of the signal.

13-6.4
Pulse Repetition Rate The *pulse repetition rate* determines the time between pulses, which in turn sets the *maximum range* to be accommodated. A repetition rate of 400 pulses per second results in a period of 2500 μs. This permits a maximum range of (2500/2)300 m or 375 km. The minimum range is determined by the width of the pulse. A 1 μs interval represents a round trip range of 150 m.

13-6.5
Duty Cycle The ratio of pulse width to period is the *duty cycle* of the system. This is related to the *peak power* of transmission. Assuming a fixed *average power* of the transmitter, the smaller the duty cycle the farther the transmission can reach.

13-6.6
Carrier Frequency The choice of carrier frequency is determined by the application. Location may be a factor, since a stationary transmitter can incorporate a larger antenna than a mobile unit. The frequency relates inversely to the size of the antenna. The power

to be transmitted depends on available power sources. These vary for different frequencies. Higher frequencies ($>$ X-band) are poor choices for weather detection.

13-6.7
Radar Receiver The receiver is usually a *superheterodyne* type with the video outptut (echo signal) applied to a display. The input may contain one or more RF amplifiers located close to the receiving antenna to improve signal-to-noise ratio. Another type of receiver used for radar systems, is the *video* receiver. The video receiver eliminates the RF, mixer, local oscillator, and IF amplifier and feeds the echo signal directly to a video detector.

13-6.8
Control Circuits Also included in a radar system are *pulse-forming networks*, *pulse generators*, *gating circuits*, and *synchronizing circuits* to sync the receiver as the pulse is transmitted.

13-6.9
Indicators The indicator is usually a cathode ray oscilloscope (scope). The type of display is determined by the choice of radar system. It is either an *A-scope* or *Planned Position Indicator* (*PPI*) display. The A-scope is the type of display commonly used in the electronics laboratory. The trigger for the sweep is the transmitted pulse and the echo signal appears as a vertical signal along the sweep at a point proportional to the range. The PPI display is the one shown at airports and on military equipment. The distance of the echo signal from the center of the tube represents the range. The angle of the pip off the vertical line of the scope represents the bearing angle of the target.

13-6.10
Radar Duplexer Pulsed radars usually have a single antenna that is shared by the receiver and transmitter sections. The coupling device is a *duplexer* that switches the antenna to the transmitter high-power output during transmission and back to the receiver at the end of the transmitted pulse.

Depending on power requirements, the duplexer may be a gas-tube switch, called a TR (transmit-receive) cell. A gas contained in the duplexer ionizes at the instant of applied transmitted power and provides a path to the antenna. At the conclusion of the transmission, the gas deionizes and the antenna is reconnected to the receiver.

Low power radar systems can use semiconductor diode switches. The PIN diode is a popular choice. The diodes can be made parallel to increase current rating. The diode is forward biased for the transmission period and reverse biased for reception.

The ferrite circulator characteristic also lends itself to duplexer action. The transmitter signal is restricted to a single path leading to the antenna. The antenna input is limited to a single path leading to the receiver.

13-6.11
Radar Antennas
The most common radar antenna is some form of parabolic antenna. It may be a dish, a pillbox or a full-blown space-probing antenna. The requirement may be high-gain narrow beamwidth for tracking radars, wide beamwidth for search radars, azimuth (horizontal) transmission, vertical (elevation) transmission, or circular (helical) transmission.

The polarization of the transmission may be specified, since the receiver antenna must accommodate the transmission. Circular transmission minimizes this problem, but is less efficient.

13-6.12
Search Radar
A search radar must cover a large section. This can be accomplished with conical scanning. The antenna is made to *mutate* about an axis as it scans the field. The same effect can be accomplished electronically by the use of multifeeds (horns) to the antenna. They are activated as a phased array, each in turn.

13-6.13
Tracking Radar
After the target has been acquired by the search radar, the mission is transferred to the tracking radar. This functions on the basis of a highly directive (pencil) beam. As the target moves, the echo signal indicates the direction and activates a servo system. The servo moves the antenna to keep the echo signal nulled. In military use, the servo error signal would activate the aim of guns and missiles. These are called *fire control* radar.

13-6.14
Doppler Radar
Doppler radar is based on the principle of *doppler frequency shift*. This is simply the fact that the frequency of the echo signal will shift from the original transmission frequency. The amount of frequency shift varies with the radial velocity of the target. As the target moves toward the receiver, the frequency will increase, and similarly decrease for motion away from the receiver. The velocity of the target (*range rate*) is indicated by the deviation in frequency.

Doppler radar is useful for selecting a small moving target in a large background (mountain) environment. Normally the mountain echo would swamp the weak target echo. In doppler systems, the constant repetitive echo signal of the mountain is readily cancelled.

Doppler radar is useful in determining the speed of an aircraft for navigation purposes. In this case the radar is in motion and the target is stationary. Doppler radar is used by police for monitoring the speed of a passing automobile. Indeed recent technology has resulted in a small handheld unit, much to the consternation of the speeder.

13-6.15
FM-CW Radar
Doppler offers velocity information but not distance (range). By combining CW and FM, it is possible to calculate the distance by comparing the echo frequency to the time at which that specific frequency was transmitted. Since the rate of change of the FM modulation is known, the comparison is relatively straightforward. The frequency difference is converted to time, which in turn is converted to range.

13-6.16
Miscellaneous Radar Systems
Early warning radars used by the military, such as the BMEWS radar in Alaska and Scotland, have a particular problem of scanning a large sector for a small high velocity target (missile).

Radar aboard naval vessels searching the horizon for low flying aircraft must differentiate the target echo from the echos of high waves (sea clutter).

Beacon radar is a system in which the conventional radar *interrogates* the beacon radar with a special *question* or code. The beacon radar then responds with a particular message. This same principle is used for IFF (identification of friend or foe) radar in military aircraft.

MTI (moving target indication) radar is a form of pulsed doppler. The pulse indicates range and the doppler indicates velocity. The doppler feature also permits separation of the weak echo from a large stationary target.

Track-While Scan radar can track many targets at the same time. During each scan the target position is noted. The change in position on successive scans indicates the path of travel of the target. This is the principle of *Air-Traffic Control* radar.

Commercial airliners try to avoid turbulent sectors by flying above or around the turbulence. The *Weather-Avoidance* radar operating in the C-band and X-band is commonly used for this purpose.

**13-7
Summary**
There are many types of communications systems other than the conventional AM, FM, and TV. Some of these are pulse modulation systems, including PAM, PPM, PDM, and PCM. Single sideband systems conserve both frequency spectrum and power. Telemetry systems are primarily for the communication of multiplexed signals. Radar systems can detect a distant target and define its velocity and coordinates.

Now return to the objectives and self-evaluation questions at the beginning of the chapter and see how well you can answer them. If you cannot answer certain questions, place a check next to each of them and review appropriate parts of the text. Then answer the questions and solve the problems below.

**13-8
Questions**

Q13-1 Define *Pulse Duration Modulation* (PDM).

Q13-2 Name three types of communications systems that use *SSB* transmission.

Q13-3 Explain the function of a *balanced modulator* in a SSB system.

Q13-4 Name three types of *filters* used in SSB systems.

Q13-5 Explain the method of *DSB transmission* where each sideband is another signal.

Q13-6 What is a *pilot carrier*?

Q13-7 Explain the *phase-shift method* of SSB generation.

Q13-8 Name three types of *SSB* receivers.

Q13-9 Define *telemetry*.

Q13-10 Identify the major blocks of a telemetry system.

Q13-11 Identify five fields in which telemetry is used.

Q13-12 Name five types of mechanical transducers.

Q13-13 Name five weather parameters commonly monitored by telemetry.

Q13-14 Identify five types of medical measurements that can be transmitted by telemetry.

Q13-15 Name five additional industries that commonly use telemetry in their processes.

Q13-16 Name ten principles of operation of transducers.

Q13-17 Identify five significant parameters of a transducer.

Q13-18 Define *commutating*.

Q13-19 Explain the sequence of *subcarriers* in *frequency multiplexing*.

Q13-20 List five functions of radar systems.

Q13-21 If a pulsed radar system uses a 1 μs pulse width, what is the minimum range that a target can be detected?

Q13-22 Define *duty cycle* of a radar system.

Q13-23 Explain the characteristics of an *A-scope* radar display.

Q13-24 What is the common type of radar antenna?

Q13-25 Define a *search* radar.

Q13-26 Define a *tracking* radar.

Q13-27 Explain the advantage of *FM-CW* radar.

Q13-28 What is the significance of *sea clutter*?

Q13-29 Explain the operation of a *beacon* radar.

Q13-30 What is the advantage of the MTI radar?

Appendix A **Filters**

The design of the frequency filters described in Ch. 2 are detailed in this section, along with illustrative examples.

A-1
Low-Pass
Constant k filter
If the product of the filter shunt impedance (Z_2) and the filter series impedance (Z_1) is constant at all frequencies, the filter is called a *constant k* filter. For the networks of Fig. A-1 the design criteria are as follows:

$$f_c = \frac{1}{\pi\sqrt{LC}} \qquad \text{hertz (Hz)} \qquad (A\text{-}1)$$

$$L = \frac{R_L}{\pi f_c} \qquad \text{henries (H)} \qquad (A\text{-}2)$$

$$C = \frac{1}{\pi f_c R_L} \qquad \text{farads (F)} \qquad (A\text{-}3)$$

where: f_c is the cut-off frequency, Hz
R_L is the terminating resistance, Ω

Example A-1

A constant k filter is to be terminated with a 100 Ω antenna and is to have a cutoff frequency of 2 MHz. Calculate the L and C values.

Solution

$$L = R/\pi f_c = \frac{100}{\pi \times 2 \times 10^6} = 15.92 \ \mu\text{H} \qquad (A\text{-}2)$$

$$C = \frac{1}{\pi f_c R} = \frac{1}{\pi \times 2 \times 10^6 \times 100} = 1592 \ \text{pF} \qquad (A\text{-}3)$$

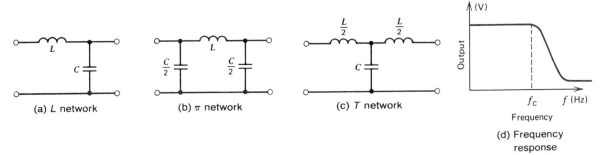

Figure A-1 Low-pass constant k filter and frequency response.

A-2 Low-Pass m Derived Filter The constant k filter characteristics can be improved by adding an element to the section that provides infinite attenuation at a frequency designated (f_∞). This improved filter is called an m derived filter (Fig. A-2).

The value of m given by Eq. (A-4) can be between 0 and 1, and is generally used as $m = 0.6$.

$$m - \sqrt{1 - (f_c/f_\infty)^2} \qquad \text{(A-4)}$$

where: m is the design decimal fraction

f_∞ is the frequency at which infinite attenuation takes place

For the m derived filter the constant k equations are modified as follows:

$$L_1 = \frac{mR}{\pi f_c} \qquad \text{henries (H)} \qquad \text{(A-5)}$$

$$C_1 = \frac{m}{\pi f_c R} \qquad \text{farads (F)} \qquad \text{(A-6)}$$

$$L_2 = \frac{m}{\pi f_c R} \qquad \text{henries (H)} \qquad \text{(A-7)}$$

$$C_2 = \left(\frac{1 - m^2}{4m}\right) \frac{1}{\pi f_c R} \qquad \text{(A-8)}$$

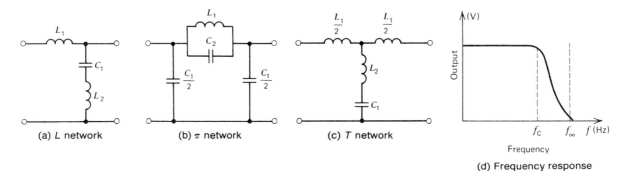

(a) L network (b) π network (c) T network (d) Frequency response

Figure A-2 Low-pass *m* derived filters and frequency response.

Example A-2

Given an *m*-derived π network low-pass filter with a cutoff frequency of 5 MHz and a termination of 50 Ω. Assuming an $m = 0.6$, calculate f_∞, L_1, C_1, and C_2.

Solution

$$m = \sqrt{1 - (f_c/f_\infty)^2} \tag{A-4}$$

This results in the relationship

$$f_\infty = f_c \sqrt{\frac{1}{1 - m^2}} = 5 \times 10^6 \sqrt{\frac{1}{1 - (0.6)^2}}$$

$$= 5 \times 10^6 \sqrt{\frac{1}{0.64}} = \frac{5 \times 10^6}{0.8} = \mathbf{6.25\ MHz}$$

$$L_1 = \frac{mR}{f_c} = \frac{0.6 \times 50}{\pi \times 5 \times 10^6} = \mathbf{1.91\ \mu H} \tag{A-5}$$

$$C_1 = \frac{m}{\pi f_c R} = \frac{0.6}{\pi \times 5 \times 10^6 \times 50} \tag{A-6}$$

$$= 0.6/785.4 \times 10^6 = \mathbf{763.9\ pF}$$

$$C_2 = \left(\frac{1 - m^2}{4m}\right)\frac{1}{\pi f_c R} = \frac{1 - (0.6)^2}{4 \times 0.6} \times \frac{1}{785.4 \times 10^6} \tag{A-8}$$

$$= \frac{0.64}{2.4} \times \frac{1}{785.4 \times 10^6} = \mathbf{339.5\ pF}$$

**A-3
High-Pass
Constant k Filters**
In a similar manner it is possible to set up the L and C elements to pass the high frequencies and attenuate the low frequencies. This is called a *high-pass* filter. The general configurations of the high-pass constant k filter L, T, and π networks, and the frequency response are shown in Fig. A-3.

The design criteria for the high-pass constant k filters are given by the following equations.

$$f_c = \frac{1}{4\pi\sqrt{LC}} \tag{A-9}$$

$$L = \frac{R}{4\pi f_c} \tag{A-10}$$

$$C = \frac{1}{4\pi f_c R} \tag{A-11}$$

Example A-3
Given a T configuration, high-pass constant k filter with a cutoff frequency of 2 MHz and a 70 Ω termination. Calculate L and C.

Solution

$$L = \frac{R}{4\pi f_c} = \frac{70}{4\pi \times 2 \times 10^6} = \textbf{2.785 } \mu\textbf{H} \tag{A-10}$$

$$C = \frac{1}{4\pi f_c R} = \frac{1}{4\pi \times 2 \times 10^6 \times 70} = \textbf{568.4 pF} \tag{A-11}$$

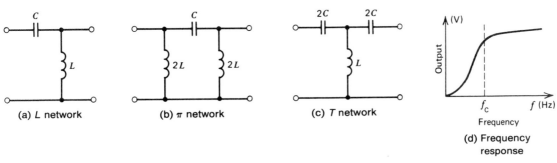

(a) L network   (b) π network   (c) T network   (d) Frequency response

Figure A-3 High-pass constant k filters and frequency response.

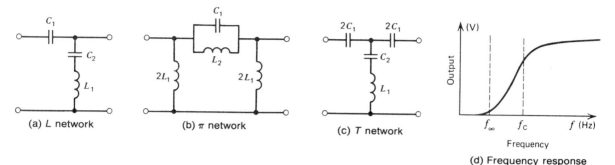

(a) L network   (b) π network   (c) T network   (d) Frequency response

Figure A-4 High-pass m derived filters and frequency response.

A-4
High-Pass m Derived Filter

The high-pass m derived filter is shown in Fig. A-4. The applicable formulas are the following:

$$m=\sqrt{1-(f_\infty/f_c)^2} \tag{A-12}$$

$$L_1=\frac{R}{4\pi f_c m} \tag{A-13}$$

$$C_1=\frac{1}{4\pi f_c mR} \tag{A-14}$$

$$L_2=\frac{mR}{(1-m^2)\pi f_c} \tag{A-15}$$

$$C_2=\frac{m}{(1-m^2)\pi f_c R} \tag{A-16}$$

Example A-4

Given a π configuration, high-pass m derived filter, with a cutoff frequency of 9 MHz and a 100 Ω termination. Assume $m=0.7$ and calculate L_1, L_2, and C_1.

Solution

$$L_1=\frac{R}{4\pi f_c m}=\frac{100}{4\pi\times9\times10^6\times0.7}=\textbf{1.263 }\boldsymbol{\mu}\textbf{H} \tag{A-13}$$

$$C_1=\frac{1}{4\pi f_c mR}=\frac{1}{4\pi\times9\times10^6\times0.7\times100}=\textbf{126.3 pF} \tag{A-14}$$

$$L_2=\frac{mR}{(1-m^2)\pi f_c}\quad\frac{0.7\times100}{\left[1-(0.7)^2\right]\pi\times9\times10^6}=\textbf{4.854 }\boldsymbol{\mu}\textbf{H} \tag{A-15}$$

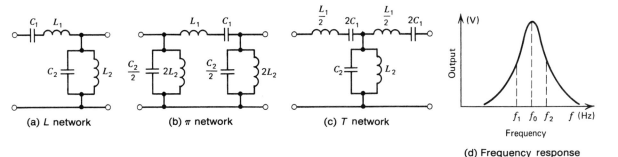

(a) L network   (b) π network   (c) T network   (d) Frequency response

Figure A-5 Bandpass constant k filters and frequency response.

A-5
Bandpass Constant
k Filters

It is also possible to configure L and C elements to accept a range or band of frequencies. This network is called a *bandpass filter*. The general configurations of the bandpass L, T, and π networks, and the frequency response are shown in Fig. A-5.

The design criteria for the bandpass constant k filters are given by the following equations:

$$L_1 = \frac{R}{\pi(f_2 - f_1)} \qquad \text{henries (H)} \qquad \text{(A-17)}$$

$$L_2 = \frac{(f_2 - f_1)R}{4\pi f_1 f_2} \qquad \text{henries (H)} \qquad \text{(A-18)}$$

$$C_1 = \frac{f_2 - f_1}{4\pi f_1 f_2 R} \qquad \text{farads (F)} \qquad \text{(A-19)}$$

$$C_2 = \frac{1}{\pi(f_2 - f_1)R} \qquad \text{Farads (F)} \qquad \text{(A-20)}$$

where: f_2 is the higher frequency limit of the bandpass (Hz)
f_1 is the lower frequency limit of the bandpass (Hz)

Example A-5
Given a T configuration bandpass constant k filter with the higher frequency limit at 1200 kHz and the lower frequency limit at 800 kHz. The termination is 100 Ω. Calculate the values of L_1, L_2, C_1, and C_2.

Solution

$$L_1 = \frac{R}{\pi(f_2 - f_1)} = \frac{100}{\pi(1200 - 800) \times 10^3} = \textbf{79.58 } \mu\textbf{H} \quad \text{(A-17)}$$

$$L_2 = \frac{(f_2 - f_1)R}{4\pi f_1 f_2} = \frac{(1200 - 800) \times 10^3 \times 100}{4\pi \times 1200 \times 10^3 \times 800 \times 10^3} \quad \text{(A-18)}$$

$$= \frac{400 \times 10^5}{1208 \times 10^{10}} = \textbf{3.316 } \mu\textbf{H}$$

$$C_1 = \frac{f_2 - f_1}{4\pi f_1 f_2 R} \quad \text{(A-19)}$$

$$= \frac{400 \times 10^3}{4\pi \times 1.2 \times 10^6 \times 0.8 \times 10^6 \times 100} = \textbf{331.6 pF}$$

$$C_2 = \frac{1}{\pi(f_2 - f_1)R} = \frac{1}{\pi \times 400 \times 10^3 \times 100} = \textbf{7958 pF} \quad \text{(A-20)}$$

The bandpass filter can be designed as an *m* derived filter. In that case *two* additional infinite attenuation frequencies (f_{∞_1} and f_{∞_2}) are introduced. The networks become more elaborate and the equations more complex.

A-6
Bandstop
(Band-Reject)
Filters
The final filter type to be considered is the *bandstop* (band-reject, band-eliminate) filter. This filter will pass all frequencies except those in a prescribed band of frequencies. The general configuration of the bandstop constant *k*, *L*, *T*, and *π* networks, and the frequency response are shown in Fig. A-6.

The design criteria for the bandstop constant *k* filters are given by the following equations:

$$L_1 = \frac{(f_2 - f_1)R}{\pi f_1 f_2} \qquad \text{henries (H)} \qquad \text{(A-21)}$$

$$L_2 = \frac{R}{4\pi(f_1 - f_2)} \qquad \text{henries (H)} \qquad \text{(A-22)}$$

$$C_1 = \frac{1}{4\pi(f_1 - f_2)R} \qquad \text{farads (F)} \qquad \text{(A-23)}$$

$$C_2 = \frac{f_2 - f_1}{\pi R f_1 f_2} \qquad \text{farads (F)} \qquad \text{(A-24)}$$

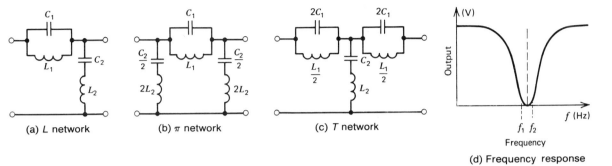

(a) L network (b) π network (c) T network (d) Frequency response

Figure A-6 Bandstop constant k filters and frequency response.

Example A-6
Given a π configuration constant k bandstop filter with the higher frequency limit at 400 kHz and the lower frequency limit at 350 kHz. The termination is 300 Ω. Calculate the values of L_1, L_2, C_1, and C_2

Solution

$$L_1 = \frac{(f_2 - f_1)R}{\pi f_1 f_2} = \frac{(400 - 350) \times 10^3 \times 300}{\pi \times 350 \times 10^3 \times 400 \times 10^3} \qquad \text{(A-21)}$$

$$= \frac{15 \times 10^6}{4.398 \times 10^{11}} = 34.11 \ \mu\text{H}$$

$$L_2 = \frac{R}{4\pi(f_2 - f_1)} = \frac{300}{4\pi \times 50 \times 10^3} = 477.5 \ \mu\text{H} \qquad \text{(A-22)}$$

$$C_1 = \frac{1}{4\pi(f_2 - f_1)R} \qquad \text{(A-23)}$$

$$= \frac{1}{4\pi \times 50 \times 10^3 \times 300} = 5305 \ \text{pF}$$

$$C_2 = \frac{f_2 - f_1}{\pi R f_1 f_2} \qquad \text{(A-24)}$$

$$= \frac{50 \times 10^3}{\pi \times 300 \times 400 \times 10^3 \times 350 \times 10^3} = 378.9 \ \text{pF}$$

The bandstop filter also lends itself to m derived filter design. Here again the two frequencies at infinite attenuation would be involved with greater complexity of configuration and equation.

Smith Chart

B-1
Smith Chart Uses

The Smith chart is widely used in the design of transmission line sections and attenuation calculations. The determination of the degree of mismatch of transmission line sections for frequencies adjacent to the design frequency is readily accomplished. The admittance of any load impedance is derived directly from the chart with minimal calculation. The Smith chart can accommodate any load impedance and any transmission line characteristic impedance. The Smith chart demonstrates the validity of Eq. (8-9) for the $\lambda/4$ matching section. It also clearly demonstrates the change from resistive to positive or negative reactance or susceptance as either the length of the $\lambda/4$ section or the frequency is changed. The Smith chart is shown in Fig. B-1.

At first glance the Smith chart seems to be an unholy mess of unrelated arcs, circles and lines, but inspection of one parameter at a time quickly clarifies the confusion. The chart is in a sense a "city map" where each location represents a particular load. The initial problem is to locate any specified load on the chart. The specific load impedance or admittance is not read onto the chart directly. What is located on the chart is a *normalized* load impedance. This is simply the ratio of load impedance Z_L to characteristic impedance, Z_0.

$$z_L = \frac{Z_L}{Z_0} \qquad (B-1)$$

where z_L is the *normalized* load impedance.

The Smith chart will now be dissected into its component parts. Figure B-2 emphasizes some of the *resistive* elements of the chart.

The *smallest* circle represents the *largest* value of *normalized* load *resistance*. A load resistance of 5000 Ω that terminates a transmission line of 100 Ω characteristic impedance would result in a normalized load resistance of 5000/100 or 50. In that case

IMPEDANCE OR ADMITTANCE COORDINATES

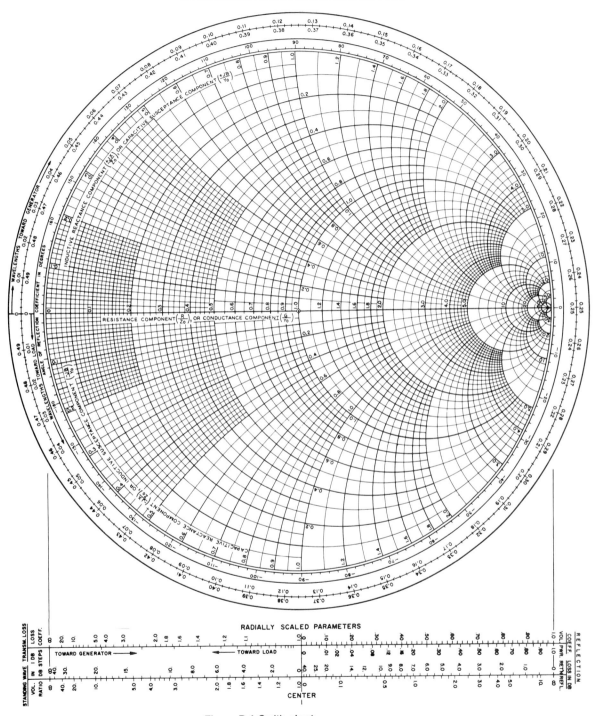

Figure B-1 Smith chart.

IMPEDANCE OR ADMITTANCE COORDINATES

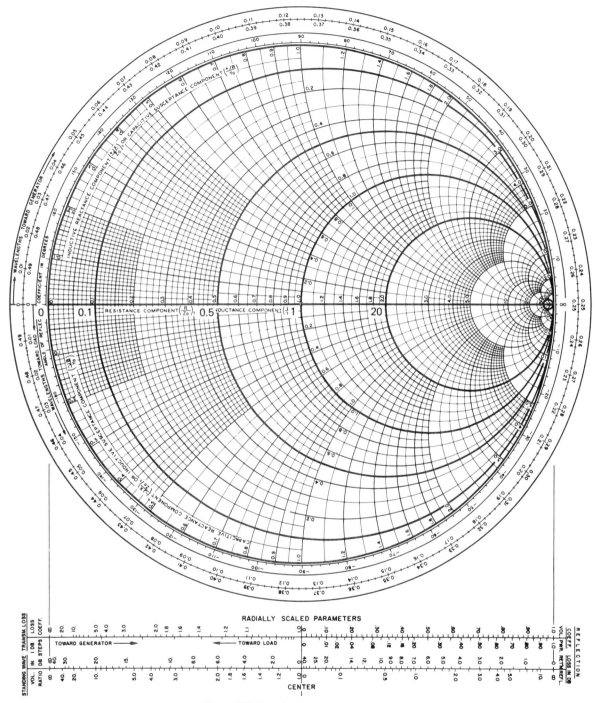

Figure B-2 Resistive elements of Smith chart.

it would be located some place on the 50 circle. Similarly an R_L of 6000 Ω and a Z_0 of 300 Ω would fall on the 6000/300 or 20 circle. The *unity* circle also includes the center of the chart. Whenever R_L and Z_0 are equal, the point would appear on the unity circle. Circles to the *right* of *center* are *greater* than unity. Circles to the *left* of *center* are *less* than unity. The *outermost* circle or perimeter represents *zero*. This would be an R_L of zero or a short-circuited load. The right-hand end of the center line represents the *infinity* circle, which reduces to a single point.

The Smith chart also accommodates admittance of load. The resistive element of the admittance would still appear on the chart except that you are plotting conductance.

The value of the conductance may prove to be considerably less than unity. Nevertheless the value would fall on one of the resistive circles.

The other significant parameter of the load impedance is the reactive element. This is represented by the series of arcs emanating from the right-hand side of the circle. Some of these arcs are shown in Fig. B-3.

The reactive element representations on the chart add an additional degree of complexity since they represent both positive and negative values. The centerline represents the *zero* reactance or susceptance, which is the case for a *pure resistance* load condition. Again the right-hand end of the center line represents the infinity arc, which reduces to a point. The arcs in the upper half of the circle represent loads with inductive reactance $(+jX/Z_0)$ or capacitive susceptance $(+jB/Y_0)$. The arcs below the center represent capacitive loads $(-jX/Z_0)$ or inductive susceptance $(-jB/Y_0)$.

Any normalized load impedance or load admittance can be located by the intersection of a resistance/conductance circle and a reactance/susceptance arc.

Example B-1

Given a transmission line with characteristic impedance of 100 Ω, locate the following loads on a Smith chart.

a. $Z_L = 200$ Ω
b. $Z_L = (300 + j50)$ Ω
c. $Z_L = (75 - j150)$ Ω
d. $Z_L = (0 + j400)$ Ω

IMPEDANCE OR ADMITTANCE COORDINATES

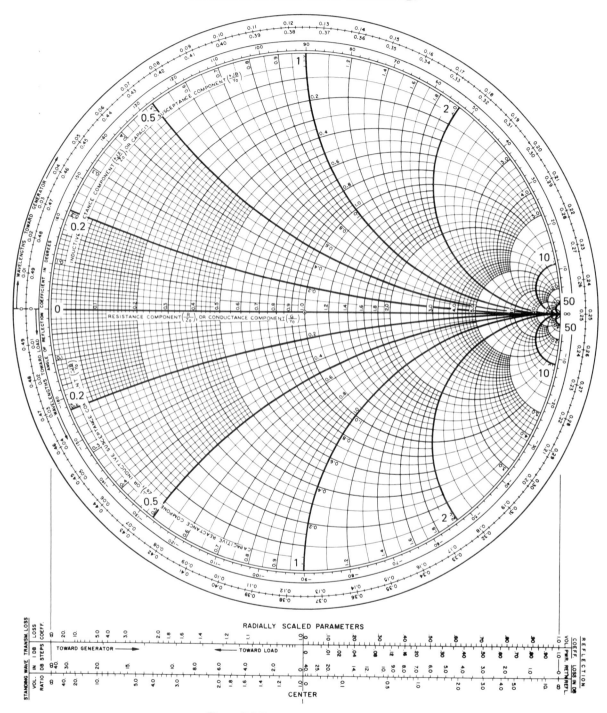

Figure B-3 Reactive elements of Smith chart.

Solution

a. $z_L = Z_L / Z_0 = \dfrac{200 + j0}{100} = (2 + j0)\ \Omega$ (Point A)

b. $z_L = \dfrac{300 + j50}{100} = (3 + j0.5)\ \Omega$ (Point B)

c. $z_L = \dfrac{75 - j150}{100} = (0.75 - j1.5)\ \Omega$ (Point C)

d. $z_L = \dfrac{0 + j400}{100} = (0 + j4)\ \Omega$ (Point D)

Refer to Fig. B-4 for location of these four points on a Smith chart.

Example B-2

Given a transmission line with a characteristic impedance of 200 Ω, locate the following loads on a Smith chart as normalized admittances.

a. $Y_L = (0 - j0.01)\ \mathrm{S}$

b. $Y_L = (0.005 + j0.003)\ \mathrm{S}$

c. $Y_L = (0.02 - j0.006)\ \mathrm{S}$

d. $Y_L = (0.003 + j0)\ \mathrm{S}$

e. $Z_L = (200 - j200)\ \Omega$

f. $Z_L = (75 + j300)\ \Omega$

Solution

Refer to Fig. B-5.

$$Y_0 = 1/Z_0 = 1/200 = \mathbf{0.005\ S}$$

a. $Y_L = Y_L / Y_0 = \dfrac{0 - j0.01}{0.005} = (0 - j2)\ \mathrm{S}$ (Point A)

b. $Y_L = \dfrac{0.005 + j0.003}{0.005} = (1 + j0.6)\ \mathrm{S}$ (Point B)

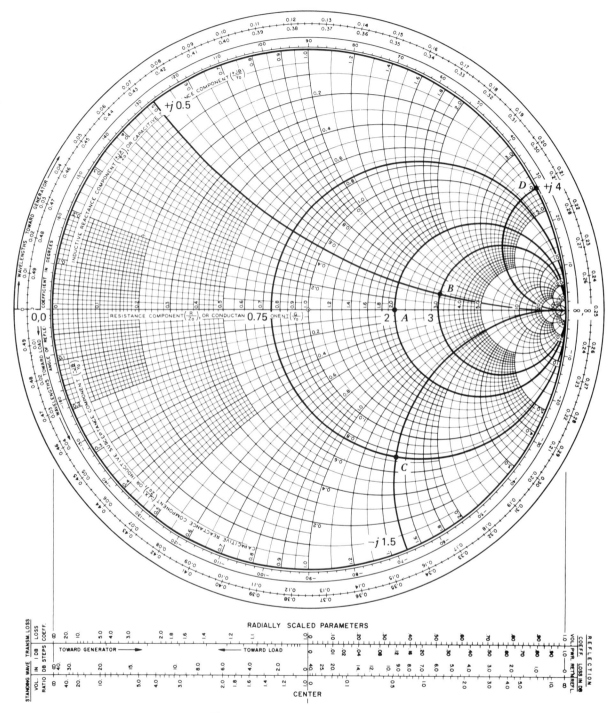

Figure B-4 Smith chart for Example B-1.

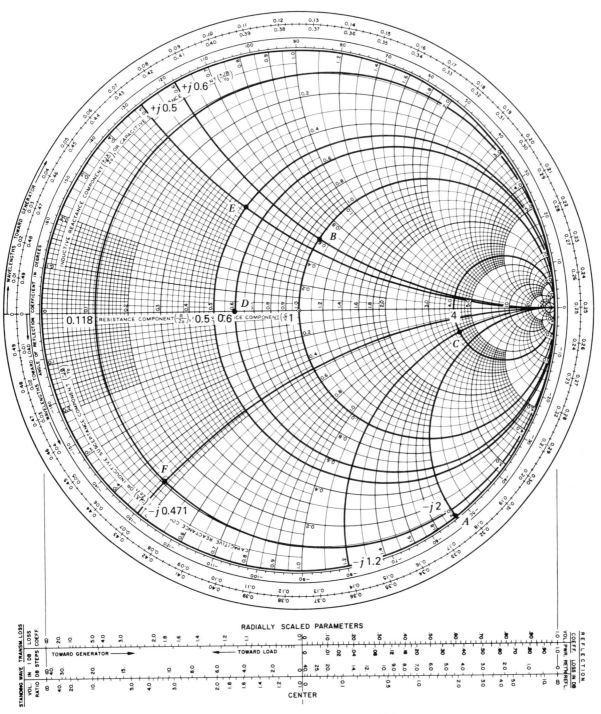

Figure B-5 Smith chart for Example B-2.

c. $Y_L = \dfrac{0.02 - j0.006}{0.005} = (4 - j1.2)\ \text{S}$ (Point C)

d. $Y_L = \dfrac{0.003 + j0}{0.005} = (0.6 + j0)\ \text{S}$ (Point D)

e. $z_L = Z_L / Z_0 = \dfrac{200 - j200}{200} = (1 - j1)\ \Omega$

$Y_L = 1/Z_L = \dfrac{1}{1 - j1} = \dfrac{1(1 + j1)}{(1 - j1)(1 + j1)}$

$= \dfrac{1 + j1}{1 \times 1 - j^2 \times 1 \times 1} = \dfrac{1 + j1}{1 + 1} = (0.5 + j0.5)\ \text{S}$ (Point E)

Note: Solution can also be obtained by converting denominator to polar form, dividing and converting the answer to rectangular form.

f. $z_L = \dfrac{75 + j300}{150} = (0.5 + j2)\ \Omega$

$Y_L = \dfrac{1}{Z_L} = \dfrac{1}{0.5 + j2} = \dfrac{0.5 - j2}{(0.5)^2 + (2)^2} = \dfrac{0.5 - j2}{0.25 + 4}$

$= \dfrac{0.4}{4.25} - j\dfrac{2}{4.25} = (0.118 - j0.471)\ \text{S}$ (Point F)

Referring back to Fig. B-1, note that the *outer* circle of the Smith chart is divided into units of wavelengths. Both sets of markings start at the left-hand end (∞, ∞) and comprise a half wavelength. The outer marking increases from zero to 0.5λ in a clockwise direction. This represents the direction *away* from the load and *toward the generator*. The inside of the same circle is numbered in the opposite direction (counterclockwise), also from zero to 0.5λ and represents the direction *toward the load* and away from the generator. The significance of this information is demonstrated by the solution of appropriate problems.

The next inner circle labeled "Angle of Reflection Coefficient in Degrees" starts with zero at the right hand $(0,0)$ end of the circle and divides each half circle into 180°. The last scales to be noted, running horizontally below the circle, have various functions. The *left*-hand side of the *bottom* line correlates standing wave ratio and decibels and relates them to the SWR of the load located in the Smith chart. The *right*-hand side of the *bottom* line defines reflection losses in decibels.

The *upper* line, *left*-hand side identifies transmission loss, correlating loss coefficient and decibels and relating these to the SWR indicated in the Smith chart. The last group of figures on the *right*-hand side of the *upper* line identifies the coefficient of reflection correlating this in voltage and power ratios and relating them to the SWR indicated by the Smith chart.

B-2 Calculations For a Quarter Wavelength Impedance Match A resistive load of incorrect value can be matched to the transmission line by means of the technique suggested by Eq. (8-9). A load consisting of resistance, and reactance can be matched to the line by methods using the Smith chart. The basic approach is to step away from the load to a fractional wavelength distance where the line impedance appears as a pure resistance. We know that a transmission line appears to be R, L, or C in a sequential pattern as you move down the line away from the load.

The simplest explanation is to go through the steps of the solution of a problem. Figure B-6 indicates the general approach.

Position A is the location of the complex load. The length l from the load brings you to point B. The impedance seen looking back toward the load at point B should appear as a pure resistance of some value not necessarily equal to Z_0. The $\lambda/4$ section of Z_0' is inserted at point B. This terminates the main transmission line properly, and avoids the formation of standing waves on the main line.

The sequence of calculations is illustrated by solving a problem.

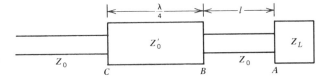

Figure B-6 A quarter-wavelength matching section for a complex load.

Example B-3

Given a transmission line with a characteristic impedance of 100 Ω and a load impedance $Z_L = (50 + j150)$ Ω, design a quarter wavelength impedance matching section.

Solution

Refer to Fig. B-7.

1. Normalize the load

$$z_L = \frac{Z_L}{Z_0} = \frac{50 + j150}{100} = 0.5 + j1.5$$

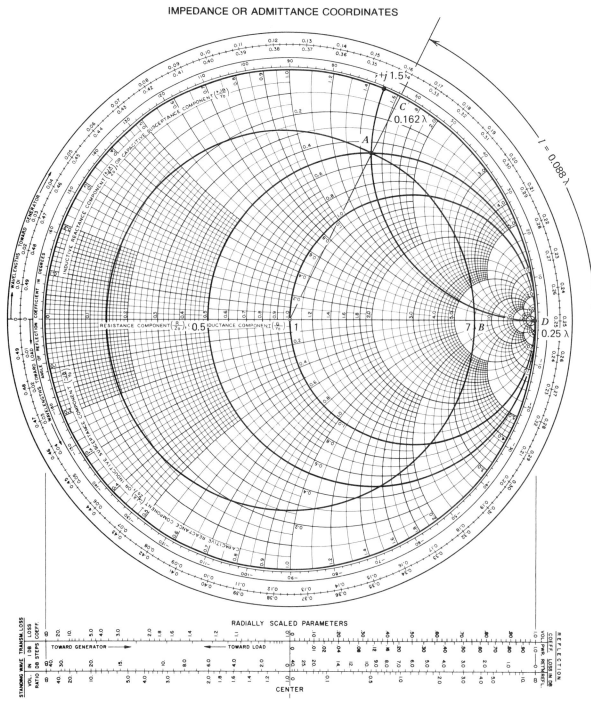

RADIALLY SCALED PARAMETERS

Figure B-7 Smith chart for Example B-3.

2. Locate z_L on Fig. B-7 (point A)

3. Using pt. A and the center of the circle as the radius draw the SWR circle about the center.

4. The SWR value will be at the point where the circle intersects the straight line (pt. B at $r=7$, therefore SWR$=7$).

5. Draw a radial line from center through pt. A to circumference (pt. C, 0.162λ).

6. The wavelength distance, going away from the load, between pt. C and pt. D is $0.25-0.162=0.0882$. This is the distance from load at which the line looks resistive and the λ/4 section may be inserted.

7. To determine the value of characteristic impedance of the inserted λ/4 section, calculate the resistance seen at the end of length l. This is the normalized value of resistance times the characteristic impedance. $R=r\times Z_0=7\times100=700$ Ω. Therefore

$$Z_0'=\sqrt{Z_0 R}\ =\sqrt{100\times700}\ =\textbf{264.6 Ω}$$

Note: If the frequency of the signal is specified, the distance l could be translated into centimeters, using:

$$\lambda=v_c/f=\frac{3\times10^{10}}{f}\qquad\text{cm}\qquad\qquad(8\text{-}1)$$

and distance from load$=l\times\lambda$

Example B-4

Given a transmission line with $Z_0=300$ Ω and a load $Z_L=(450-j150)$ Ω, determine the required locations and value of the λ/4 section required for impedance matching, if the signal frequency is 600 MHz.

Solution

Refer to Fig. B-8.

1. Calculate z_L and locate pt A on the chart.

$$z_L=Z_L/Z_0=\frac{450-j150}{300}=1.5-j0.5$$

2. Draw SWR circle and note that SWR$=1.85$ at point B. This is the *unmatched* SWR.

3. Extend a radius from center through pt A to circumference at pt C. The reading on the "toward generator" scale is 0.296λ.

4. At point D on the SWR circle, the line impedance is a pure resistance. The normalized r is 0.54. The actual resistance is $r\times Z_0=$

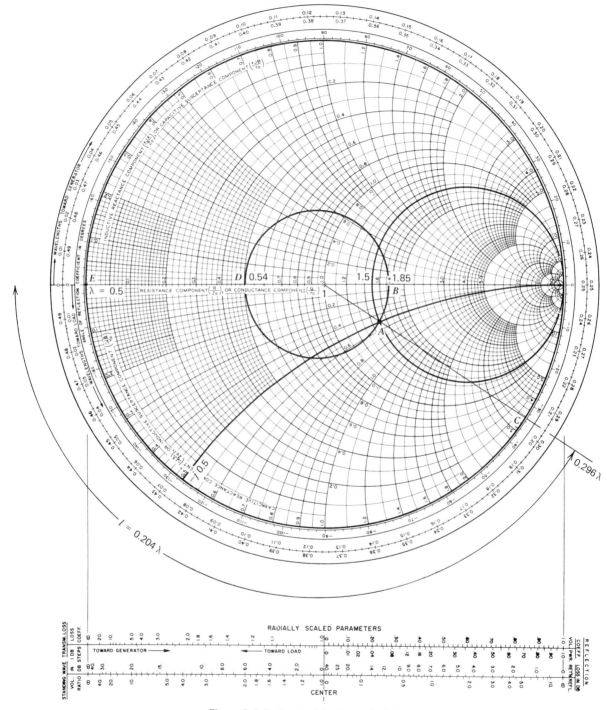

Figure B-8 Smith chart for Example B-4.

$0.54 \times 300 = \mathbf{162}$ Ω. Point D corresponds to point E at 0.5λ. The distance from the load is the arc C-E corresponding to a required $l = 0.5 - 0.296 = \mathbf{0.204\lambda}$.

5. The distance is readily converted to centimeters.

$$\lambda = \frac{v_c}{f} = \frac{3 \times 10^{10}}{600 \times 10^6} = \mathbf{50 \ cm/wavelength} \qquad (8\text{-}1)$$

$$l = 50 \times 0.204 = \mathbf{10.2 \ cm}$$

6. Inserting the $\lambda/4$ impedance matching section will transform the resistance of point D ($R = 162$ Ω) to the required main line resistance of 300 Ω. The required Z_0' will be:

$$Z_0' = \sqrt{Z_0 R} = \sqrt{300 \times 162} = \mathbf{220 \ \Omega}$$

It is also possible to analyze a $\lambda/4$ section problem by a sequence that must be used to determine the effect of frequency variation on the SWR. The procedure is shown in Sec. B-4.

B-3
Calculations For
a Matching Stub

The advantage of the matching stub design over the $\lambda/4$ section is the use of the *same* type of line for the stub as the main transmission line. In addition it is possible to design multistub sections for impedance matching over a wider range of frequencies. The connection of the stub to the line is shown in Fig. B-9.

The stub is connected in parallel with the transmission line at a distance l_1 from the load. The length of the short-circuited stub is l_2. Point B is selected to provide an admittance $y = 1 \pm jB$ where the conductance component is unity, meaning $R = Z_0$ and the main line is matched insofar as the resistive component is concerned. The susceptance component ($\pm jB$) can be any value and is either positive or negative. The length of the short-circuited stub is selected to provide a conjugate susceptance $\pm jB$ that cancels the reactance seen at the line where the stub is joined to the line. The sequence of steps is given in the following example.

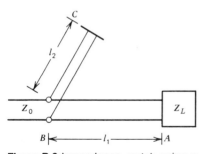

Figure B-9 Impendance match using a short-circuited matching stub.

Example B-5
Given a 150 Ω transmission line terminated in a load $Z_L = 200 - j300$. Determine the location and length of a short-circuited matching stub.

Solution

The sequence is shown on Fig. B-10.

The conversion of z_L to y_L is a simple procedure on a Smith chart, since a $\lambda/4$ section inverts the impedance at one end to an admittance at the other end.

a. Calculate $z_L = \dfrac{Z_L}{Z_0} = \dfrac{200 - j300}{150} = 1.33 - j2$ (point A)

b. Draw the SWR circle through pt A. Note that the SWR *before* impedance matching is a high 4.9!

c. Extend the radial line from pt. A through the center to the other side of the SWR circle (pt B), and out to the outer perimeter, point C at 0.057λ. Point B $(0.23 + j0.36)$ is the normalized load admittance equal to the reciprocal of the normalized load impedance or $1.33 - j2 = 1/0.23 + j0.36$.

d. Extend a radial line from center through the intersection of the SWR circle and the $r = 1$ circle point $D(1 + j1.8)$ and continue the line to the outer perimeter, point E at 0.183λ. The distance from load to junction of stub and transmission line is

$$0.183 - 0.057 = 0.126\lambda = l_1$$

e. The final step is the determination of the *actual* length of the stub. Since the susceptance seen at the junction is $+j1.8$, the susceptance to be contributed by the stub is $-j1.8$. At point F $(jB = -j1.8)$ the outer perimeter reads 0.33λ. The length of the matching stub is determined by the arc starting at the right-hand side (∞, ∞) and rotating clockwise to point F: $l_2 = 0.33 - 0.25 = 0.08\lambda$.

Example B-6

Design a short-circuited matching stub for a load $Z_L = (150 + j225)$ Ω for a 75 Ω line at 500 MHz.

Solution

Refer to Fig. B-11.

a. $z_L = \dfrac{150 + j225}{75} = 2 + j3$ (point A)

b. Draw SWR circle. Note that the uncompensated SWR $= 7$.

c. Extend point A radius through the center to admittance point B $(0.15 - j0.23)$ and point C (0.464λ).

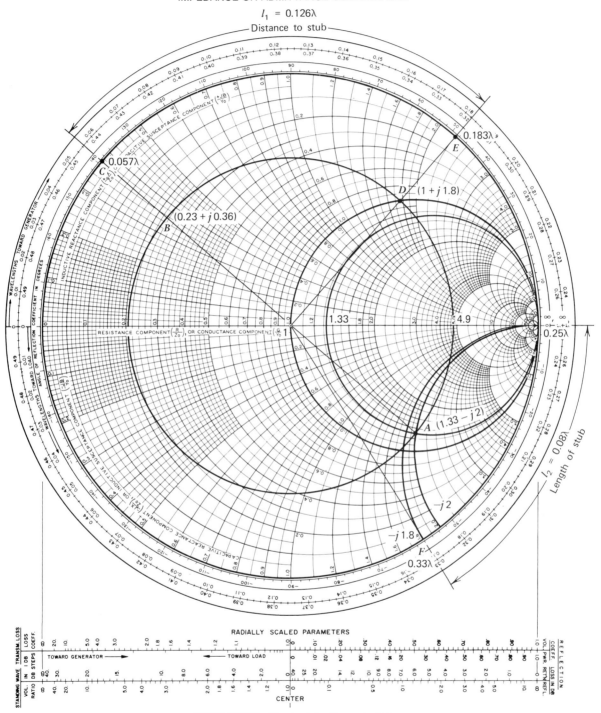

IMPEDANCE OR ADMITTANCE COORDINATES

$l_1 = 0.126\lambda$

Distance to stub

RADIALLY SCALED PARAMETERS

Figure B-10 Smith chart for Example B-5.

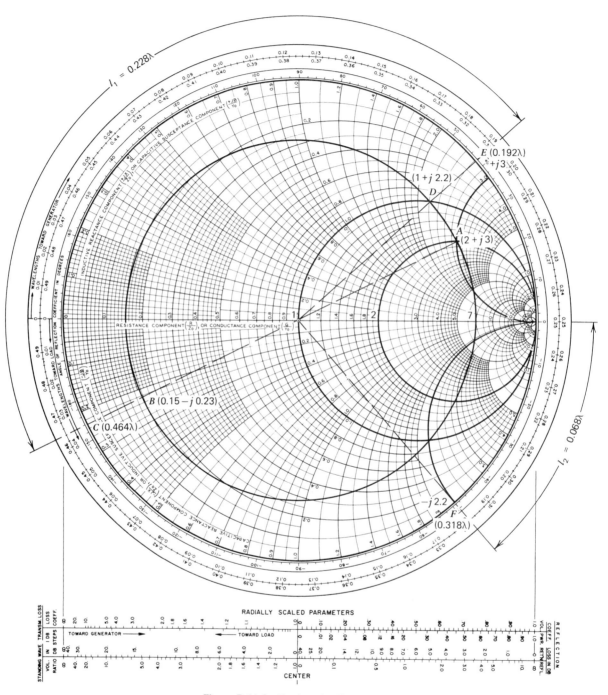

Figure B-11 Smith chart for Example B-6.

d. Note intersection of $r=1$ circle and SWR circle at point D $(1+j2.2)$. Draw the extended radius through point D to perimeter, point E (0.192λ). Length to stub is $0.036+0.192=0.228\lambda$.

$$\lambda = \frac{v_c}{f} = \frac{3\times10^{10}}{5\times10^8} = \textbf{60 cm/wavelength}$$

$l_1 = 0.228\lambda = 0.228$ wavelengths $\times 60$ cm/wavelength $= \textbf{13.7 cm}$

e. Note point F $(-j2.2)$ on perimeter at 0.318λ. The length of the stub is

$l_2 = 0.318 - 0.25 = \textbf{0.068}\boldsymbol{\lambda}$

$l_2 = 60\times0.068 = \textbf{4.08 cm}$

B-4
Impedance Mismatch
with Frequency
Variation
The $\lambda/4$ section and the stub lengths are designed for a specific frequency. If the carrier is shifted in frequency, or if the side-bands of the carrier are a significant percentage of carrier frequency, the impedance match is *no longer valid*. This results in standing waves on a transmission line that originally had been designed to be flat.

Example B-7

Given $Z_L = (225 - j37.5)$ Ω, $Z_0 = 75$ Ω and $f = 800$ MHz. Design a $\lambda/4$ impedance matching section and determine the mismatch if the frequency is increased 10%.

Solution

Refer to Fig. B-12.

a. $z_L = \dfrac{225 - j37.5}{75} = \textbf{3} - \boldsymbol{j}\textbf{0.5}$ \quad (point A).

b. Draw a SWR circle, extend the radius to point B (0.261λ), and note that SWR $= 3.1$.

c. Determine distance to $\lambda/4$ section at point C (0.5λ):

$l = 0.5 - 0.261 = \textbf{0.239}\boldsymbol{\lambda}$

$$\text{Length} = \left(\frac{v_c}{f}\right)l = \frac{3\times10^{10}}{8\times10^8} \times 0.239 = \textbf{8.96 cm}$$

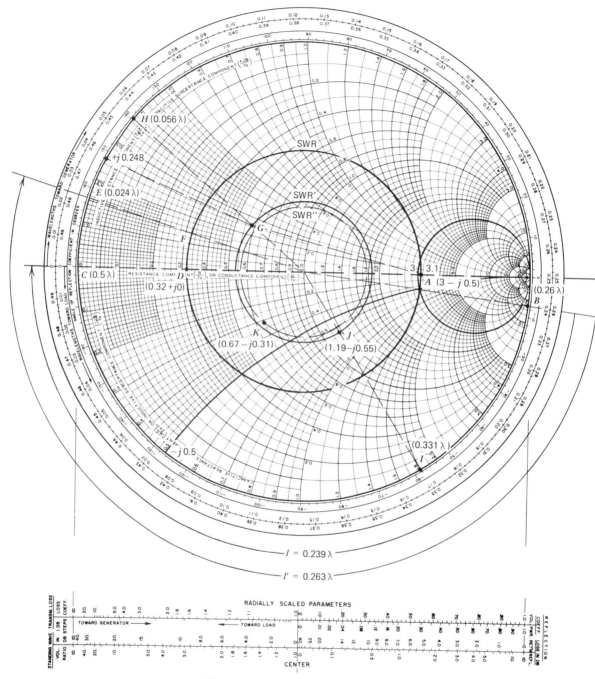

Figure B-12 Smith chart for Example B-7.

d. Note point D, $(0.32+j0)=(r+j0)$

Calculate $Z_0'=\sqrt{Z_0 \times R}=\sqrt{Z_0 \times (Z_0 r)}$

$$=\sqrt{(75)^2 \times 0.32}=\sqrt{1800}=\textbf{42.4 }\Omega$$

e. At $f=1.1 \times 800=880$ MHz, the line segment l appears 10% *longer*.

$l'=1.1 \times 0.239=0.263\lambda$. Draw arc l' starting from point B to point E (0.024λ).

f. Draw radial line to point E. Note the intersection with SWR circle at point F $(0.33+j0.14)$.

g. The impedance presented to the $\lambda/4$ section is no longer a pure resistance.

$$Z_L'=Z_0(z_F)$$

$$Z_L'=75(0.33+j0.14)=\textbf{25}+\textbf{\textit{j}10.5}$$

h. The $\lambda/4$ section *also* appears to be 10% longer or $1.1 \times 0.25\lambda=0.275\lambda$. Normalizing the Z_L' in terms of Z_0'

$$z_L'=\frac{25+j10.5}{42.4}=0.59+j0.248 \quad \text{(point } G\text{)}$$

i. Draw z_L' (SWR)$'$ circle.

j. Draw radial line through point G to point H (0.056λ).

k. Locate arc 0.275λ away from point H $(0.056+0.275)$ to point I (0.331λ).

l. Draw radial line to point I. Note intersection with z_G (SWR)$'$ circle at point J $(1.19-j0.55)$. This is the normalized impedance presented to the main transmission line. The actual impedance is

$$Z_L''=Z_0'(1.19-j0.55)=42.4(1.19-j0.55)=\textbf{50.5}-\textbf{\textit{j}23.3}$$

m. Normalizing Z_L'' in terms of $Z_{0'}$

$$z_L''=\frac{Z_L'}{Z_0}=\frac{50.5-j23.3}{75}=0.67-j0.31 \quad \text{(point } K\text{)}$$

n. Plot point K and draw the (SWR)$''$ circle. Note that by coincidence point K is practically on the z_G (SWR)$'$ circle and the (SWR)$''$ is approximately 1.75. Therefore the properly matched (SWR$=1$) system at 800 MHz is *unmatched* at 880 MHz with a SWR of **1.75**.

If the load had been specified in terms of $Z_L = R + j2\pi fL$ or $Z_L = R - j(1/2\pi fC)$, the modified frequency would necessitate a modification of Z_L.

Example B-8

Given $Z_L = (30 + j50)$ Ω and $Z_0 = 150$ Ω, design a $\lambda/4$ section for a frequency of 2 GHz. Determine the SWR mismatch for a frequency of 1.8 GHz.

Solution

Refer to Fig. B-13.

a. $z_L = \dfrac{30 + j50}{150} = 0.2 + j0.33$ (point A)

b. Draw SWR circle through point A (SWR = 5.2).

c. Draw radial line through point A to point B (0.052λ).

d. Distance from load to $\lambda/4$ section.

$l = 0.25 - 0.052 = \mathbf{0.198\lambda}$

$$\text{length} = \left(\frac{v_c}{f}\right)l = \left(\frac{3 \times 10^{10}}{2 \times 10^9}\right) \times 0.198 = 15 \times 0.198$$

$$= \mathbf{2.97\ cm}$$

e. $Z_0' = \sqrt{Z_0 R} = \sqrt{Z_0 (Z_0 r)} = \sqrt{(150)^2 \times 5.2} = \mathbf{342\ \Omega}$

f. At 1.8 GHz, l appears 10% shorter.

$l' = 0.9 \times 0.198 = 0.178\lambda$

This length brings you to $0.052 + 0.178 = \mathbf{0.23\lambda}$ (point C).

g. Draw radial line through point C intersecting the SWR circle at point D ($3.9 + j2.4$). This represents the impedance seen as a load by the $\lambda/4$ section and is equal to:

$Z_L' = Z_0(3.9 + j2.4) = 150(3.9 + j2.4)$

$\qquad = \mathbf{585 + j360}$

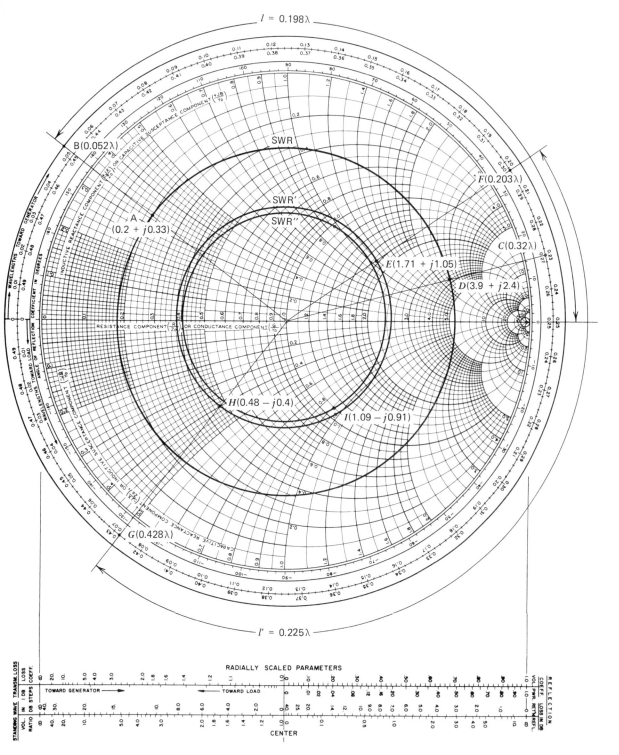

Figure B-13 Smith chart for Example B-8.

h. Normalizing Z'_L in terms of Z'_0,

$$z'_L = \frac{585 + j360}{342} = 1.71 + j1.05 \qquad \text{(point } E)$$

i. Draw (SWR)' circle using point E.

j. The $\lambda/4$ section is 10% less at the lower frequency.

$$l' = 0.25 \times 0.9 = 0.225\lambda$$

Extend radial line through point E to point F (0.203λ).

k. Adding the modified $\lambda/4$ (0.225λ) to point F, $0.225 + 0.203 = 0.428\lambda$, brings you to point G.

l. Draw radial line through point G. Note intersection with SWR' at point H $(0.48 - j0.4)$. This is the normalized impedance presented to the main transmission line. The actual impedance is

$$Z''_L = Z'_0(0.48 - j0.4)$$

$$= 342(0.48 - j0.4)$$

$$= (164 - j137) \ \Omega$$

m. Normalizing the line load in terms of Z_0

$$z''_L = \frac{164 - j137}{150} = 1.09 - j0.91 \qquad \text{(point } I)$$

Locate point I on chart and draw the (SWR)'' circle. Note SWR = **2.4** yielding the conclusion that a properly matched system (SWR = 1) at 2 GHz is mismatched (SWR = 2.4) at 1.8 GHz.

The short-circuited stub design also involves two lengths, l and l_2 that will perform differently at varied frequencies.

Example B-9
Perform a short-circuited stub design for $Z_0 = 200 \ \Omega$, $Z_L = (40 - j100)\Omega$, $f = 500$ MHz. Calculate SWR for 600 MHz.

Solution

Refer to Fig. B-14.

a. $z_L = \dfrac{40 - j100}{200} = (0.2 - j0.5) \ \Omega \qquad \text{(point } A)$

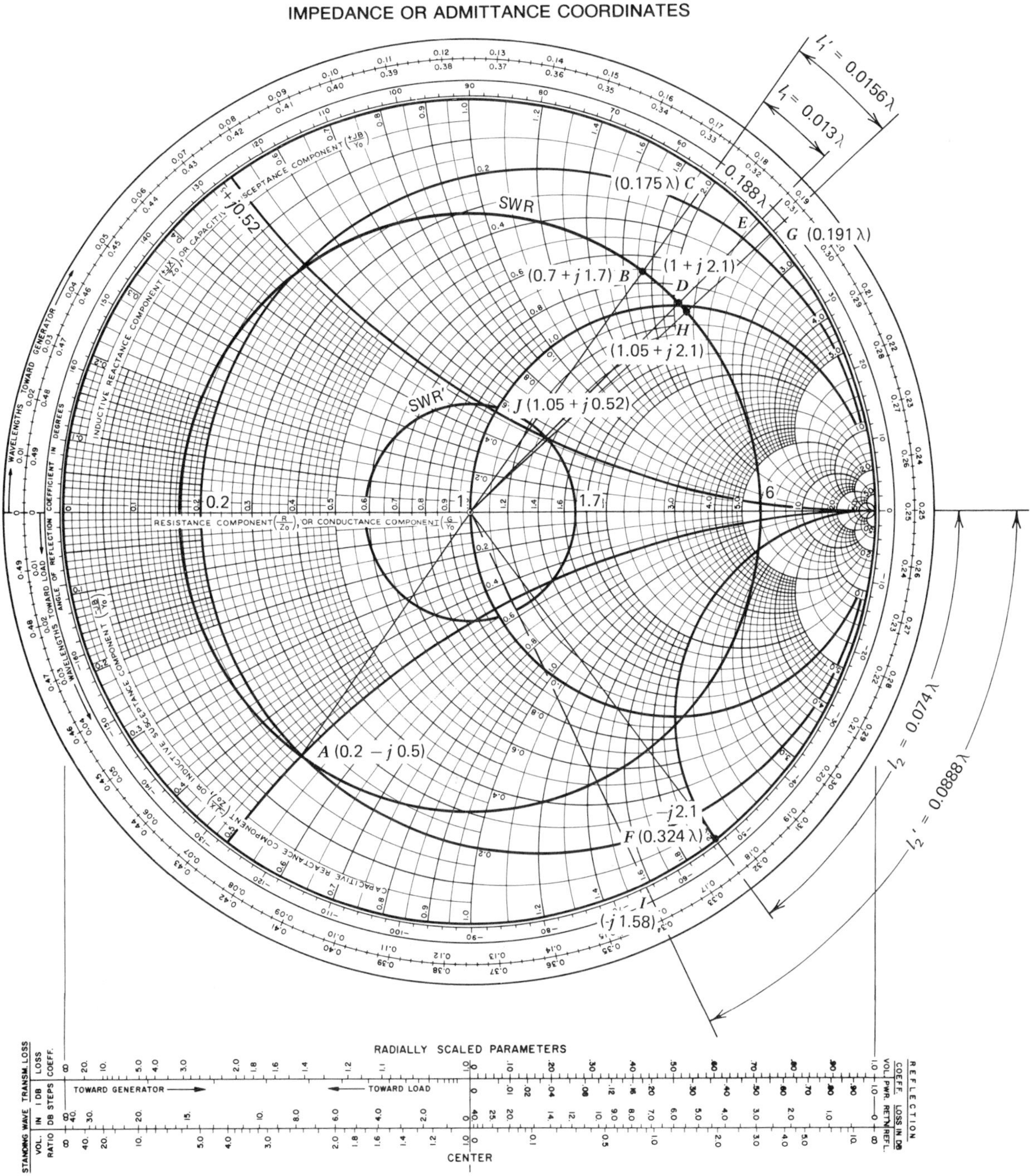

IMPEDANCE OR ADMITTANCE COORDINATES

Figure B-14 Smith chart for Example B-9.

b. Plot Point A, draw SWR circle, and note SWR $= 6$.

c. Extend radial line through the admittance point B

$(Y_L = 0.7 + j1.7)$ to point C (0.175λ).

d. At intersection of SWR circle and $r = 1$, note point D $(1 + j2.1)$. Extend the radial line through point D to the perimeter, point E (0.188λ).

e. The distance from load to stub

$$l_1 = 0.188 - 0.175 = 0.013\lambda$$

$$\text{length} = \frac{3 \times 10^{10}}{5 \times 10^8} \times 0.013 = 0.78 \text{ cm}$$

f. The length of short-circuited stub l_2 is the arc from 0.25λ (∞, ∞) to the wavelength corresponding to $jB = -j2.1$ point F (0.324λ).

$$l_2 = 0.324 - 0.25 = 0.074\lambda$$

$$\text{length} = 60 \times 0.074 = 4.44 \text{ cm}$$

g. At $f = 600$ MHz, l_1 and l_2 will appear to be 20% too long.

$$l_1' = 1.2l_1 = 1.2 \times 0.013 = 0.0156\lambda$$

$$l_2' = 1.2l_2 = 1.2 \times 0.074 - 0.0888\lambda$$

h. Draw arc l_1' from point C to point G at $0.175 + 0.0156 = 0.191\lambda$.

i. Draw radial line through point G. Note the intersection with SWR circle at point H $(1.05 + j2.1)$. This is the admittance presented to the line by l_1 at the higher frequency.

j. Draw arc l_2' starting at 0.25λ, ending at point I.

$$(0.25 + 0.0888) = 0.3388\lambda$$

k. The total admittance seen at the stub junction is the admittance offered by the length l_1 and the stub. This will be plotted at point J.

$$Y_{\text{total}} = 1.05 + j2.1 - j1.58 = 1.05 + j0.52 \qquad (\text{point } J)$$

l. Plot point J and draw the modified (SWR)′ circle. Note the SWR is 1.7, which makes the design still useful at 600 MHz.

Example B-10

This example assumes a 5% decrease in frequency. Perform a short-circuited stub design given $Z_L = (40 + j100)$ Ω, $Z_0 = 100$ Ω.

Solution

Refer to Fig. B-15.

a. $z_L = \dfrac{40 + j100}{100} = 0.4 + j1$ (point A)

Plot point A and draw SWR circle. Note that the unmodified SWR = 5.

b. Extend radial line from point A through center to point B ($0.35 - j0.85$), and point C (0.382λ).

c. Draw radial line through the intersection of $r = 1$ circle and SWR circle at the point that is clockwise (toward generator) from point C. This is point D ($1 + j1.8$).

d. Extend radial line to perimeter point E (0.183λ). The location of stub from the load

$$l_1 = 0.118 + 0.183 = 0.301\lambda$$

e. Locate $-j1.8$ on perimeter, point F, corresponding to 0.33λ. Therefore the length of the short-circuited stub is $l_2 = (0.33 - 0.25) = 0.08\lambda$.

f. At 5% decrease in frequency, the electrical length of l_1 and l_2 decreases 5%. Therefore,

$$l_1' = 0.95 l_1 = 0.95 \times 0.301 = 0.286\lambda$$

$$l_2' = 0.95 l_2 = 0.95 \times 0.08 = 0.076\lambda$$

g. Start at point C and lay out arc l_1' to point G at

$$0.286 - 0.118 = 0.168\lambda$$

Draw radial line to point G. Note intersection with SWR circle at point H ($0.72 + j1.5$). This is the admittance at the junction contributed by l_1.

h. Lay out arc l_2' starting at 0.25λ to point I at $0.25 + 0.076 = 0.326\lambda$. This length corresponds to a susceptance of $-j1.93$.

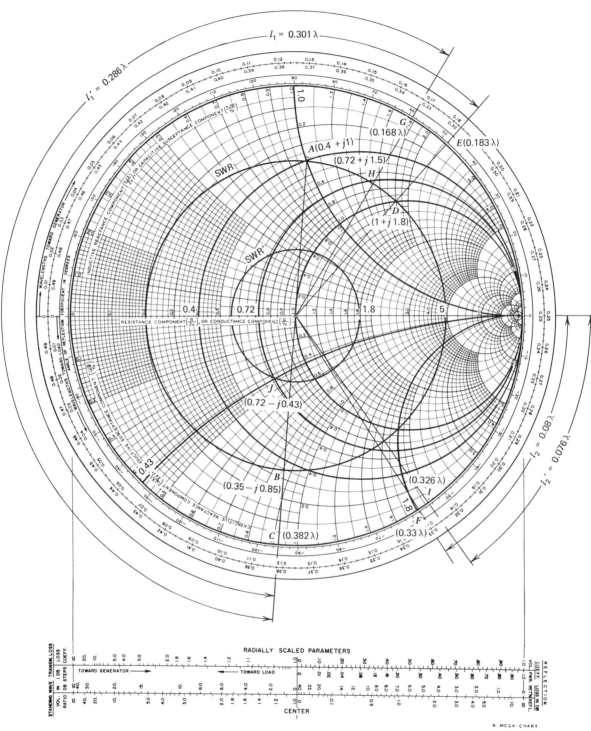

Figure B-15 Smith chart for Example B-10

A MEGA-CHART

i. The total admittance at the junction is

$Y_T = 0.72 + j1.5 - j1.93 = 0.72 - j0.43$ (point J)

j. Plot Y_T (point J), draw (SWR)′ circle. Note that the *modified SWR* is 1.8: Even a 5% frequency variation will change what had been a matched *flat* line to a resonant line.

B-5   The Smith chart can be used in the solution of various prob-
Miscellaneous Problems lems. This section solves a few problems not previously considered.

Example B-11
Given a transmission line system with a SWR of 1.5 and $Z_0 = 100$ Ω.
The impedance seen 1.6λ away from the load is $(70 - j20)$Ω. Determine Z_L.

Solution

Refer to Fig. B-16.

a. Draw SWR = 1.5 circle.

b. 1.6λ is the same as 0.1λ.

c. Normalized impedance at a distance of 0.1λ is $\dfrac{70 - j20}{100} = 0.7 - j0.2$
   (point A), equivalent to 0.444λ   (point B)

d. Rotating point B 0.1λ toward load, point C (0.344λ), locates point D
   $(1.08 - j0.42)$.

e. $Z_L = 100(1.08 - j0.42) = (108 - j42)$ Ω.

Example B-12
Given a transmission line system with a SWR of 3.5 and a Z_0 of 50 Ω.
The impedance seen 0.21λ away from the load is $(0.36 + j0.5)$Ω. De-
termine Z_L.

Solution

Refer to Fig. B-17.

a. Draw SWR = 3.5 circle.

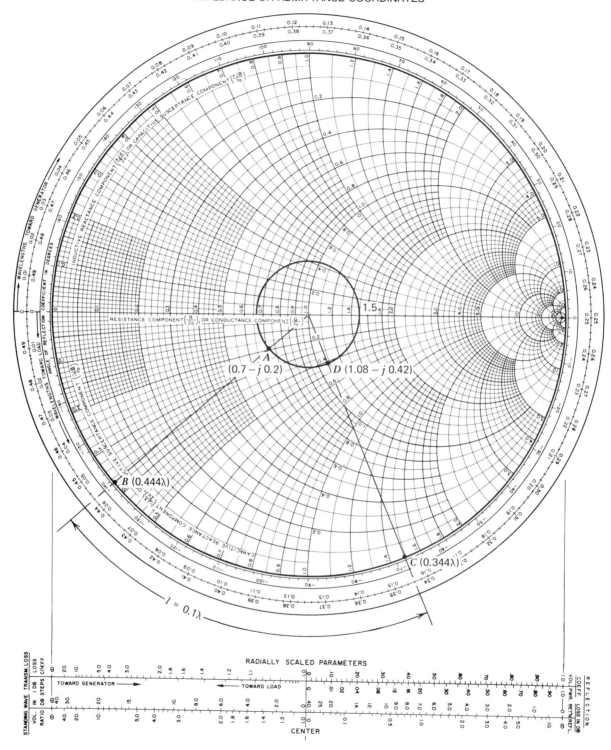

Figure B-16 Smith chart for Example B-11.

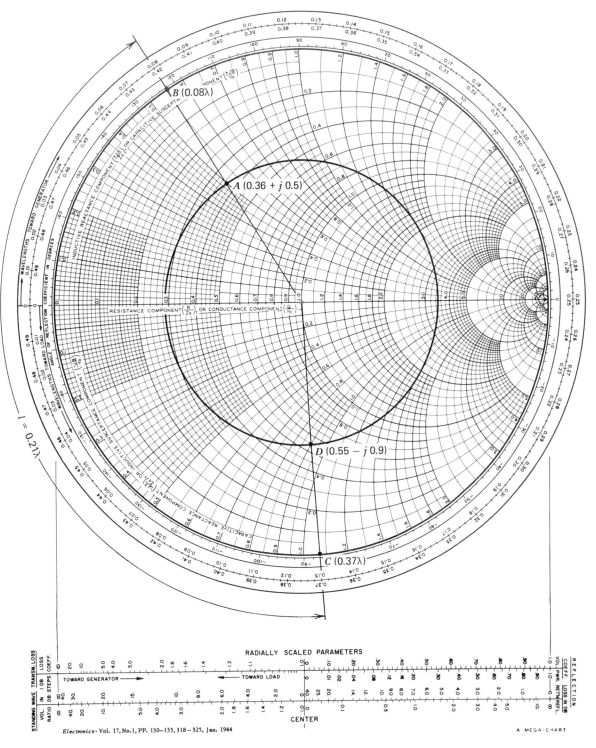

Figure B-17 Smith chart for Example B-12.

b. Plot $0.36 + j0.5$ (point A). Note point A corresponds to point B (0.08λ).

c. Point C is $0.08 - 0.21 = 0.37\lambda$. Note point C corresponds to point D $(0.55 - j0.9)$.

d. $Z_L = 50(0.55 - j0.9) = (27.5 - j45) \ \Omega$.

Another problem that lends itself to Smith chart solution is the determination of the value of an unknown impedance using a slotted line, a probe, and a detector that senses and displays VSWR directly. The characteristics of a slotted line are detailed in Sec. 8-12. The slotted line is inserted in series with the transmission line. Its length is calibrated in centimeters. Various readout devices are employed with the slotted line to measure the amplitude of the signal at any point along the slotted line.

The load impedance measurement is accomplished in two steps. First the line is terminated with a short-circuit load. An input signal is applied and a *minimum voltage* point is correlated to the position on the slotted line. This position is called the *reference minimum*. The short circuit is then replaced by the unknown load, and a new minimum position is located. This is the *impedance minimum*. Note is made of the direction of shift of one to the other relative to location of load. The VSWR under load is then measured.

The distance between minima, which is measured in centimeters, is converted to wavelengths. The SWR circle is drawn. Starting at the left-hand side $(0,0)$, we draw the arc in the appropriate direction. The radial line intersection with the SWR circle is noted $(z_L = r + jX)$. This normalized load is then converted to actual impedance $Z_L = [Z_0(r + jX)]$.

The above procedure is described in the following examples.

Example B-13

Given the following data for the laboratory experiment to determine the value of an unknown impedance load terminating a 50-Ω transmission line: the frequency is 500 MHz, the *short-circuit minimum* occurs at 10 cm, the minimum with the unknown load occurs at 24 cm (away from the load), and the VSWR is 2.3, at the impedance minimum for the unknown load.

Solution

Refer to Fig. B-18.

a. Draw SWR circle $= 2.3$.

b. The shift in minima $= 24 - 10 = 14$ cm. This is equal to a fractional wavelength determined by:

$$\lambda = \frac{3 \times 10^{10}}{5 \times 10^8} = 60 \text{ cm}$$

$$\therefore 14 \text{ cm} = \frac{14}{60} = 0.233\lambda$$

e. Starting at $(0,0)$, rotate 0.233λ toward generator (point A).

d. Note intersection with SWR circle, point B $(2.2 + j0.4)$.

e. Calculate $Z_L = 50(2.2 + j0.4) = (110 + j20)\Omega$.

Example B-14

In the use of a slotted line to determine the impedance of an unknown load, terminating a 75 Ω transmission line using a frequency of 800 MHz, the following data was obtained: short circuit minimum at 42 cm, minimum with load at 8 cm, shift toward load, VSWR $= 6$. Determine load impedance.

Solution

Refer to Fig. B-19.

a. Draw SWR circle $= 6$.

b. The shift in minima $= 42 - 8 = 34$ cm, toward the load.

c. $\lambda = \dfrac{3 \times 10^{10}}{8 \times 10^8} = 37.5$ cm.

Therefore shift $= 34/37.5 = 0.907\lambda = 0.407\lambda$

d. Starting at $(0,0)$, rotate 0.407λ toward load (point A).

e. Note intersection with SWR circle at point B:

$(0.25 + j0.64)$

f. Calculate $Z_L = 75(0.25 + j0.64)$

$$= (18.75 + j48) \ \Omega$$

IMPEDANCE OR ADMITTANCE COORDINATES

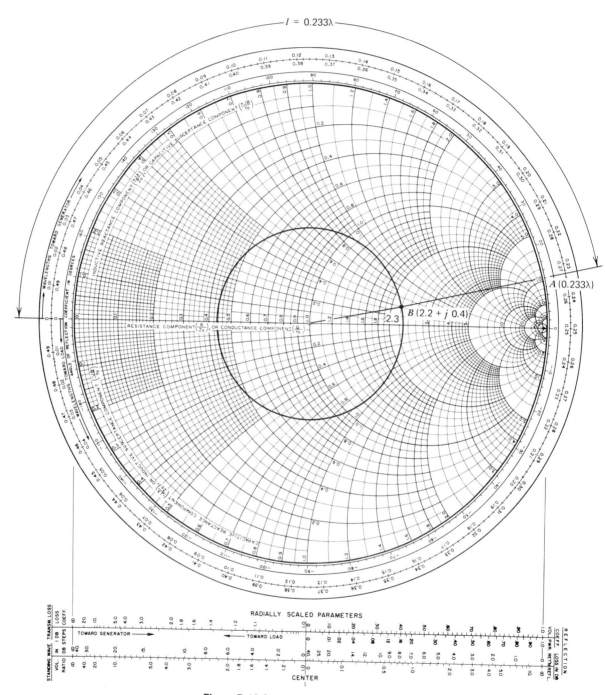

Figure B-18 Smith chart for Example B-13.

324

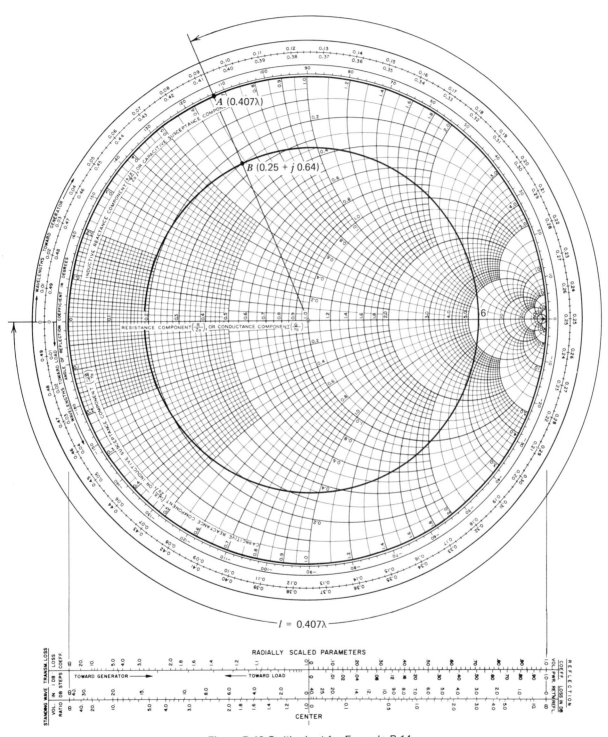

RADIALLY SCALED PARAMETERS

Figure B-19 Smith chart for Example B-14.

A practical transmission line must cause some weakening of the signal as the signal travels down the line. This weakening is described as an *attenuation* of the signal and the loss is specified in decibel units (dB). The Smith chart can be used to determine the attenuation of a signal or the effect of attenuation on the impedance seen at any point on a line. The SWR circle of a transmission line with attenuation is represented by a *spiral* (rather than a circle). Therefore a correction must be added to the solutions offered by the methods we have considered. These corrections are demonstrated by the following illustrative examples.

Example B-15

The impedance seen at a specific point (A) on a 75 Ω transmission line is $(75+j50)$ Ω. Determine the impedance 10 cm closer to the load if the line attenuation between the two points is 2 dB and the signal frequency is 800 MHz.

Solution

Refer to Fig. B-20.

a. Normalized impedance at point

$$A = \frac{75+j50}{75} 1+j0.67$$

b. Plot point A. Draw SWR circle. Note point A corresponds to 0.149λ (point B).

c. At $f=800$ MHz, $\lambda = \frac{3\times10^{10}}{8\times10^{8}} = 37.5$ cm. Therefore, 10 cm $= 10/37.5$ $= 0.267\lambda$. Draw arc toward load with $l=0.267\lambda$ (point C). Note that point D $(0.78-j0.55)$ is the normalized impedance seen at a point 0.267λ away if no attenuation is assumed.

d. From left-hand edge of SWR (point E) drop a perpendicular line to the TRANSM LOSS 1 DB STEPS line of the horizontal scales (point F).

e. Moving two divisions (2 dB) on this scale toward the load (to the left), (point G), draw a perpendicular line back to $x=0$ line (point H).

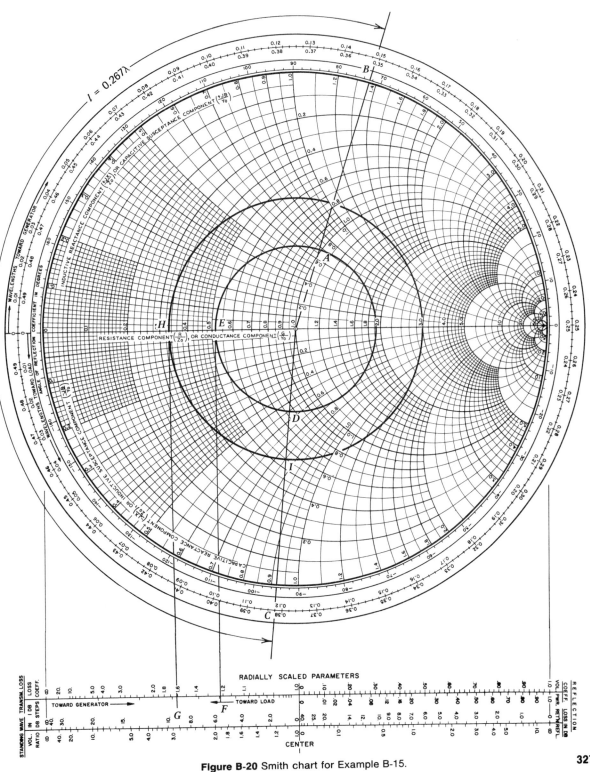

Figure B-20 Smith chart for Example B-15.

f. At point H draw new SWR circle. Note intersection with radial line CD at point I $(0.57 - j0.75)$. This is the normalized impedance seen at a point 10 centimeters from point A toward the load.

g. Impedance $= 75(0.57 - j0.75)$

$$= (42.8 - j56.3) \ \Omega$$

Example B-16

The *normalized* impedance measured at a point 8.2λ from the load terminating the transmission line is $0.5 - j0.75$. Assuming the attenuation of the line is 1 dB per wavelength, determine the normalized impedance measured at a point 6.1λ from the load.

Solution

Refer to Fig. B-21.

a. Plot $0.5 - j0.75$ (point A) and draw SWR. Note point B (0.385λ).

b. Lay out arc $8.2 - 6.1 = 2.1 = 0.1\lambda$ from point B to point C (0.285λ). Note unattenuated impedance at point D $(2.2 - j1.5)$.

c. Drop perpendicular from point E to point F. Note point G, two divisions (2 dB) from point F.

d. Draw perpendicular from point G to point H at reactance equal zero line.

e. Draw SWR using point H and note intersection with DC radial line at point I $(1.6 - j3.8)$. This is the normalized impedance seen at the specified point with attenuation included.

There are many other types of charts, nomographs, and tables that can be used in the solution of transmission line problems. A chart can also be designed for a specific type of transmission line, such as a 50 Ω line. Mastery of the Smith chart problems covered in this chapter should enable readers to readily adapt to any specific methods they may encounter in industry.

IMPEDANCE OR ADMITTANCE COORDINATES

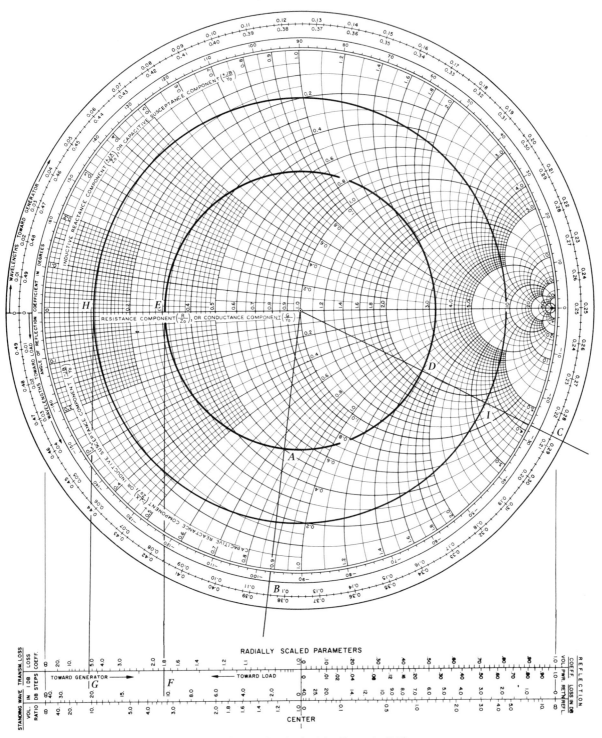

RADIALLY SCALED PARAMETERS

Figure B-21 Smith chart for Example B-16.

329

Glossary

Amplitude modulation. Variation of the amplitude of the carrier frequency to correspond to a modulating signal.

Antenna array. A grouping of antenna elements to accomplish a specified gain and/or directivity.

Antenna beamwidth. The angular separation between the two half-power points on the power density radiation pattern.

Armstrong oscillator. A type of tunable RF oscillator that uses magnetic coupling for the feedback path.

Attenuator. A device that absorbs energy, thus reducing the power levels.

Automatic frequency control. A method of maintaining an oscillator on frequency.

Automatic gain control. A method of maintaining the output signal at a constant level.

Balanced modulator. A circuit that mixes RF and audio and results in sidebands without the carrier.

Bandpass filter. A circuit that passes a prescribed band of frequencies and attenuates all other frequencies.

Beat frequency oscillator. An oscillator used in superhet receivers to receive CW or SSB transmission.

Bessel functions. A mathematical table that defines the amplitudes of the sidebands of an FM signal.

Buffer. An amplifier that acts to isolate an oscillator stage from the rest of the transmitter.

Buncher cavity. A microwave cavity that modifies the flow of electrons to form bunches.

Capture effect. The tendency of an FM receiver to stay tuned to the stronger of two signals at the same frequency.

Carrier. The FCC allocated frequency of a broadcast station.

Cathode modulation. A type of modulation where the modulating signal is inserted into the RF stage through the cathode leg.

Characteristic impedance. The impedance of a transmission line that is infinitely long.

Choke flange. A type of flange used to provide the connection of waveguide sections without discontinuities.

Coaxial line. An unbalanced line with a center wire in an outer shield supported by a dielectric.

Colpitts oscillator. A tunable oscillator used at VHF that uses a tapped capacitor for the feedback path.

Converter. A stage in a superhet receiver that mixes the RF and LO signals with the IF frequency as the output.

Critical coupling. A double-tuned amplifier in which the degree of coupling results in a resistance reflected into the primary that is equal to the resistance of the primary.

Cross neutralization. A form of neutralization used in push-pull amplifiers.

Crystal oscillator. A fixed frequency oscillator that depends on the piezoelectric effect of a quartz crystal.

Cutoff wavelength. The longest wavelength (lowest frequency) that can be accommodated by a waveguide.

Deemphasis circuit. Used in the audio section of the FM receiver to attenuate the high frequencies.

Demodulation. The process of extracting the intelligence from the modulated RF.

Diode detector. A diode used for demodulation.

Directional coupler. A microwave device that extracts a sample of the forward direction signal for power measurement purposes.

Directional antenna. An antenna that transmits or receives signals in a specified direction relative to the axis of the antenna.

Doppler radar. A type of radar that depends on the frequency shift of the reflected signal to determine target velocity.

Duplexer. A device that couples the receiver and transmitter of a radar to a common antenna.

Flywheel effect. The oscillatory condition that results when an impulse of energy is inserted into an L-C tank.

Folded dipole. A 300 Ω antenna commonly used for TV reception.

Foster-Seeley discriminator. A type of FM detector using parallel diodes.

Frequency modulation. A form of modulation in which the frequency of the carrier is varied to correspond to the modulating intelligence.

Frequency multiplex. A system of ascending subcarrier frequencies each modulated by one or more signals, ultimately modulating a microwave carrier.

Frequency multiplier. An RF amplifier used to provide an output frequency that is a harmonic of the input frequency.

Grid-leak bias. A form of bias used in RF amplifiers and oscillators, which is self-adjusting with signal level.

Group velocity. The velocity of a microwave signal as it progresses through a waveguide.

Hazeltine neutralization. The neutralizing signal from the bottom of the output tank.

Helix antenna. Helical wound wire that results in a circular polarized directional microwave signal.

Heterodyne. The process of mixing two variable signals (RF and LO) to result in a fixed IF frequency.

High-level modulation. An AM transmitter that has the carrier modulated at the output of the RF power amplifier.

Horn antenna. A horn-shaped antenna that results in a directional microwave signal.

Image frequency. An undesired signal separated from the desired signal by a frequency equal to twice the IF frequency.

Isotropic antenna. A theoretical pin point antenna that radiates equally in all directions.

Johnson noise. Thermal agitation noise related to BW, temperature, and resistance of the component.

Klystron. Microwave oscillator or amplifier using cavities to modulate an electron stream.

Local oscillator. A tunable oscillator used in the superhet receiver to provide a mixing signal to the converter.

m Derived filter. An L-C network that provides well-defined frequency cutoff points.

Magnetron. A microwave oscillator that uses the interaction of magnetic and electric fields in a complex cavity.

Marconi antenna. A $\lambda/4$ vertical antenna that uses reflected ground to provide the missing $\lambda/4$.

Overcoupling. A degree of coupling beyond a critical point, which results in a double-peak frequency response.

Overmodulation. Modulation over 100%, which results in the generation of spurious frequencies.

Parabolic antenna. A directional microwave antenna commonly used for radar.

Partition noise. Caused by the random variation in the distribution of current among the elements of an amplifier.

Piezoelectric effect. A mechanical vibration to electrical signal conversion effect, associated with quartz crystals.

Preemphasis circuit. Used in the FM transmitter to amplify the high frequencies.

Pulse modulation. Transmission of a carrier in bursts or pulses.

Pulse amplitude modulation. Variation of the amplitude of the transmitted pulse to correspond to a modulating signal.

Pulse time modulation. Variation of the time of occurrence of the transmitted pulse to correspond to a modulating signal.

Push-pull amplifier. Two amplifiers connected for alternate polarity inputs and outputs.

Quarter-wave transformer. A $\lambda/4$ length of transmission line selected to match the source and load impedance.

Quartz crystal. Provides the piezoelectric effect for oscillators and filters.

Radiation pattern. A measure of the radiated energy in each direction.

Rat race junction. A microwave hybrid junction used for mixing or directing more than one signal.

Ratio detector. An FM detector that does not require limiter stage to precede it.

Reactance modulator. Simulates an L or C reactance, the amount of which is varied by a modulating signal.

Reciprocity principle. An antenna will function equally well as a transmitting or receiving antenna.

Reflected wave. The signal in a transmission line or waveguide that is not absorbed by the load will return to the source as a reflected wave.

Reflection coefficient. The ratio of voltage reflected from the load to the voltage applied to the load.

Reflector. An element in a multielement antenna that acts to reflect a signal to the driven element.

Resonant lines. A transmission line that is not properly terminated.

Rhombic antenna. A directional, terminated antenna, in the shape of a rhomboid.

Selectivity. The ability of a receiver to accept a signal and reject adjacent signals.

Sensitivity. Defines the weakest signal that can be received.

Single sideband suppressed carrier. A form of transmission commonly used to conserve bandwidth and power.

Slotted line. Inserted in series with a transmission line to measure standing wave ratio.

Smith chart. A chart used for microwave transmission line calculations.

Split stator. A dual capacitor used in push-pull amplifiers.

Stagger tuning. A method of broadening the bandwidth by tuning cascaded IF amplifiers to different frequencies.

Standing waves. An improperly terminated transmission line has energy reflected back from the load, which interacts with the forward signal and sets up nodes and antinodes.

Standing wave ratio. The ratio of peak to node of a standing wave.

Stubs. Shorting elements used with transmission lines to effect an impedance match.

Superheterodyne. A receiver that mixes a variable RF input with a correspondingly variable LO to provide a fixed frequency IF.

TE mode. A form of microwave transmission in which the electric field is perpendicular to the direction of propagation.

TM mode. A form of microwave transmission in which the magnetic field is perpendicular to the direction of propagation.

Transducer. A device used for converting a nonelectrical parameter to a current or voltage equivalent.

Transmission line. A conduit for passage of UHF and microwave signals.

Traveling wave tube. A microwave amplifier that uses a helical structure for velocity modulation of an electron beam.

Tunnel diode. A microwave oscillator that uses the negative resistance characteristic for operation.

Twin lead. A parallel-wire transmission line commonly used as 300 Ω TV cable.

Twist. A microwave waveguide accessory used to twist the plane of the signal.

Varactor diode. Used as a variable capacitor device for tuners.

Velocity modulation. The form of modulation of the electron beam used in microwave amplifiers and oscillators.

Vestigial sideband. The type of transmission used for TV where the entire upper sideband is transmitted, but only a part of the lower sideband.

Waveguide. A transmission line for microwave signals.

Wavelength. The distance between two successive peaks of a signal.

White noise. Noise that appears at all frequencies.

Yagi-Uda antenna. A multielement antenna commonly used for TV reception.

Index

traveling-wave, 227
Tuned amplifiers, 47
Tuned-input tuned-output oscillator, 84
Tunnel diode, amplifier, 233
    oscillator, 233
Twin lead, 166
Twist (waveguide), 203

Varactor diode, 231
Vehicle speeding radar, 281
Velocity, group, 186
    light, 162
    phase, 186
Velocity modulation, 219
Vertical antenna, 247
Vestigial sideband, 111
VHF, 3, 185
VSWR, 171
VVC diode, 231

Waveguides, advantages, 184
    attenuators, 210
    bends, 203
    characteristic impedance, 187
    circular, 195
    corners, 203
    coupling, 203, 205
    cutoff wavelength, 187, 191
    detectors, 210
    dominant mode, 187
    ferrite devices, 212
    field configurations, 193, 199
    flanges, 209
    group velocity, 186
    guide wavelength, 186
    irises, 208
    joints, 209
    junctions, 209
    magic tee, 206
    measurements, 213
    modes, 187, 190, 191, 197
    phase velocity, 186
    rat race, 207
    rectangular, 185
    resistive loads, 210
    sizes, 195
    tapers, 210
    TE field, 190
    tee junctions, hybrid, 206
        magic, 206
        series, 204
        shunt, 204
    terminations, 207
    TM field, 191
    twist sections, 203

window, 208
Wavelength, cutoff, 187, 191
    free-space, 162
Weather avoidance radar, 282
White noise, 5
Windows, microwave, 207
Yagi-Uda antenna, 250